BELIEF THAT BEHAVES

THE BOOK OF EPHESIANS

DAVID JEREMIAH

with Dr. David Jeremiah

Contents

Introduction

It was a dream come true for Roman Yurkov. As a 35-year-old car salesman from Tula, Russia, Yurkov had his share of financial troubles—including a gambling habit. Like most people in his community, he was doing his best to get by.

Then one day in May 2020, Yurkov was surprised to see that 95 million rubles (approximately 1.3 million dollars) had been deposited into his bank account. The deposit had come through his online bookie, which caused Yurkov to believe—or maybe to hope—that this windfall was the result of a wager paying off in a big way.

Still feeling somewhat skeptical, Yurkov called his bank. To his surprise, employees there told him there were no issues with his account. The money was real, and it was really his.

For Roman Yurkov, this unexpected turn of events represented an incredible blessing—and he set about blessing himself in every way possible. On the night of May 31 and into the morning of June 1, Yurkov made 220 separate transactions. Among the items he purchased on that spending spree were four separate apartments, a new iPhone, a BMW, and a Mercedes.

"I bought everything I wanted," he said later. "Well, only I didn't buy the plane."

Sadly, Roman Yurkov's story does not have a happy ending. His bank later became aware of some discrepancies in its accounting. In November 2020, Yurkov's account—which amazingly still held about $540,000—was blocked. The following month, he was arrested on charges of stealing from a bank. Despite continued protestations of his innocence, the court found Yurkov guilty of "taking advantage of a malfunction in the bank's software" and sentenced him to six years in prison.[1]

For Roman Yurkov, the dream turned into a nightmare. Why? Because his hopes for the future rested on resources he did not actually possess. He relied on that which is inherently unreliable.

Of course, he's not the only one. Our world is centered on the pursuit of what is temporary. That goes beyond wealth and finances. Society constantly pushes us to chase power and authority. Our culture is obsessed with fame and notoriety. Our communities convince us that the right relationships will eventually open the right doors—pathways to purpose and meaning.

But power can be pulled away in a moment. Fame is fickle. And relationships founded on self-indulgence quickly turn toxic. Worse yet, even if we were to exert ourselves for decades and fiercely hold on to everything we attain—our money, our reputation, our connections, and more—there is still the inescapable reality of the grave. No matter what we achieve or accomplish or acquire in this life, we will lose it when this life comes to an end.

Every blessing this world offers is a blessing we cannot keep.

That's why I'm excited to join with you in studying the book of Ephesians. Ephesians highlights for us a treasure trove of spiritual blessings we can never lose! No wonder this epistle remains one of the best-known and most-beloved letters in all of Scripture.

Located on the eastern side of the Aegean Sea, Ephesus was a major city in the region known to the ancient world as Asia Minor, or sometimes just Asia. Today, Ephesus would be located in Turkey. (It was destroyed by the Goths in A.D. 262.)

A large and prosperous city in its day, Ephesus was famous for its sprawling temple dedicated to the Roman goddess Diana, or Artemis as she was known to the Greeks. This magnificent structure was one of the seven wonders of the ancient world— but architecture wasn't the only source of the temple's popularity. Housing a large number of prostitutes known as priestesses, men routinely made their way to its inner chambers to "worship." Such a practice is just one of the reasons why Ephesus had a reputation for debauchery.

Paul first visited Ephesus during his second missionary journey (A.D. 49–52). During those years, he also visited the Greek city of Corinth where he met a wonderful couple named Aquila and Priscilla. Like Paul, these two were Jews by birth but had come to accept Jesus as the Messiah. Also like Paul, Priscilla and Aquila made their living as tentmakers. Because of these commonalities, they developed a fast friendship with Paul. They even joined him when he left Corinth and set sail for—can you guess?—Ephesus.

Once in Ephesus, Paul "entered the synagogue and reasoned with the Jews" (Acts 18:19) as was his custom. But he did not remain there for long, wanting to return to Jerusalem in time for an upcoming feast. Priscilla and Aquila did remain, however. In fact, they are the unsung heroes of the book of Ephesians because they led the church after Paul departed. They even trained up a young man named Apollos who became a great leader and a mighty evangelist for the church.

Paul returned to Ephesus as part of his third missionary journey and stayed in that city for about three years. Partnering once more with Priscilla and Aquila, the church exploded with growth. In fact, so many people believed in Jesus that the local silversmiths—who created idols in the image of Diana—became enraged and started a riot! After that event, Paul left the city for Macedonia and likely never returned.

Ephesians is known as one of Paul's prison epistles because he wrote it as a prisoner in Rome around A.D. 62, years after his third missionary journey (A.D. 53–57). Happily, Paul didn't contact the Ephesians in order to correct a major heresy or solve a crisis, which was the case with many of his epistles. Paul wrote Galatians to counter the practices of the "Judaizers," for example, who demanded that Gentile Christians be circumcised. And he wrote 1 Corinthians to address the major issue of sexual misconduct in the church.

The book of Ephesians, on the other hand, is remarkably free from controversy. Rather than offering correction, it is filled with encouragement. Specifically, Paul sought to remind the believers in Ephesus—and by extension, those of us who are believers today—about the many blessings they had received through Christ.

Here is a brief list of the blessings we will explore together in these pages:

- The blessing of salvation
- The blessing of being empowered by God
- The blessing of inclusion in the Body of Christ
- The blessing of inner strength
- The blessing of unity
- The blessing of spiritual transformation
- The blessing of work
- And much more.

If you are a Christian, the blessings described throughout the book of Ephesians are already yours. They've already been deposited into your account, and all the numbers check out. There will be no accounting errors or reassessments. As we walk through these pages together, I want to remind both you and me about our true wealth—an inheritance that is not vulnerable to the fluctuations of the stock market. It's not touched by inflation. And it cannot be lost through corruption and greed at the top.

In other words, your blessings as a believer in Jesus are secure, and they are ready for you to use. Even today—even right this moment. These resources are enough to cover all your past debts, to meet all your present liabilities, and to provide for all of your future needs.

Are you ready to learn more? Let's study together everything we have been given in Christ!

BLESSED BE THE GOD
AND FATHER OF OUR
LORD JESUS CHRIST,
WHO HAS BLESSED
US WITH EVERY
SPIRITUAL BLESSING
IN THE HEAVENLY
PLACES IN CHRIST.

EPHESIANS 1:3

CHAPTER 1

Eight Spiritual Blessings

EPHESIANS 1:3-14

It was a sad day in the Williams' household when they learned their neighbor, Ken Watson, had passed away. Ken's death wasn't a surprise—he was 87 and had suffered setbacks in his health. But Owen Williams and his wife knew that Ken's passing would be especially difficult for their young daughter, Cadi.

You see, Cadi was only two years old at the time, but she had a special connection with Mr. Watson. The elderly man treated her more as a granddaughter than a neighbor, even making a special effort to deliver Christmas presents for the child each year. His passing would leave an empty place not only within their neighborhood and street but also in Cadi's heart.

Thankfully, that's not the end of the story. It turns out Ken Watson had one more trick up his sleeve. Or, to say it more accurately, one more gift to give.

Shortly after Ken's death, his daughter stopped by the Williams' home carrying a large bag. She said it was for Cadi. Inside were fourteen gifts Ken had purchased for his friend—fourteen wrapped presents to bless the young girl over the next fourteen Christmases.

"I kept reaching into the bag and pulling out more presents," Owen Williams said. "You could have knocked me over with a feather. It was quite something."[1]

Try to imagine Ken Watson as he purchased all fourteen of those gifts and carried them back to that street—back to his home. Think of him making the effort to wrap each gift with his own failing fingers, knowing that younger fingers would one day rip through the paper with delight and think of him with fondness on Christmas mornings far into the future.

Can you see the smile on his face?

What about young Cadi? Can you picture her eyes lighting up during a distant Christmas morning when she opens yet another mystery gift from "Grandpa Ken"? What emotions will she feel when her parents once again tell her the story of the man who cared for her so much that he took steps to show that care not only in his present but also far into her future?

When you think about it, giving and receiving gifts is one of those universal experiences within the human race. Even the crustiest character on his or her worst day can be reached by the wonder of receiving a meaningful gift from a loved one—or from a stranger. And while there are certainly grinches walking about who resist the joy of generosity and philanthropy, I'm glad to say they are few and far between. Most of us understand and embrace the gladness of giving.

That theme of giving and receiving, of blessing and being blessed, is at the heart of the book of Ephesians. This letter reveals the avalanche of blessings you and I have received from our Heavenly Father—blessings that outstrip even our wildest imaginings.

Ephesians is all about the blessing of God on our lives. It's also about our behavior. In fact, the book is easy to outline around those two themes. The first three chapters are about what we believe, and the last three chapters are about how we behave. Paul is telling us that our behavior is grounded in God's blessing. That is why I have titled this book *Belief That Behaves*.

The passage of Scripture that we are going to study in this chapter is the longest sentence in the Bible. If you read it in the Greek language, there are no periods from the beginning of verse 3 all the way to the end of verse 14. I know that's true because when I was in seminary in Greek class, I had to diagram those verses, and the diagram ran off the first page and onto a second. Everything modifies everything else, and the whole sentence just keeps going on and on.

I used to wonder why Paul would include such a long sentence in an epistle, but I think I understand it now. I believe Paul started dictating to the Ephesians about all the blessings God has for us, and he got so excited he couldn't even take a breath. He just kept going, one right after the other, until he exhausted everything he had to say.

Paul started with the blessings connected to eternity past, he carried them out all the way through our present lives, and then he ended up in eternity future. As a result, this list of gifts is sequential. Each one reinforces the one that came before and introduces the one that comes after.

I want to follow Paul's example in this chapter. There is so much packed into these verses that I could write numerous books about them alone. But if I did that, you would miss out on the blessing of seeing everything in one incredible picture. So hang on! Let's take a whirlwind tour through some of the gifts we have received from our good and gracious God.

We Are Chosen

Paul began the Bible's longest sentence by telling us—every person who has accepted the free gift of salvation through Jesus Christ—that we have been chosen. Notice what it says in verse 4: "Just as He chose us in Him before the foundation of the world, that we should be holy and without blame before Him in love."

The Bible tells us that God is love, and love cannot live alone. And so God determined to bring to Himself a group of people that He would choose to come and spend eternity with Him. Scripture says He chose these people for Himself "before the foundation of the world."

Now I know I am treading on some very controversial territory here when I write about being chosen. Maybe you already have that word *election* stuck in your throat. What does it mean when it says Almighty God chose us? Well, I've studied this carefully in the Greek language and in all the commentaries, and I figured it out. Are you ready to hear what it means? It means God has chosen us!

Whether we like it or not, whether we can understand it or not, the Word of God says that before there was a world, before you and I existed, before there was anything, in the heart of Almighty God, He had thoughts about us. He pictured our faces. He understood our hearts. He fashioned the ins and outs of our minds. And then, knowing everything about who we would be and what we would become, He chose us.

He chose you.

You ask, "How did I get chosen and somebody else didn't?" I will never be able to comprehend that. This truth is a mystery that I cannot explain, but it is still truth. It is still God's Word.

Now please, don't get arrogant about this because it really has nothing to do with you or me. We don't have anything we can offer to God and say, "God chose me because He needs me." No, He chose me in spite of me. He chose you because of Jesus Christ—because you are in Christ.

The Bible says it. We can't contradict it. I'm unfaithful if I don't teach it. Whatever you might think about this truth, Almighty God has chosen you.

We Are Adopted

The second blessing Paul revealed to us is that not only are we chosen, but we are also adopted. Verse 5 says God chose us, "having predestined us to adoption as sons by Jesus Christ to Himself, according to the good pleasure of His will."

There's another of those dangerous words: "predestined." But notice Paul doesn't use that word in the way many people use it today. Paul was not saying that in eternity past God predestined the entire outcome of your life so that you don't have free will and don't have the ability to make any real choices. No, the word "predestined" means to set boundaries around something so that it stays on a certain course.

Here's what the Bible says: God chose you in eternity past, and then He predestined—He predetermined in His sovereignty—that you would be adopted as a son or daughter within His household.

This is a critical truth because adoption in the ancient world was different than how we experience adoption today. In Paul's day, children didn't really have any legal rights or status until they reached a certain age—until they became mature. When that time came, the child would be brought forth and officially recognized as an adult, which meant they were granted all the rights and privileges they deserved as an adult within that family.

So what God communicated through this passage of Scripture is that when He chose us in the past, He determined that we would be adopted into His family as mature sons and mature daughters. We would have all of the rights and privileges associated with a member of His family.

That's wonderful news, of course, but here's the really astounding thing: The Bible says because we have been adopted as mature sons and daughters in the family of God, we have the same status with Almighty God as Jesus Christ. We are joint heirs with Him, which means everything Christ has with the Father, we have with the Father.

Try to let that reality sink in. You have been chosen by God. You have been blessed not just with inclusion in His household but also with full adoption as a son or daughter. You are legally and spiritually His child.

We Are Accepted

In July 2021 a video featuring a young man named Kurt Kinley from Normal, Illinois, went viral. At the time of filming, Kurt was 21 years old and working two jobs. He also has Down syndrome. The video captures the moment Kurt opens an acceptance letter from a local community college.

As Kurt takes the letter out of the envelope, you can see the anticipation on his face—as well as the fear. His head swivels from side to side as he reads the first few sentences, and then he raises his arms in triumph. "I'm in! Yeah!" Kurt's laughter and shouts of joy are quickly drowned out by his family and friends gathered around.

After a moment of filming Kurt literally bouncing with joy, his mom asks him to read the letter out loud. Standing with his father, Kurt dutifully reads the first sentence. "We are pleased to inform you that you have been accepted to …"

But that's as far as he gets. Breaking down in tears, Kurt is overwhelmed at the idea that he has been accepted.[2]

As you look around the world today, it's clear that Kurt Kinley is not the only person looking for—in truth, desperate for—acceptance. That's the case for all of us. Acceptance from our parents. Acceptance from our friends and coworkers. Acceptance from the world, which now includes the shadowy specter of social media. And yes, acceptance from God.

Thankfully, those of us who have chosen to follow Jesus can rest assured on that last count. As Paul makes clear in verses 5 and 6, we have already been accepted by our Heavenly Father: "Having predestined us to adoption as sons by Jesus Christ to

Himself, according to the good pleasure of His will, to the praise of the glory of His grace, *by which He made us accepted in the Beloved*" (emphasis added).

Notice that word "Beloved." That is a term that refers to Jesus Christ. There are two times in Scripture when heaven opened and Almighty God said, "This is My beloved Son, in whom I am well pleased" (Matthew 3:17; 17:5). Paul was teaching that you and I, who were chosen and adopted, have also been accepted because of Jesus Christ. We have been accepted in the Beloved.

There is a little bit of poetry I learned a long time ago. It goes like this:

> *So near, so very near to God,*
>
> *I cannot nearer be;*
>
> *for in the person of his Son*
>
> *I am as near as he.*
>
> *So dear, so very dear to God,*
>
> *More dear I cannot be;*
>
> *The love with which he loves the Son,*
>
> *such is his love for me.*[3]

Don't you love that gift? Isn't that a blessing worth treasuring? Almighty God accepts you in the same way He accepts His beloved Son.

We Are Redeemed

Look at the next verse in the longest sentence in the Bible: "In Him we have redemption through His blood, the forgiveness of sins, according to the riches of His grace" (Ephesians 1:7). "Redemption"—that's a word we hear a lot in church, but what does it mean?

In the Greek language Paul used to write this letter, to redeem something meant to buy it back or cause it to be set free. We think of redemption primarily as a theological concept, but it carried more of a financial association in the ancient world. Why? Because redemption always required a price to be paid.

My wife, Donna, and I have had the privilege of traveling around the country. Some years back we stopped in a Southern city and stayed at a hotel. While we were checking in, the concierge said, "Be sure you go and see the market."

I asked, "Why is that so important?" After all, there are markets just about everywhere.

I'll never forget his answer. He said, "Well, just about a block from this hotel is one of the old slave markets where they used to sell and buy slaves. But now they've turned it into a kind of flea market, and you ought to go down there and see."

Well, we went down to see. And I have to tell you, I had the eeriest feeling while we were there. I was walking through a place that represented one of the worst moments in the history of our nation—a period in which men and women created in the image of God were bought and sold like pieces of property. Just like the various goods being marketed and purchased at that flea market today.

That's a terrible thought. A terrible image. But I want you to keep that image in mind as you read Romans 6:17-18: "But God be thanked that though you were slaves of sin, yet you obeyed from the heart that form of doctrine to which you were delivered. And having been set free from sin, you became slaves of righteousness."

The Bible says you and I used to be slaves on the slave market of sin. But one day Almighty God came down to buy us back. Do you know what He used for collateral? The precious blood of Jesus Christ. He brought the precious blood of Christ— the blood that was spilled on the altar of the Cross—and He bought us back so that we could be free from sin.

He redeemed us.

We Are Enlightened

We've come halfway through Paul's extraordinary enumeration of the blessings we have received from God, so let's take a quick inventory. Because of our salvation through Christ, we are chosen, we are adopted, we are accepted, we are redeemed—and now, fifth, we are enlightened.

Verse 7 mentions the "riches" of God's grace, "which He made to abound toward us in all wisdom and prudence, having made known to us the mystery of His will, according to His good pleasure which He purposed in Himself" (verses 8-9). There are two phrases there I want you to notice. First, God's riches and grace "abound toward us in all wisdom and prudence." And then, God has "made known to us the mystery of His will."

Did you know that before you became a Christian, you could not understand God? That's what Scripture says: "But the natural man does not receive the things of the Spirit of God, for they are foolishness to him; nor can he know them, because they are spiritually discerned" (1 Corinthians 2:14).

I've had people tell me all throughout my ministry that they can't understand the Bible. They tried to read it, but they just couldn't follow it. Maybe they tried to pray, but they never found a connection with God. Then those same people became born again, and all of a sudden everything changed. Scripture became clearer. God was present. One guy told me, "Somebody must have rewritten the Bible in the time it took me to get saved, because all of a sudden Scripture started making sense."

That's funny, but that's also what the Bible says. We can't understand God or appreciate His Word when we are disconnected from His presence.

When we are saved, however, one of the gifts God gives us is an enlightened mind that allows us to better comprehend Him and connect with Him. As Paul wrote in Ephesians, we are blessed with "wisdom and prudence." We become attuned to "the mystery of His will."

We Obtain an Inheritance

Paul still wasn't out of breath as he dictated Ephesians 1:3-14, which means there are yet more gifts for you and me to unwrap. The next comes in verses 11-12: "In Him also we have obtained an inheritance, being predestined according to the purpose of Him who works all things according to the counsel of His will, that we who first trusted in Christ should be to the praise of His glory."

As followers of Jesus, we have an inheritance that is reserved especially for us.

Now remember that because we are mature sons and daughters in God—because we have been adopted into His family—we've already received all the rights and privileges that come with that legal status. And one of those rights and privileges is an inheritance. This is a special blessing each of us will receive one day.

What is that inheritance? I don't know for sure. Paul didn't elaborate on the details in the middle of his super sentence. But the apostle Peter did offer a little more in terms of a description of that blessing: "Blessed be the God and Father of our Lord Jesus Christ, who according to His abundant mercy has begotten us again to a living hope through the resurrection of Jesus Christ from the dead, to an inheritance incorruptible and undefiled and that does not fade away, reserved in heaven for you" (1 Peter 1:3-4).

I read a sad story about a woman named Cathy from Astoria, Oregon, who passed away inside a homeless shelter. Much of Cathy's life was difficult. She was addicted to drugs and suffering from mental health issues. She was alone and disconnected, having spent years on the street with no safe place to call home.

In other words, Cathy needed help.

The saddest part of her story is that help was available. Cathy's mom had passed away some years before, leaving her daughter just over $884,000 in inheritance money deposited in a state bank. People had tried to connect Cathy with the money she was owed. There were newspaper ads, and even a private investigator hired to locate her. But Cathy was never found, and the money remained unclaimed at the time of her death.[4]

That won't happen with the inheritance God has promised to us. It is "incorruptible" and "reserved in heaven for you."

We Are Sealed

So far in this chapter we've seen the ways God expressed His love for us in the past. He chose us and predestined us for adoption "before the foundation of the world" (verse 4). We've also seen some of the ways God plans to take care of us in the future. He redeemed us from the power of sin, and He has set apart an inheritance for us that is secure in heaven.

You may be wondering: *What about right now? God loved me in the past and He has plans for my future, but what about today?*

Read verses 13-14: "In Him you also trusted, after you heard the word of truth, the gospel of your salvation; in whom also, having believed, you were sealed with the Holy Spirit of promise, who is the guarantee of our inheritance until the redemption of the purchased possession, to the praise of His glory."

When you became a Christian, the Holy Spirit came to live within your heart. Not physically within the muscle that beats in your chest, of course, but the Holy Spirit connected with what makes you "you" in a way that is both real and immediate—He merged with you and transformed you into something different. A new creation.

That same Holy Spirit serves as a seal that you are God's. He is the guarantee that tells you no matter what is happening in your life, things are going to be okay. God is with you.

The best way I can explain it is what happens when you send a piece of registered mail. When you go to the post office, you fill out a form and give them the letter, and then they stamp a seal on that letter so that nobody can open it without the recipient knowing what happened. The seal provides a guarantee for the authenticity of that letter.

Well, the Bible says the Holy Spirit is the guarantee that what God promised from the past He's going to fulfill in the future. How do I know I'm going to get what God has for me? The Holy Spirit lives in my heart. How do I know the Holy Spirit lives in my heart? Because He witnesses with my spirit that I'm a child of God.

The same is true for all who follow Christ.

We Are Secured

We have been pulling gifts from our spiritual stocking throughout this chapter, but now we've reached the final one. As followers of Jesus, we are chosen, adopted, accepted, redeemed, enlightened, given an inheritance, sealed—and now, finally, we are secured. Look again at verse 14, which describes the Holy Spirit as "the guarantee of our inheritance until the redemption of the purchased possession, to the praise of His glory."

Some older translations of Scripture replace that word "guarantee" with "earnest"—the "earnest of our inheritance" (KJV). The idea, of course, is similar to the practice of offering earnest money in modern real estate.

When you go to make an offer on a home today, you typically include some kind of financial payment alongside that offer. We call it earnest money. By making that payment, you are showing the seller that your offer is serious. You are putting your money where your mouth is.

In a similar way, the Holy Spirit is the earnest money for the inheritance God has secured for each of us in heaven. By blessing us with His Spirit, God has put His money where His mouth is. He has provided part of our inheritance so that we can rest assured—and rest secured—in His provision and care throughout all eternity.

To say all of that in another way, once we receive the blessing of the Holy Spirit in our life, our salvation is secured. The Spirit is proof positive that you and I will be in heaven one day.

I once heard about an old man who was asked to give his testimony in the church where he grew up. So he did. He talked about God until he didn't have anything more to say. He talked about how God had loved him, how God had called him, how God had found him, how God had cleansed him, and how God had filled him. He gave a glorious testimony.

When he finished, there was another man in that church who felt like it was his responsibility to correct the old man's testimony. (God seems to plant two or three of those types of people in every church, though I'm not sure why.) This fellow went up to the old man and said, "I liked your testimony—except you only talked about God's part. You didn't tell anybody about your part."

The old man thought for a moment before he said, "Well, I'll tell you what my part was. I ran away from God as fast as I could, and He ran after me. That's the way it worked."

That's about the way it works for most of us, isn't it? We didn't come begging to God. God came after us, and He made us His own. Before the foundation of the world, He chose us. Then He adopted us into His family. Then He accepted us in the Beloved. Then He redeemed us and forgave us. Then He gave us an inheritance, and He sealed that inheritance through His Holy Spirit.

Cadi Williams was blessed by her neighbor with fourteen gifts for fourteen future Christmases; you and I have been blessed by Almighty God with gifts that will last for all eternity. Let's never forget that! And let's never stop blessing the One who has showered us with so many blessings!

CHAPTER 2

The Secret to Spiritual Power

EPHESIANS 1:15-23

Hurricane Andrew struck the southern tip of Florida as a Category 5 storm in 1992. It was one of the most powerful storms to strike the United States in recorded history, and it caused great devastation across the Caribbean and Gulf regions. Many people were killed, many homes were destroyed, and a huge number of homes were cut off from utility services for weeks—even months.

One home was cut off from the electric grid for fifteen years.

That home belonged to an elderly woman named Norena. After being scammed by an unscrupulous contractor, Norena's house did not qualify for being reconnected to the power grid; it was not up to code. But Norena could not afford to pay for the necessary repairs.

So she simply went about her life. For fifteen years Norena endured the Florida heat without air-conditioning. She showered without hot water. She made do with the reality of being disconnected.

I'm thankful to report that someone eventually discovered the truth of Norena's plight. After a phone call to city officials in Cutler Bay, her hometown, Norena's power was restored. She was reconnected in a matter of hours.[1]

It's a sad reality that many Christians in today's world are disconnected from their source of power—not electricity but spiritual power. They have learned to endure and make do in a powerless situation. Thankfully, like Norena, these followers of Jesus can be reconnected to God's power through a renewed knowledge of and connection to Christ. That is the subject of this chapter.

As a reminder, Paul began the letter we know as Ephesians by expressing a wonderful list of the blessings we have been given through Christ. Because of Jesus, we have been chosen, adopted, and accepted. We are redeemed and enlightened. We have an inheritance in heaven. We have been sealed by the Holy Spirit, and we are secured for our future. Those gifts are available to us at the moment of our salvation.

How did Paul urge his readers to make use of their spiritual blessings? Not by delivering a lesson or a lecture but by praying for them. Indeed, while Ephesians 1:3-14 represent a long section of praise, verses 15-23 are a long section of prayer—one of two important prayers in this letter.

Paul spelled out the occasion for this prayer in verses 15-16: "Therefore I also, after I heard of your faith in the Lord Jesus and your love for all the saints, do not cease to give thanks for you, making mention of you in my prayers."

As always, pay attention to the word "therefore." Because the Ephesian Christians had been given such remarkable gifts by God the Father, "therefore"—for that reason—Paul regularly took the time and made the effort to pray for them. Why? So they would not waste those gifts. So they would not squander everything they had received in Christ. That was the reason for Paul's prayer.

We learn about the object or purpose of Paul's prayer in verse 17: "That the God of our Lord Jesus Christ, the Father of glory, may give to you the spirit of wisdom and revelation in the knowledge of Him." Because they had received a myriad of blessings through Christ, Paul wanted to make sure the believers in Ephesus maintained their connection to Christ—that they continued in "the knowledge of Him."

That's the background for Paul's prayer in verses 15-23. As we explore those verses together throughout this chapter, you'll see that Paul's goal was to empower his hearers—both the Christians in Ephesus and those who follow Jesus today. He wanted to empower us by helping us understand the gift of knowing and being known by Jesus Christ.

Let's not waste that gift as we continue our exploration of the book of Ephesians!

The Priority of Knowing Christ

The first way Paul sought to empower followers of Jesus through his prayer was by reminding them about the blessing of knowing Jesus—not simply knowing *about* Jesus.

We live in a world that is increasingly filled with and focused on knowledge. On facts. On information. Because of the Internet and other advances in technology, there are very few limits to what any person can understand in terms of data, dates, and definitions. It's all accessible at our fingertips at any moment, day or night.

But as I'm sure you understand, knowledge does have its limits. This is especially true when it comes to knowing other people in the context of relationships.

Here's a quick example of what I mean. There are sports fans across the world today who can tell you almost everything about their favorite athletes. They know how many touchdowns a person has scored, how fast he or she can run, how much they are being paid on their current contract, and so on. And now, because of social media, fans can research the types of clothes their favorite athletes prefer to wear, the food they like to eat, the movies they attend, and more. Even so, the vast majority of those fans have no actual connection to the athletes they admire. Those fans can collect statistics, but they have no personal knowledge. No intimacy. No relationship.

The same can be true of our connection with God, which is a major problem. Why? Because God is a Person! Our God is not a conglomeration of doctrines and dogmas for us to memorize. No, He is a Person we have the opportunity to know. And He has revealed Himself to us through Jesus Christ.

Look again at what Paul wrote in verse 17. In his prayer for the Ephesians, he specifically desired "that the God of our Lord Jesus Christ, the Father of glory, may give to you the spirit of wisdom and revelation in the knowledge of Him."

"Revelation" is an important word because without revelation there is no relationship. As human beings, all of us have been created in God's image. Yet because of our sin—because of our rebellion against God both corporately and individually—we are separated from God with no way to approach Him. That is the tragedy of the human condition apart from Christ. Yet God did not allow us to remain separated. Instead, He revealed Himself to us. He made it possible for us not only to perceive Him but also to know Him and establish a relationship with Him.

The "spirit of … revelation" Paul mentioned works in two important ways. First, God reveals Himself to us through His Word. How did we get the Bible? God, through His Spirit, revealed it to us. Yes, it's true that God used the personalities and experiences of human beings as scribes for the Scriptures. But ultimately it was the Holy Spirit working through those human authors to create the Bible in a similar way to how you or I might use a pen to create a list.

But that's not the end of God's special revelation. He has also placed His Spirit in our hearts. What that means is that any time you or I encounter God's Word, a two-way communication occurs. Almighty God has revealed the truth of Himself in His Word through the inspiration of the Holy Spirit. Then, He placed the Holy Spirit inside believers so that whenever we read His Word, we can understand it. We can be changed by it. We have "the spirit of wisdom and revelation in the knowledge of Him."

I fear many modern believers don't appreciate that gift. In today's world, we often approach the Bible primarily as a devotional experience. We sip at God's Word in the same way we sip our coffee, seeking a quick taste of encouragement or truth or inspiration. We look for a verse or a passage that will tickle our spiritual fancy—maybe something pithy we can post on social media.

Now, I want to be very careful here, because there is nothing wrong with "devotionals" or posting Scripture passages on Facebook or other social media platforms. There is nothing harmful about seeking a quick burst of wisdom or encouragement from God's Word when we need it. The Bible can be used as a devotional tool—a devotional experience—and that practice can be helpful in our lives.

But look at that word I used earlier: *primarily*. We harm ourselves and our spiritual lives when we approach the Bible *primarily* as a devotional tool or a devotional experience—as a "quick fix."

God wants more for our experiences with His Word. He wants us to find more than a sip of inspiration as we briefly skim through Scripture before moving on with the rest of our lives. Specifically, God wants us to approach the Bible in a way that enables us to know Christ. That's why He gave us His Word, to reveal Himself to us. Our primary experience with the Bible should be to saturate ourselves regularly in God's Word so that we know God Himself—so that we know Him relationally. We can know who He is and what He values when we immerse ourselves in Scripture.

The Possibility of Knowing Christ

The second way Paul sought to empower the Ephesians was by reminding them about the possibility of knowing Christ. And that's key. Because even if something is a priority—even if it's the most important thing in the world—we can't achieve a priority that is not possible.

Make no mistake: It is impossible for us to know God in and of ourselves. It is impossible for us to connect with God using our own strength or our own resources or our own righteousness. The apostle Paul made that clear later in his epistle to the Ephesians when he wrote, "At that time you were without Christ, being aliens from the commonwealth of Israel and strangers from the covenants of promise, having no hope and without God in the world" (2:12).

Hundreds of years before Paul, the prophet Isaiah offered this stark and startling picture of our spiritual situation as human beings: "Behold, the Lord's hand is not shortened, that it cannot save; nor His ear heavy, that it cannot hear. But your iniquities have separated you from your God; and your sins have hidden His face from you, so that He will not hear" (Isaiah 59:1-2).

Isaiah was writing to the Jewish residents of Judah who were expecting God to save them from their enemies despite their own rebellion against Him. Yet the principle applies to all people: Sin separates us from God.

Thankfully, there is a way to bridge that separation. Look at what Paul wrote in his prayer for the Ephesians: "That the God of our Lord Jesus Christ, the Father of glory, may give to you the spirit of wisdom and revelation in the knowledge of Him, *the eyes of your understanding being enlightened*" (1:17-18, emphasis added).

The word "understanding" can literally be translated as "heart." Paul prayed about "the eyes of your [heart] being enlightened." It's through that essential part of our being—through our heart—that we can know Jesus.

But how is it possible for you and me to know Jesus in spite of our sin? Paul explains it in a word found in verse 18—"enlightened."

I've noticed it's become more common in recent years for companies to install motion-sensing lights in their buildings. I've seen them in offices, in churches, and in homes. These aren't a security feature, like the floodlights on the outside of your house that warn you of possible intruders at night. Instead, these are the regular lights found in offices, conference rooms, and other meeting spaces. The idea is for the lights to stay off when people are not using those spaces, which saves on energy costs. But as soon as a person walks in the room, their presence is detected, and the lights come on.

Well, in our natural, sinful state, we as human beings live in spiritual darkness. We cannot even perceive spiritual things, let alone connect with God. Scripture says, "The natural man does not receive the things of the Spirit of God, for they are foolishness to him" (1 Corinthians 2:14). We are living in the dark.

But when the Holy Spirit enters our hearts, it's like walking into one of those modern conference rooms. The lights come on. Because of His presence, our hearts can be "enlightened." We can know Christ. We can understand and apply God's Word. We can grow and develop spiritually. These are blessings of unspeakable value!

The Purpose of Knowing Christ

Paul's prayer at the end of Ephesians 1 is a reminder for believers to continue developing their relationship with Christ— to know Him. That is our first priority, and that is possible because of the Holy Spirit's work in our life.

But why? What is the purpose of knowing Christ? What is the purpose of continuing to develop our relationship with Him after the moment of salvation—after our eternal future has been secured? That is the question we will explore as we wrap up this chapter.

Here's what Paul communicated about the purpose of knowing Christ:

> That you may know what is the hope of His calling, what are the riches of the glory of His inheritance in the saints, and what is the exceeding greatness of His power toward us who believe, according to the working of His mighty power which He worked in Christ when He raised Him from the dead and seated Him at His right hand in the heavenly places, far above all principality and power and might and dominion, and every name that is named, not only in this age but also in that which is to come. And He put all things under His feet, and gave Him to be head over all things to the church, which is His body, the fullness of Him who fills all in all. (Ephesians 1:18-23)

As believers, we know Jesus has saved us. We know He's forgiven us and redeemed us—we saw that in the previous chapter, and those truths are important. But the verses above offer three specific reasons for continuing to know Christ as we live out our destinies here on earth. Fair warning: These reasons might surprise you because they are not the typical teachings we hear about Christ.

To Know the Promise He Has Made to Us

The first reason Paul gave for continuing to know and deepen our connection with Jesus is "that you may know what is the hope of His calling" (verse 18). I want to focus for a moment on that word "hope." But first, a quick story.

On July 30, 2016, Luke Aikins jumped out of an airplane that was flying at 25,000 feet. For many of us, that would be a big deal—a moment of horror or exhilaration, depending on our personality type. Yet Luke is a professional skydiver. By that time in his career, he had participated in a staggering 18,000 jumps! So the act of stepping out of a plane in flight was nothing new.

What was new on this particular day, however, was Luke's equipment. More specifically, his lack of equipment. On that clear July afternoon over Southern California, Luke Aikins became the first person in history to jump out of a plane without a parachute or a wingsuit.

It took just over two minutes for Luke to plummet from the sky to the ground, reaching a maximum velocity of 120 miles per hour. A few hundred feet before impact, Luke tucked his chin to his chest and rolled over so that his eyes were facing upward. Then he struck—not the ground, but a specialized net suspended two hundred feet above the earth. Dubbed "the Fly Trap," the net absorbed and dispersed the kinetic energy of Luke's impact, allowing him to survive the fall without a scratch.

Luke Aikins's jaw-dropping stunt was the main feature of a television spectacle called *Heaven Sent*, which was broadcasted live on national television. "My whole life has been about air, aviation, flying, jumping, all that stuff," Luke said prior to his jump. "I'm out here to show that there are ways to do things that people think are insane and aren't able to be done."[2]

Can you relate to Luke Aikins? If that question shocks or surprises you, take a moment to think it through. As a believer in Jesus, you are also "heaven sent." You are hurtling through this life day after day, doing your best to steer yourself toward a specific goal: eternal life.

If I were Luke Aikins, I would do everything possible to inspect and approve "the Fly Trap" apparatus before I stepped onto that plane. I would make sure every possible scenario had been covered, and every back-up system was in place and functioning at optimal capacity.

In a similar way, you and I are relying on a measure of hope as we hurtle toward eternity. Thankfully, our hope is not in ourselves. We don't need to place or invest that hope in our own ability to build a safety net for our future, or in our government, or in humanity as a whole.

No, our hope is in God! When we talk about our future prospects, they are grounded in Him.

God has a plan for your life. And "the hope of His calling," as Paul phrased it, stretches out into the future in a way that is special and amazing. John was thinking about this hope when he wrote, "Beloved, now we are children of God; and it has not yet been revealed what we shall be, but we know that when He is revealed, we shall be like Him, for we shall see Him as He is" (1 John 3:2).

Did you know that part of the hope of your calling is that one day you are going to be with Jesus and the Bible says you are going to be like Him? You are going to be like Him in perfect righteousness. You will be holy, without sin, and blameless. Just like Him. That is part of your prospects for the future.

To Know the Pleasure He Takes in Us

The second reason for continuing to invest ourselves in knowing Christ even after salvation is so that we can continue to experience the pleasure God takes in us. Did you know God likes you? Did you know Jesus enjoys knowing you? It's true!

Continuing with verse 18, Paul wanted the Ephesians to know "what are the riches of the glory of His inheritance in the saints."

Earlier in chapter 1 Paul mentioned our inheritance in Christ, which is sealed and secure. In this passage, he reused that same word in a different way. He wrote that we—those of us who believe, those of us who make up the universal Church— are Almighty God's inheritance. We are the inheritance of Jesus Christ. What that means is that when Jesus Christ looks out over the world and sees His followers, His believers, He looks at us as His special treasure. We are His inheritance, and we are precious to Him.

I know there are many in today's world who struggle with self-esteem issues. They wonder if they are valued by others. The answer is yes! You are valued by God. As we saw in chapter 1, you are chosen and accepted. And now, Paul prayed that the

Ephesians would know the pleasure God takes in them, in us. We as followers of Jesus are the special treasure of God. He loves us so much that He gave His own Son to die for us. He purchased each one of us out of the market of sin, redeeming us with His precious blood.

Psalm 149 says it this way: "For the Lord takes pleasure in His people" (verse 4). Remember that the next time you are feeling a little discouraged. God takes pleasure in you, in knowing you. His love didn't end when you accepted Him. You became a part of His forever family at that moment, and you please Him even now.

To Know the Power He Can Release in Us

As Paul prayed for the Christians in Ephesus (and by extension for us), he wanted them to know the prospects God had in store for them, he wanted them to know the pleasure God takes in them, and he wanted them to know and experience the power that God desired to release in them and through them.

In fact, as you read the end of Paul's prayer in verses 19-23, which is also the end of Ephesians 1, you can see it is all about power.

Jesus Christ is the source of your power as a Christian. And He wants that power to be exhibited in your life. I think Almighty God is grieved when He sees Christians walking around constantly defeated all the time, always falling on their faces.

I remember hearing somebody say that the Christian life is falling down and getting up, falling down and getting up, falling down and getting up—all the way to heaven. Well, that may be true, but I'm not sure that's the way it should be. Obviously, we do fall down. But we fall down a whole lot more than we should, and we stay down a lot longer than we ought.

Why do I say that? Because we have power through Christ! And Paul says that power is wrapped up and illustrated in four ways.

First is the power of Christ's resurrection. Paul wrote about "the exceeding greatness of His power toward us who believe, according to the working of His mighty power which He worked in Christ when He raised Him from the dead" (verses 19-20). The same power that was evident when Christ came out of the grave is available to you and to me.

Believe me, that is a lot of power! The Greek word Paul used to describe that power is *dynamis*, which describes something with latent or inherent power—especially the power for performing miracles. That power is made possible by the resurrection of Jesus, and that power is available to us.

Second is the power of Christ's ascension. Verse 20 reminds us that God brought Christ out of the grave "and seated Him at His right hand in the heavenly places." Think about that. Almighty God didn't just raise Jesus from the depths of the grave up to ground level. No, He raised Him from the depths of the grave up to ground level, then took Him all the way to heaven in glory.

That is the same power you and I have in our lives.

Third is the power of Christ's exultation. Look again at verses 21-22: God exalted Jesus "far above all principality and power and might and dominion, and every name that is named, not only in this age but also in that which is to come. And He put all things under His feet, and gave Him to be head over all things to the church."

That's similar to the fourth expression of power Paul wanted the Ephesians to remember, and that's *the power of Christ's position*. Verses 22-23 say, "And He put all things under His feet, and gave Him to be head over all things to the church, which is His body, the fullness of Him who fills all in all."

Plug Into the Power of God

There is nobody above Jesus. He is over every name, every principality, every power, every authority. There is no one to whom He answers. He is the ultimate power in the universe. And we're in Christ! His power is available to us.

Paul wanted his readers to see that Christ has conquered everything, so why should we be afraid? Why should we live in defeat? Jesus is the King of kings. Satan and sin and the grave are all defeated enemies. As Paul wrote in Philippians 2: "Therefore God also has highly exalted Him and given Him the name which is above every name, that at the name of Jesus every knee should bow, of those in heaven, and of those on earth, and of those under the earth, and that every tongue should confess that Jesus Christ is Lord, to the glory of God the Father" (verses 9-11).

You know what that says to me? If Almighty God is the ultimate power and He's my friend through Jesus Christ, then there's not anything in my life He can't handle. Not a thing. Let me tell you what I mean.

There is no sinner who is beyond His rescue. I've heard people say they are convinced they could never be saved because of the depth of their sins. But let me ask you this question: If Jesus

Christ has been exalted to the right hand of the Father and there is no power that is greater than Him and He is our resource, is He able to rescue that person who is really messed up?

Absolutely!

You may think, *I'm not sure I'm even a candidate for salvation. I don't even know how you get into the candidate status.*

Well, you are a candidate because Almighty God through Jesus Christ wants to show His power in your life. Sometimes He does that by taking someone who is so far down, deeper than in the grave, and He exalts that person, lifts him up, and brings him into a saving relationship.

There is a verse in the book of Hebrews that I love. The reason I love this verse is because it uses a little phrase that is special to me: "He is able." The word "able" is a power word. It means God's got power. He can do it.

Here is the whole verse: "He is also able to save to the uttermost those who come to God through Him, since He always lives to make intercession for them" (Hebrews 7:25).

If you wonder if you are savable, let me just say to you: Almighty God says Jesus Christ is able to save you! There's no one who is beyond rescue with God. Almighty God is able to lift you up, and you can become part of His family.

There is no saint who is beyond recovery. Sometimes after being redeemed and forgiven, the life of a Christian gets entangled in sin—they think they've blown it with God; they think there is no recovery. They act like a person whom God has cured of cancer but who can't trust Him to heal a common cold.

God has already done the biggest thing by forgiving our sins, yet some people can't seem to trust Him to restore them when they stumble and fall. Christ's power is sufficient not only to rescue you but also to restore you no matter what you've done.

In his book *The Divine Conspiracy*, the late philosopher Dallas Willard described growing up as a child in a rural area of Missouri that had no electricity. But then one year, the Rural Electrification Administration extended its network of power lines into Willard's community, bringing the possibility of electrical power to the households and farms there.

Willard recollects the completely new style of life that electrical power represented. He was given a whole new view on daylight and darkness. Hot and cold. Work and leisure. Even so, embracing that new lifestyle meant turning away from the old.

"We had to turn away from kerosene lamps, lanterns, iceboxes and cellars and toward all that electricity could provide for us." Everything was available for connection to this new world—yet some in Willard's community would not embrace it. "The power that could make our lives far better was right there in front of us. Strangely, some did not accept it. Some did not want to change."[3]

In the same way, God's power is available to us all. The big question is, will you pour your life into believing it, understanding it, and taking the practical steps involved in relying on it? Will you plug into the power of God?

FOR BY GRACE YOU HAVE
BEEN SAVED THROUGH
FAITH, AND THAT NOT OF
YOURSELVES; IT IS THE
GIFT OF GOD, NOT OF
WORKS, LEST ANYONE
SHOULD BOAST.

EPHESIANS 2:8-9

CHAPTER 3

Salvation Pure and Simple

EPHESIANS 2:1-9

LynLee Boemer is known throughout the medical community as the baby who was born twice. Her story began when LynLee's mother, Margaret, visited her doctor for a routine ultrasound when she was sixteen weeks along in her pregnancy. Doctors saw something out of place on the scan. After review, they determined Margaret's baby was afflicted with a sacrococcygeal teratoma—a tumor growing from her tiny tailbone.

By the time Margaret Boemer was 23 weeks along, the tumor was almost as large as LynLee herself. The situation was grim. "LynLee didn't have much of a chance," said Margaret. "The tumor was shutting her heart down and causing her to go into cardiac failure, so it was a choice of allowing the tumor to take over her body or giving her a chance at life. It was an easy decision for us: We wanted to give her life."

Dr. Darrell Cass and his team at the Texas Children's Fetal Center got to work. First, they performed an emergency surgery to gain access to LynLee within her mother's womb. In a technical sense, baby LynLee was "born" during that surgery. She was removed from the womb. "The fetus is outside, like completely out," Dr. Cass explained. "All the amniotic fluid falls out. It's actually fairly dramatic."

Once the tumor was removed, the surgeons placed LynLee back in her mother's womb and took extra care to seal everything up as tightly as possible. "It's kind of a miracle you're able to open the uterus like that and seal it all back and the whole thing works," said Cass.

A miracle indeed! Returned to the womb, baby LynLee remained there for another three months before doctors removed her once more through a C-section. Her second birth was much less dramatic than her first, and her parents took home a healthy, happy baby just a few weeks later.[1]

While the concept of a second birth may seem new or surprising to many people, it should not be so for followers of Christ. Remember what Jesus declared to Nicodemus in John 3: "Most assuredly, I say to you, unless one is born again, he cannot see the kingdom of God" (verse 3).

In this way, little LynLee Boemer offers a dramatic picture of the Christian doctrine we call salvation. And it's that doctrine— that wonderful blessing of salvation—that we're going to explore here as we take a closer look at the beginning of the second chapter in Paul's epistle to the Ephesians.

Paul concluded his prayer at the end of Ephesians 1 by focusing on God's power as expressed through Jesus Christ—

the power of Jesus' resurrection, His ascension to heaven, His exultation, and His position over every other name or power or principality. Then in Ephesians 2, Paul worked to remind the believers in Ephesus about how they had been changed because of that same power.

That's an important nuance as we look through verses 1-9 together in this chapter. Paul wasn't writing to non-believers in an effort to push them toward salvation. Instead, he was writing to Christians—to people who had already been saved—so that they would remember everything God had done for them.

What we're about to explore together in Ephesians 2:1-9 may be the most concise presentation of the Gospel in all of God's Word. If you want to know what it means to become a Christian, to experience the blessing of salvation, these verses are the place to look.

The Reason for Salvation

First, let's address the reason why salvation is necessary in the first place. Why is it that we must be rescued by someone other than ourselves? Why is it that God Almighty has to reach down to save us? Why can't we, as many of the other religions of the world teach, continue to climb up upon our own good works and ultimately earn God's favor?

Paul answered those questions in verses 1-3:

And you He made alive, who were dead in trespasses and sins, in which you once walked according to the course of this world, according to the prince of the power of the air, the spirit who now works in the sons of disobedience,

among whom also we all once conducted ourselves in the
lusts of our flesh, fulfilling the desires of the flesh and of
the mind, and were by nature children of wrath, just as
the others.

These verses are as blunt as they are powerful. Through five
definitive terms, Paul established once and for all why human
beings must rely on God for salvation. I want to focus on each of
those terms together.

We Were Dead

First of all, we are unable to save ourselves because we are
spiritually dead without Christ. Ephesians 2:1 says, "And you He
made alive, who were dead in trespasses and sins."

According to God's Word, every human being who does
not have a relationship with God through faith in Jesus Christ
is spiritually dead. They are dead toward God and the things of
God. That means they can't communicate with God—they are
deaf to His voice and His guidance. As we saw in the previous
chapter, that means they cannot understand God's Word. The
Bible is foolishness to those who are not spiritually alive.

Paul said we were "dead in trespasses and sins." There is a
connection between those concepts. Sin and death are partners,
which is why Paul wrote in another epistle that "the wages of sin
is death" (Romans 6:23). Apart from Christ we are dead in our
sins, and that condition begins at birth.

R. Kent Hughes notes, "The Biblical view is that man is not
well or sick but dead—'dead in [his] trespasses and sins.' All
man's self-help will avail nothing! You can play reveille in the

Arlington National Cemetery for a whole year, but you will get no response from the dead soldiers there."[2]

We Were Deceived

Not only were we spiritually dead before we encountered Christ, but we were deceived. We were living out a lie. Having already mentioned our trespasses and sins, Paul added, "You once walked according to the course of this world, according to the prince of the power of the air" (Ephesians 2:2).

Because we were dead in our trespasses and sins, we walked according to the course of this world. That means we walked within the guidelines and the boundaries of the system that operates our world. We were like zombies—dead men and women walking around, living our lives according to whatever the ruler of this world wanted us to do.

That brings up an interesting question: Who is in charge of this world? Who is running the show right now on planet Earth?

Many people would answer that question by pointing to God. And in a technical sense, they are correct. God is sovereign over the entire universe. He is the Creator and Sustainer of all things, which means He does have control over all things. On the ultimate level, He is in charge of our world.

But on a practical level, God has given control of this world over to Satan—"the prince of the power of the air." Satan is the prince, and the demons at his command are "the power of the air." Satan has a whole system of evil at work in the world today. In fact, when you read the book of Daniel, you get the impression that there are demons assigned to specific nations and regions all over our world.

So, the system and the machinations of our world are currently ruled by evil forces, and we were a willing participant in that system before we became saved. Most of us didn't realize what was going on. We thought we were just living our lives, trying to do our best. But we were participating in a Satan-led rebellion against God.

We were deceived.

We Were Disobedient

Not only were we deceived, but we were also actively disobedient to God. At the end of verse 2, Paul mentioned "the spirit who now works in the sons of disobedience." Before we encountered Christ, we actively and willingly rejected what we knew to be right.

Do you remember the old slogan from Burger King? "Have it your way." Those commercials used to be all over both radio and television. "When you have it your way, it just tastes better."

Before salvation, we wanted to have it our own way when it came to just about every aspect of our lives, including our eternal destinies. That's why you still have people walking around today saying, "I deserve to go to heaven because I'm a good person. I'm a good husband and father. I donate money to charity." Those who are outside of God's plan are desperate to create their own rules and their own system of morality.

Now, when Paul talked about "the sons of disobedience," he wasn't only referring to our disobedience against God. He was also referring to our failure to meet our own systems. When people say they deserve eternal life because they are a good person, that means they are setting a standard for themselves—to be good. But we cannot even match our own standards!

Before Christ, we were disobedient to God and disobedient even to the moral systems we were trying to build.

We Were Defiled

In verse 3, Paul continued to use strong words and blunt images to describe our lives apart from Christ. He said we were sons and daughters of disobedience, "among whom also we all once conducted ourselves in the lusts of our flesh, fulfilling the desires of the flesh and of the mind."

In other words, we were defiled. We were driven by our "lusts" and by "the desires of the flesh."

Importantly, Paul was not limiting these descriptions to sex and sexuality. The word "lusts" refers to any kind of unbridled desire—throwing ourselves into doing whatever we want in any number of circumstances. How many people today do you see living only for themselves and caring only for their own selfish needs? That's the way we are until God gets a hold of us.

Now, you might say, "Aren't there great philanthropists who don't follow Christ?" Yes, there are. But if you go behind their gift to explore their motives, you will discover that even the best things we do apart from God are self-centered and self-serving.

The Bible says, "All our righteousnesses are like filthy rags" (Isaiah 64:6). Apart from God, we are defiled.

We Were Doomed

Now at this point in the chapter, I can imagine you might be feeling discouraged. Maybe even upset. Maybe you're thinking,

I didn't read this book, Dr. Jeremiah, to hear you tell me I'm dead, deceived, disobedient, and defiled!

I understand! And the very good news is that you and I are none of those things—not any longer. Remember, Paul was describing what the Ephesians (and by extension us) were like before they experienced the blessing of salvation through faith in Jesus Christ. He was writing to believers, and he was encouraging them to look back over their shoulders and remember what their lives used to be like.

The fifth factor that defines the lives of unbelievers is that they are doomed. Paul said not only are unbelievers defiled by the desires of the flesh, but also "by nature children of wrath, just as the others" (verse 3).

Whenever you feel tempted to take pride in the fact that you're a Christian, remember where you came from. Each one of us was separated from God with no hope of rescue. We were children of wrath. We were doomed.

That's the reason why God had to reach into our lives and make a pathway for our salvation.

The Remedy of Salvation

Oh, how I love the way Paul started the next section of his letter in verse 4! In verses 1-3, he described all the reasons why we have no hope apart from Christ—that we were dead, deceived, disobedient, defiled, and doomed. We were afloat in an ocean of our own sin with no way to get ourselves back to shore. We were done.

"But God." In many ways, those are the two greatest words in Scripture. You could say those two words summarize the entire theme and message of God's Word.

- Adam and Eve were lost forever because of their sin—but God.

- Noah deserved to be drowned along with the rest of the world—but God.

- Jonah did nothing to deserve a second chance—but God.

- Humanity deserved complete and total wrath after crucifying the Savior of the world—but God.

The late James Montgomery Boice said, "If you understand those two words—'but God'—they will save your soul. If you recall them daily and live by them, they will transform your life completely."[3]

Throughout all of history, God has made all the difference. While the reason we need salvation is spelled out in Ephesians 2:1-3, the first two words of verse 4 point to our only hope: "But God." He is our remedy.

Speaking of remedy, the NPR broadcaster Ira Glass made some news a few years back when he claimed to have discovered the secret recipe for Coca-Cola. Glass had stumbled across an article from the *Atlanta Journal-Constitution* written in 1979 that contained a photograph from an old book of pharmacist recipes. Coca-Cola was originally a medicinal recipe sold at drug stores, and Glass believed he had found the original ingredients.

"I am not kidding," Glass told his radio listeners on *This American Life*, rustling a piece of paper into his microphone. "One of the most famously guarded trade secrets on the planet: I have it right here and I am going to read it to you. I am going to read it to the world."[4]

It's unlikely we'll ever know whether the recipe Ira Glass read on the radio was actually the secret to Coca-Cola's success. But as we read through Ephesians 2:4-9, we can discover something infinitely better: the recipe for God's remedy of salvation. That recipe has five key ingredients, and I want to highlight them for you here.

Here is the full recipe for the salvation we have been offered through Christ:

> But God, who is rich in mercy, because of His great love with which He loved us, even when we were dead in trespasses, made us alive together with Christ (by grace you have been saved), and raised us up together, and made us sit together in the heavenly places in Christ Jesus, that in the ages to come He might show the exceeding riches of His grace in His kindness toward us in Christ Jesus. For by grace you have been saved through faith, and that not of yourselves; it is the gift of God, not of works, lest anyone should boast. (Ephesians 2:4-9)

Rich Mercy

As you can see, the first ingredient in that recipe is "mercy." Paul reminded his readers that God is "rich in mercy."

Now, "mercy" is a term we use frequently in our society, and it means withholding a penalty that is deserved. That's mercy. Many people talk about their desire for justice in our culture. "We want justice!" Trust me, my friend, when it comes to God and our eternal future, we don't want justice. We want His mercy.

Thankfully, God has extended that mercy to us freely. We don't even have to ask for it—we can simply receive it. We can avoid receiving what we deserve.

There is a wonderful psalm from the Old Testament that illustrates God's mercy in a lovely way. Here it is, written by the hand of David under the inspiration of the Holy Spirit:

> The Lord is merciful and gracious,
> Slow to anger, and abounding in mercy.
> He will not always strive with us,
> Nor will He keep His anger forever.
> He has not dealt with us according to our sins,
> Nor punished us according to our iniquities.
> For as the heavens are high above the earth,
> So great is His mercy toward those who fear Him;
> As far as the east is from the west,
> So far has He removed our transgressions from us.
> (Psalm 103:8-12)

God Almighty is rich in mercy, which is why mercy is the first ingredient in His remedy for our salvation.

Great Love

The second ingredient is love. Notice what Paul said later in verse 4: "But God, who is rich in mercy, because of His great love with which He loved us."

Why has God given us His mercy? Because He loves us. Why does He love us? Because God is love. Remember, it's not because of anything we've done that God reached out to offer us His remedy of salvation. You and I don't deserve to be loved—not by God. But He loves us anyway. Scripture makes that clear.

The world's most famous Bible verse is all about that love: "For God so loved the world that He gave His only begotten Son, that whoever believes in Him should not perish but have everlasting life" (John 3:16). Romans 5:8 says, "But God demonstrates His own love toward us, in that while we were still sinners, Christ died for us." And 1 John says, "In this the love of God was manifested toward us, that God has sent His only begotten Son into the world, that we might live through Him. In this is love, not that we loved God, but that He loved us and sent His Son to be the propitiation for our sins" (4:9-10).

Do you see the reason why we aren't stuck in our death and disobedience and defilement? Only because God is rich in mercy and He has great love.

Rich Grace

The third ingredient in God's not-so-secret formula for salvation is grace. In fact, three times Paul talked about God's great grace. In verse 5 he said, "By grace you have been saved." In verse 7 he said, "That in the ages to come He might show the exceeding riches of His grace." And in verse 8, "For by grace you have been saved."

I just showed you that God's mercy prevents us from receiving what we deserve. Well, God's grace is the other side of the coin—it means God blesses us by giving us what we don't deserve. God keeps back the penalty we've earned for ourselves, and then He gives us His own righteousness, which we could never hope to achieve.

As always, Christ is the vehicle through which we have received God's grace. As I've mentioned many times, grace can be defined as "God's Riches At Christ's Expense."

Isn't it interesting that Paul was so effusive about God's grace in these verses? He mentioned in several times, almost as if he couldn't contain himself when he got close to that subject. Can you guess why that may have been the case? Yes, because Paul needed a lot of grace! Just like you and me, Paul had transgressed against Almighty God in major ways.

Denise Banderman tells the story of taking a final exam at Hannibal-LaGrange College in Missouri. When she arrived at class, all of the students were anxiously doing their last minute review. The teacher arrived and told the nervous students that they were responsible for everything they had covered in class and everything they had read in the book—something Denise knew she could never achieve.

Then the teacher handed out the test face down before instructing everyone to start. To Denise's amazement, when she turned over the test, every answer was filled in. Her name was even written on the exam in red ink. The bottom of the last page said: "This is the end of the exam. All the answers on your test are correct. You will receive an A …. The reason you passed the test is because the creator of the test took the test for you. All the work you did in preparation for this test did not help you get the A. You have just experienced … grace."

Then the professor said, "Some things you learn from lectures, some things you learn from research, but some things you can only learn from experience. You've just experienced grace. One hundred years from now, if you know Jesus Christ as your personal Savior, your name will be written down in a book, and you will have had nothing to do with writing it there. That will be the ultimate grace experience."[5]

Look at what Paul wrote to Timothy: "Although I was formerly a blasphemer, a persecutor, and an insolent man; but I obtained mercy because I did it ignorantly in unbelief. And the grace of our Lord was exceedingly abundant, with faith and love which are in Christ Jesus" (1 Timothy 1:13-14).

You and I may never have physically persecuted God's people, but we share Paul's desperate need for God's grace.

Free Gift

The fourth ingredient in God's recipe for salvation is not so much an ingredient but rather a price: free. Paul wrote, "For by grace you have been saved through faith, and that not of yourselves; it is the gift of God" (Ephesians 2:8).

I know it sounds too good to be true. I know we've been told over and over that there's no such thing as a free lunch. But the reality remains the same: God has offered the gift of salvation to any who would receive it, including you and me. And He has offered it for free.

Of course, like any gift, salvation must be accepted.

My wife, Donna, gave me a watch for Christmas a few years back. I love this watch. It was a beautiful gift, and I treasure it to this day.

But suppose on that Christmas morning, right after I opened the watch for the first time, I placed it back in its box. Then I rewrapped it in the lovely paper she had picked out. Suppose I said, "Sweetheart, this is a wonderful watch. I really love it. But I'd like you to hold on to it for now, and maybe someday in the future when I really need to know what time it is, I'll decide to take it."

How would she respond? Such a thing would have broken her loving heart. She's already paid for a gift and taken the time to prepare it for me and give it to me with love. *Why won't he take it?*

The same is true with God's free gift of salvation. The price has already been paid through the blood of Jesus Christ. The gift has been offered—every person in the world can accept forgiveness for his or her sin and find security for his or her eternal future. But that decision must be made. The gift must be accepted.

How do we accept the gift of salvation? What does that look like? Well, that's the final ingredient in God's remedy for our life.

Through Faith

We receive the gift of salvation through faith. We cannot receive that gift by "works"—by our own efforts to earn God's approval. Paul went to great lengths to explain that truth to the Ephesians. "For by grace you have been saved through faith, and that not of yourselves," he wrote. "It is the gift of God, not of works, lest anyone should boast" (2:8-9).

You say, "That's great Dr. Jeremiah. But what is faith? What does that look like to accept God's gift of salvation through faith?"

There's a little acrostic I often use to explain what faith is:

Forsaking
All
I
Trust
Him

Faith means you bet eternity on Jesus Christ. It means not just saying you believe in Him but living like it—following in His footsteps as a disciple. Faith means we forsake our will and our priorities for life so that we can follow God's will and obey His priorities.

Charles Spurgeon described faith this way:

Your condition is like that of a child in a burning house, who, having escaped to the edge of the window, hung on by the windowsill. The flames were pouring out of the window underneath, and the poor lad would soon be burnt, or falling would be dashed to pieces; he therefore held on with the clutch of death. He did not dare to relax his grasp until a strong man stood underneath, and said, "Boy! Drop! Drop! I'll catch you." Now, it was no saving faith for the boy to believe that the man was strong—that was a good help towards faith—but he might have known that and yet have perished; it was faith when the boy let go and dropped down into his big friend's arms.

There are you, sinner, clinging to your sins or to your good works. The Savior cries, "Drop! Drop into my arms!" It is not doing, it is leaving off doing. It is not working, it is trusting in that work which Jesus has already done. Trust! That is the word, simple, solid, hearty, earnest trust. Trust and it will not take an hour to save you, the moment you trust you are saved.[6]

That is our remedy for salvation. Those are the ingredients: rich mercy, great love, and great grace all wrapped into a free gift that we receive through faith. As you can see, salvation is all about God. It was purchased by Him and offered by Him, and our only part is to receive.

I'm sure you remember the story of the Chilean miners who were trapped beneath two thousand feet of rock in the fall of 2010. Thirty-three men were underground when a main tunnel collapsed and sealed them inside a mountain. These men had very few rations and very little hope. For two months, they prayed for someone to save them.

On the surface, Chilean rescue teams worked desperately to do just that. Working round the clock and consulting with NASA, the rescuers developed a thirteen-foot-tall capsule that allowed them to drill into the mountain. First a communication line, then a tunnel. No one had ever tried this method before, and no one knew if it would succeed.

Thank God, it did. On October 13, 2010, the miners began to emerge from the ground. They were saved!

I like the way Max Lucado describes that moment:

No one returned the rescue offer with a declaration of independence: "I can get out of here on my own. Just give me a new drill." They had stared at the stone tomb long enough to reach the unanimous opinion: "We need help. We need someone to penetrate this world and pull us out." And when the rescue capsule came, they climbed in.

Would you do the same? Climb into the capsule of grace. Let God pull you out. Trust in his strength. It's easy as A-B-C.[7]

CHAPTER 4

Created for Good Works

EPHESIANS 2:10

Chadwick Boseman was one of the greatest actors of his generation. Before he died an untimely death from colon cancer in 2020 at the age of only 43, he received two Screen Actors Guild Awards, a Golden Globe Award, a Critics' Choice Movie Award, and a Primetime Emmy Award, among other accolades. He was probably best known for playing Jackie Robinson in *42* and the Black Panther in the Marvel Cinematic Universe.

What was the secret to Boseman's extraordinary life? A part of the answer can be found in the following counsel he delivered to the graduating class of Howard University, his alma mater, in May 2018: "You would rather find purpose than a job or a career. Purpose crosses disciplines. Purpose is an essential element of you. It is the reason you are on the planet at this particular time in history. Your very existence is wrapped up in the things you are here to fulfill."[1]

Calvin Miller wrote the following in his book *Into the Depths*: "I have no way to prove this, but I have a feeling that they live the longest who know why they are alive in the first place. We not only find out who we are when we move into the depths but we also find out what God has for us to do. Then, glory of glories ... we discover they are one and the same. What God has for us to do is who we are. It is better to live a decade and know why we are alive than to live a century without any clue."[2]

How about you? Have you discovered what God wants you to do with your life? I believe He has a special purpose for each one of us, and when we find out what that is, we will no longer need an alarm clock to get us out of bed in the morning. Why? Because our heart will be filled with enthusiasm and joy to do the things He has created us to do.

The Bible says, "For we are His workmanship, created in Christ Jesus for good works, which God prepared beforehand that we should walk in them" (Ephesians 2:10).

For hundreds of years, Christians have been living out Ephesians 2:10. In the third century, Tertullian wrote that the Christians of his day gave generously and without compulsion to a common fund that provided for the needs of widows, the physically disabled, orphans, the sick, those in prison, and even for the release of slaves.

Throughout the Middle Ages, the church sponsored orphanages, built schools, and fed the hungry. In the 1800s, believers such as A. H. Francke and George Müller provided homelike environments for unwanted children.

Also in the 1800s, a group of Christians in Great Britain worked tirelessly to reform child labor practices. At roughly the same time, statesman William Wilberforce and his fellow Christians were fighting for the abolition of slavery in the British Empire.

It's been the influence of Christians in society that has built hospitals, halted infanticide, discouraged abortion, inspired relief societies, and enhanced the arts.

Now it's our turn. Today, I want to walk with you through just one verse in the Bible—Ephesians 2:10. Here we discover six secrets to living the life for which we were created.

The Secret of Authority

"For we are His workmanship."

In the Greek language, the first word in verse 10 is the word "His." This is an unusual placement, but Paul had a purpose in writing it this way. He was putting the emphasis squarely on God. We are His workmanship. Meaning, we are His tools.

Even our good works are under the authority of the Lord. He has the right to deploy us as He pleases, but He never does so without our best interests in mind. He is the Lord of the universe, the Lord of the Church, and the Lord of our lives.

In the Gospels, Jesus affirmed His authority on many occasions, including the authority to require our obedience. He told His disciples, "Not everyone who says to Me, 'Lord, Lord,' shall enter the kingdom of heaven, but he who does the will of My Father in heaven" (Matthew 7:21). He asked the multitudes,

"Why do you call Me 'Lord, Lord,' and not do the things which I say?" (Luke 6:46)

And of course, Jesus' authority was a key theme of His Great Commission in Matthew 28:18-19. "And Jesus came and spoke to them, saying, 'All authority has been given to Me in heaven and on earth. Go therefore and make disciples of all the nations, baptizing them in the name of the Father and of the Son and of the Holy Spirit.'"

Our good works are to be done according to the Word of God and according to the will of God. Since it is possible to do good works according to our own definition of "good" and not God's, it is important that we know the heart of the Father and pursue the good works He has clearly declared "good" in His Word.

In the New Testament, that phrase "good works" is used fifteen times. Most of the time, we are not given any specific instructions on what these good works entail. But on four occasions we get a glimpse into what a life of doing good to the glory of God looks like.

First, Jesus said, "Many good works I have shown you from My Father" (John 10:32). Meaning, to know the types of good works that are according to God's will, we can study the life and ministry of Jesus! And then do what He did.

Second, in Paul's discussion about providing for widows, he defined good deeds this way: "If she has brought up children, if she has lodged strangers, if she has washed the saints' feet, if she has relieved the afflicted, if she has diligently followed every good work" (1 Timothy 5:10). One chapter later, he wrote, "Be rich in good works, ready to give, willing to share" (6:18).

And finally, in his letter to Titus, Paul said, "Let our people also learn to maintain good works, to meet urgent needs" (3:14).

"To meet urgent needs." That's probably the simplest description of a good work. As you go about your day, simply be on the lookout for the needs around you and the ways you can fill them. This you have been commanded to do by Jesus Christ, your Savior.

The Secret of Identity

Before we can demonstrate God's love to others, we must know where we stand in Christ. Knowing who we are in Him helps us demonstrate His love to others. We see that as we continue with Ephesians 2:10. "We are His workmanship, created in Christ Jesus."

My favorite translation of this phrase is F. F. Bruce's: "We are his work, his masterpiece." This might be the most exalted description of a Christian in all of the Bible. We are a work of art. We are God's masterpieces!

A masterpiece is a work done with extraordinary skill. It is the artist's supreme achievement. That's you and me.

In his book *Shaped by the Cross*, Ken Gire tells the story of Michelangelo's masterpiece the *Pieta*, which is a sculpture of Mary with the dead Christ in her arms. The *Pieta* was commissioned on August 27, 1498. For the sculpture, Michelangelo searched the quarries for months for just the right type of stone. Once the stout cube of marble arrived in his studio, the artist went to work. He labored for almost two years, sweating over it in the sweltering heat of summer and shivering over it in the biting cold of winter. He believed his figures were trapped inside the marble, and that if he listened to the stone, he could chip away everything that wasn't a part of the final sculpture.

When Michelangelo finally finished the *Pieta*, he was only 24. His final touch was to chisel his name on the ribbon attached to Mary's garment. He wrote, "Michelangelo of Florence made this." It was the only sculpture he ever signed.

From its overall structure to its smallest detail, the *Pieta* is a work of unsurpassed beauty. As one contemporary of Michelangelo wrote: "It would be impossible for any craftsman or sculptor—no matter how brilliant—ever to surpass the grace or design of this work."[3]

If Michelangelo had his *Pieta*, God has us.

If da Vinci had his *Mona Lisa*, God has us.

If Shakespeare had his *Hamlet*, God has us.

Paul goes on to say that we were "created in Christ Jesus" for good works. Our old identity was marred by sin, disobedience, and the lust of the flesh. But in Christ we have been recreated and given a new identity: "If anyone is in Christ, he is a new creation; old things have passed away; behold, all things have become new" (2 Corinthians 5:17).

There's an old parable about a man who found a young eagle who had fallen out of his nest. The man took it home and put it in his barnyard where it soon learned to eat and behave like the chickens. One day a biologist passed by the farm and asked why the king of all birds was confined to live with the chickens. The farmer replied that since he had given it chicken feed and trained it to be a chicken, it had never learned to fly. It was no longer an eagle.

"It has the heart of an eagle," replied the biologist, "and can surely be taught to fly." He lifted the eagle toward the sky and said, "You belong to the sky. Stretch out your wings and fly." The eagle, however, was confused. He did not know who he was, and seeing the chickens eating their food, it jumped down to be with them again.

Next, the biologist took the bird to the roof of the house and urged it again to fly. But the eagle was afraid of his unknown self and jumped down once more for the chicken food.

Finally, the biologist took the eagle out to a high mountain. There he held the king of the birds high above him and encouraged it again, saying, "You are an eagle. You belong to the sky. Stretch out your wings and fly." The eagle looked around, back towards the barnyard and up to the sky. Then the eagle began to tremble. Slowly, it stretched his wings, and with a triumphant cry, soared away into the heavens.

Sometimes, we can be so preoccupied with who we were that we are afraid to become who we really are. You aren't a chicken or an eagle. You are God's masterpiece! And you were designed to soar through life doing good works.

Do you see yourself as God sees you? A new creation in Christ. The light of the world. A masterpiece destined to do good things for His glory.

That's the secret of identity.

I have known and loved Pat Williams for over fifty years. He was one of the founders of the Orlando Magic of the National Basketball Association and one of the most well-read and well-written people on planet Earth. When I was visiting Orlando, he gave me a copy of a little book he had written on success. It is written in a motivational style and includes his lifetime research on what makes successful people tick.

Here is what he wrote: "Successful individuals have learned to apply their greatest talent to the pursuit of their strongest passion in life. They are doing not only what they do well, but what they love most."[4]

Every believer has been given a gift, a God-given ability for doing good works. That same God gives us a love for what He calls us to do.

The Secret of Responsibility

As we learned last chapter, the New Testament is very clear about the nature of salvation. It is not the result of man's efforts but of the grace of God. I have noticed, however, that in many of the passages where the doctrine of salvation apart from good works is found, the doctrine of salvation unto good works is also found. Here are two examples:

- "For by grace you have been saved through faith, and that not of yourselves; it is the gift of God, not of works, lest anyone should boast" (Ephesians 2:8-9).

- "Not by works of righteousness which we have done, but according to His mercy He saved us, through the washing of regeneration and renewing of the Holy Spirit" (Titus 3:5).

If we are not careful, we can make such an issue of the fact that our salvation is not by works that we carry over the "not by works" concept into the rest of our life. We forget that

Ephesians 2:8-9 is followed by Ephesians 2:10: "For we are His workmanship, created in Christ Jesus for good works, which God prepared beforehand that we should walk in them."

Titus 3:5 is followed by Titus 3:8, which says, "This is a faithful saying, and these things I want you to affirm constantly, that those who have believed in God should be careful to maintain good works. These things are good and profitable to men."

In other words, we are not saved *by* good works, but we are saved *for* good works. Those two different prepositions make all the difference in the world!

Warren Wiersbe has written, "It is too bad that many believers minimize the place of good works in the Christian life. Because we are not saved by good works, they have the idea that good works are evil, and this is a mistake."[5]

Paul wrote to the Christians in Corinth, "God is able to make all grace abound toward you, that you, always having all sufficiency in all things, may have an abundance for every good work" (2 Corinthians 9:8). The very purpose of the Bible is so that we may be "thoroughly equipped for every good work" (2 Timothy 3:17). And, perhaps most powerfully, Paul said that one of the reasons Christ died for us is so that we would be passionate about doing good: "[He] gave Himself for us, that He might redeem us from every lawless deed and purify for Himself His own special people, zealous for good works" (Titus 2:14).

As a response to God's grace, you and I are responsible to do the good works He has given us. Let's be like Dorcas in the book of Acts. Let's be people who are "full of good works" (Acts 9:36).

The Secret of Ability

The next phrase in Ephesians 2:10 is critical but often overlooked. We are created in Christ Jesus for good works, "which God prepared beforehand."

The word "prepared" was taken from the ancient custom of sending servants ahead of a king to prepare the road for the royal caravan. The servants were responsible to secure the road and ensure that the king arrived at his destination safe and on time.

In Ephesians 2:10, Paul turned the picture on its head. It is God, the King of kings, who goes ahead of His servants to prepare the road for us. He strategically places us in situations and circumstances where we can use our talents and resources to help others.

I remember reading that when Amy Carmichael was a little girl, she earnestly prayed that God would turn her brown eyes into blue ones, for she longed for blue eyes. Later in life, she became a missionary in the slums of India, and she came to understand why brown eyes were important for her. When rescuing girls from Hindu slavery, Amy often had to cover herself with a scarf that revealed only her eyes. Blue eyes would have betrayed her identity in that brown-eyed nation.

So learn to thank God for the body and personality He has given you, for no one else is exactly like you—and for God's good reasons!

Paul also wrote about our unique abilities in his epistle to the Romans. "Through the grace of God we have different gifts. If our gift is preaching, let us preach to the limit of our vision. If it is serving others let us concentrate on our service; if it is teaching let us give all we have to our teaching; and if our gift be the stimulating of the faith of others let us set ourselves to it. Let the man who is called to give, give freely; let the man who wields authority think of his responsibility; and let the man who feels sympathy for his fellows act cheerfully" (12:6-8, Phillips).

Here again is Pat Williams:

You are a unique and irreplaceable blend of interests, experiences, abilities, passions and talents. There is nobody else in the world like you. Every day when you get up in the morning, you have to decide how to use your passions and talents and your time to the highest possible use .... If you follow your passion and focus your talent ... you'll have something to offer that no one else has. You'll achieve a level of distinction that few other people ever know .... "You are the only person who can use your ability."[6]

If you ever question your own abilities, remember the old Danish proverb: "What you are is God's gift to you; what you do with yourself is your gift to God."

The Secret of Fidelity

Next, Paul writes in Ephesians 2:10 that God has prepared our good works "that we should walk in them."

To walk in good works means we are to do them constantly and consistently. In other words, we are to be faithful in them—faithful to seek out and accomplish good deeds on behalf of our good God.

The Bible says, "It is required in stewards that one be found faithful" (1 Corinthians 4:2).

Missionary Bertha Smith served the Lord faithfully in China until at age seventy she was forced to retire because of the policy of her mission board. She wasn't at all ready to retire. "What a pain!" she wrote. "I never dreamed that anything in this life could ever hurt like giving up work with the Chinese and returning home. I was still doing about fifteen hours of work a day, and I never became too tired to get up rested the next morning."

Bertha accepted her retirement as from the Lord, but she was convinced that God had a new work for her to begin. It wasn't long before invitations flooded in for her to speak and share the principles of revival that she had learned and observed in China. So Bertha traveled far and wide across America and around the world, carrying on an exhausting ministry of telling the story of revival.

For almost thirty more years, she served the Lord during her retirement ministry, and then she passed into glory just five months shy of her one-hundredth birthday.[7]

That's what I call a faithful life of good works!

Bertha Smith followed Jesus' command in Matthew 5:16, where He said, "Let your light so shine before men, that they may see your good works and glorify your Father in heaven."

The Secret of Availability

Finally, we reach the end of our super-verse: "For we are His workmanship, created in Christ Jesus for good works, which God prepared beforehand that we should walk in them."

Verse 10 begins with the powerful word "for," which points back to the precious verses in chapter 2. If you remember, Paul has just outlined our desperate position apart from Christ and what Christ has done to save us. In other words, we owe who we have become to the grace and kindness of God. That should create a great desire in our hearts to obey Him—to be available to serve Him wherever and however He desires.

In Scripture, a desire to be available to the Lord is often the first step a person takes after having an encounter with Him. Consider these three examples.

The prophet Isaiah said, "I heard the voice of the Lord, saying: 'Whom shall I send, and who will go for Us?' Then I said, 'Here am I! Send me'" (Isaiah 6:8).

When the angel told Mary that she would give birth to the Son of God, she responded, "Behold the maidservant of the Lord! Let it be to me according to your word" (Luke 1:38). And the angel departed from her.

And when Paul was saved on the road to Damascus, "He, trembling and astonished, said, 'Lord, what do You want me to do?' Then the Lord said to him, 'Arise and go into the city, and you will be told what you must do'" (Acts 9:6).

God is looking for willing hearts and willing hands. If we are to walk in the good works for which we were created, we must make ourselves available to Him.

We can echo Dr. A. T. Pierson, who once said, "To go as I am led, to go when I am led, to go where I am led—that has been for twenty years the one prayer of my life."[8]

That's a good prayer for me to recommend to you. Usually our willingness and availability come first, and the assignment comes next.

I read a story about a missionary candidate that illustrates what I'm talking about. It was one snowy day at 5:00 a.m., and the candidate rang the bell at a missionary examiner's home. He was ushered into the office and sat there for three hours. His examiner didn't show up. Finally, after three hours, the guy he was supposed to meet who was going to examine him came for the interview.

He said to the missionary candidate, "Can you spell?"

Rather mystified, the candidate answered, "Yes, sir."

The examiner said, "All right, spell 'baker.'"

The candidate said, "B-A-K-E-R."

"Fine, now, do you know anything about numbers?" the examiner continued.

"Yes, sir, something."

"Well, please add two plus two."

The candidate said, "Two plus two is four."

"That's fine," said the examiner. "I believe you have passed the test. I'll tell the board tomorrow."

Well, the guy was shaking his head. He got up before 5 o'clock for this? He didn't know what in the world was going on. The next day at the board meeting, the examiner reported on the interview. This is what he said:

He has all the qualifications for a fine missionary. First, I tested him on self-denial, making him arrive at my home at five in the morning. He left a warm bed on a snowy morning without any complaint. Second, I tested him on promptness. He arrived exactly at 5 o'clock. Third, I examined him on patience. I made him wait there three hours to see me. Fourth, I tested his temper. He failed to show any aggravation or anger about the issue. Fifth, I tried his humility by asking him questions that a seven-year-old child could answer, and he showed no indignation. So you see, I believe this candidate meets the requirements. He will make the fine missionary that we need.[9]

Almighty God won't lead us in a direction of giftedness unless we have a spirit of availability before Him—unless we really are saying, "Lord God, show me what You want me to do, and I'll do it, whatever it may be." When you come with that attitude toward Almighty God, He is there indeed to show you His will for your life.

In Ephesians 2:10, God has given us the purpose for which we were created. So let's take Him at His Word! Let's wake up each morning with a sense of adventure, eager to discover our assignments for the day. Let's be on the lookout for the good works He has prepared for us. And then ...

Let's get to work!

THEREFORE REMEMBER
THAT YOU, ONCE . . .
WERE WITHOUT CHRIST
. . . HAVING NO HOPE
AND WITHOUT GOD IN
THE WORLD. BUT NOW IN
CHRIST JESUS YOU WHO
ONCE WERE FAR OFF HAVE
BEEN BROUGHT NEAR BY
THE BLOOD OF CHRIST.

EPHESIANS 2:11-13

CHAPTER 5

Before and After

EPHESIANS 2:11-22

Allen Langham remembers what his life was like before Christ. Raised in an unstable and violent environment, he left home when he was just sixteen. Craving acceptance from members of the criminal underworld, he "began fighting for money, selling drugs, collecting debts for dealers," and generally bullying his way through life.

A few years later, he landed in a top-security prison in London—hating what he had become. Hopeless and at the end of himself, one day he dropped to his knees and prayed to God: "If you're real and you hear me …. Show me you are with me!"

The next morning joy replaced tears of despair. In the following days, he began praying and studying the Bible. He surrendered his rage to Jesus. He felt peace like never before.

Since that day, Allen has founded a ministry called Steps to Freedom. He speaks to rooms filled with men convicted of the most heinous crimes. He's seen God repair his relationships with his sisters, his three children, and his father.

"The refining process has been long and hard," Allen says. "But bit by bit, it's polishing me into a trophy of God's grace."[1]

Once angry and estranged from his family, now reconciled. Once without hope, now at peace. Once a bully, now a trophy of God's grace.

That brings us to Ephesians 2, where Paul encourages us to do what Allen Langham has done: remember what our lives were without Christ and what they have become with Him. In Paul's words: "Remember that you, once … were without Christ … having no hope and without God in the world. But now in Christ Jesus you who once were far off have been brought near by the blood of Christ" (Ephesians 2:11-13).

I like how one scholar describes those verses:

> Paul tells the Ephesians, that you were once separated, alienated, estranged, hopeless. Because then, and only then, will it mean something that in Christ you are reconciled, welcomed, adopted, saved. So too with us. If we are going to love Christ much, we need to remember the depths from which he saved us. If we are going to treasure all we have in him, we need to remember who we were without him.[2]

There are two words that help us understand Paul's point in the passage we will study in this chapter, which is Ephesians 2:11-22. Those words are "once" and "now."

Once We Were Far Off, Now We Are Near

Paul began this section of his letter by reminding the Gentile Christians about their lives and identities before they encountered Jesus. He asked them to remember what they "once" were.

As Gentiles, the Ephesian believers experienced a four-fold alienation.

First, before Christ, they were "called Uncircumcision by what is called the Circumcision" (verse 11). According to the old covenant of Moses, the practice of circumcision was what physically set apart God's people from the rest of the world. That separation had continued in Jewish society so that Gentiles were separated and excluded on a social level.

Second, the Gentiles were "without Christ" (verse 12). While the Jews had been expecting the appearance of the Messiah for hundreds of years, the Gentiles were isolated as national groups with no real hope of salvation—no real hope of connecting with God. They were idol worshipers, which made them spiritually separated from Christ.

Third, Paul said the Gentiles were "aliens from the commonwealth of Israel." And they were insulated culturally as "strangers from the covenants of promise" (verse 12). God had established His relationship with the Jews as His chosen people through a series of covenants—legal agreements represented by Abraham, Moses, and David. The Gentiles were excluded from that relationship prior to Christ.

Finally, Paul reminded the Gentiles in Ephesus that they had "no hope and were without God in the world" (verse 12). Can you imagine a sadder line? Can you imagine a sadder reality for our lives?

Bertrand Russell, the renowned philosopher and avowed atheist, had this to say about life apart from God:

> [Man's] origin, his growth, his hopes and fears, his loves and his beliefs, are but the outcome of accidental collocations of atoms ... no fire, no heroism, no intensity of thought and feeling, can preserve an individual life beyond the grave ... all the labours of the ages, all the devotion, all the inspiration, all the noonday brightness of human genius, are destined to extinction in the vast death of the solar system ... the whole temple of Man's achievement must inevitably be buried beneath the debris of a universe in ruins.[3]

There is no hope without Christ. There is no hope without God. That's where the Gentiles were. That's where all of us were before Jesus Christ entered our life. We were without God and without hope.

Thankfully, that's what the Gentiles were "once." That's what they used to be, and that's what we used to be. But no longer!

"But now in Christ Jesus you who once were far off have been brought near by the blood of Christ" (Ephesians 2:13).

In Christ, hopelessness has been exchanged for nearness. Isn't that interesting? To be near to God is to be near to hope. The book of Hebrews says it this way: "Hope is a strong and trustworthy anchor for our souls. It leads us through the curtain into God's inner sanctuary" (Hebrews 6:19, NLT).

That's what Dena Yohe has come to experience. In her book *You Are Not Alone*, she describes the pain and panic she endured as her daughter lapsed in and out of crises. She finally made a discovery: "The most important thing about my life wasn't how my children were doing (as important as that was) but my relationship with Jesus, my Savior .... When I chose to focus on Christ, my real hope, firm hope, was revealed."

She also wrote, "Our challenge is to loosen our grip on the fragile hopes we've been setting our hearts on. They're slippery and elusive. They slip through our fingers like sand .... Hope is the rope thrown to us by almighty God, who fastens it tightly around our waists to keep us from falling into a pit of despair. Take hold of this new kind of hope!"[4]

Yes, in Christ there is hope!

Once We Were Separated, Now We Are United

"For He Himself is our peace, who has made both one, and has broken down the middle wall of separation" (Ephesians 2:14).

Three times in Ephesians 2:11-22, the word "peace" appears. Each time Paul seems to be emphasizing not just peace between humanity and God but also peace between Jew and Gentile.

There is an important first century cultural reference in verse 14—"the middle wall of separation." On the periphery of the temple complex in Jerusalem was the court of the Gentiles where the Gentiles were allowed to gather. They could not enter into the inner court where the Jews were allowed, but at least they could gather on the outside of a barrier set up to separate Jews from Gentiles. There the Jews tried to proselytize the Gentiles.

So the Gentiles were separated from the Jews by a wall of separation. But Paul says Jesus broke down that wall.

Notice the words "both" and "one." "Both" refers to the separate groups of Jews and Gentiles; "one" refers to the Church of Jesus Christ in which the two have been made one. Through the shed blood of Jesus Christ, all the barriers which separate individuals—racial, religious, gender, social, economic—have been torn down. All who believe in Christ have been made one, not only one with God but one with each other.

"There is neither Jew nor Greek, there is neither slave nor free, there is neither male nor female; for you are all one in Christ Jesus" (Galatians 3:28).

When Jesus died on the cross, He brought us near to God and to one another. Harold Hoehner explains: "The Gentiles who once were far away from both God and the Jews have been brought near through the blood of Christ. They have come near to God and to the Jews by means of Christ's sacrificial death. Sin separates people from God and one another and only Christ's atonement can remove that sin barrier."[5]

InterVarsity Christian Fellowship sponsors the Urbana Conference every three years, drawing about fifteen thousand college students to gather and encourage each other to take on the mission of world evangelization. One year, after the main session, students dispersed to smaller groups for prayer and reflection. Among these groups were students from China, Taiwan, and Hong Kong, historically divided by deep-seated bitterness and animosity.

Despite these divisions, the Chinese students took a bold step forward and invited the other countries to join them in prayer. After some contemplation and singing, the Taiwanese students opened up their wall divider, and the Hong Kong students followed suit. In the end, about eighty students came together and mingled, breaking down the walls that once divided them.

"In Christ, we are all one family," said one leader. "And [Christ] breaks down political boundaries. In Christ, we have the desire to make the first steps to connect."[6]

Once We Were Two, Now We Are One

"Having abolished in His flesh the enmity, that is, the law of commandments contained in ordinances, so as to create in Himself one new man from the two, thus making peace, and that He might reconcile them both to God in one body through the cross, thereby putting to death the enmity" (Ephesians 2:15-16).

The way Christ tore down the wall of separation between Jew and Gentile was by abolishing "in His flesh the enmity, that is, the law of commandments contained in ordinances." The ceremonial law, prescribed by Moses, was abolished by Christ's death on the cross. Had it not been abolished, we would still be bringing lambs to church every Sunday to offer as sacrifices for our sin. The ceremonial law which the Jews had and from which the Gentiles were excluded was abolished by Christ's death. Therefore, it could no longer be a point of division between Jew and Gentiles.

God didn't make Jews become Gentiles or Gentiles become Jews. Instead, He created something new—a new person, called the Church. There are no longer Jews and Gentiles, religiously speaking, but only Christians, only believers in Christ. That is not to say there are no longer cultural distinctives which characterize the Jewish or Gentile peoples, but they do not separate us. What characterizes each group now is their unity in faith in Christ.

As Paul wrote in another epistle: "For there is no distinction between Jew and Greek, for the same Lord over all is rich to all who call upon Him" (Romans 10:12). And, "There is neither Greek nor Jew, circumcised nor uncircumcised, barbarian, Scythian, slave nor free, but Christ is all and in all" (Colossians 3:11).

Once We Were Excluded, Now We Are Admitted

"And He came and preached peace to you who were afar off and to those who were near. For through Him we both have access by one Spirit to the Father" (Ephesians 2:17-18).

Bible scholar Bryan Chapell notes that "Jesus preached to those near: the Jews in Nazareth, Capernaum, and Jerusalem; and he commissioned Peter and other disciples to continue that ministry. He also preached to those far away: speaking to a Samaritan woman at a well, comforting a Syro-Phoenician, blessing an Ethiopian eunuch through Philip, and commissioning Paul for the Gentiles."[7]

Jesus' message to both those who were near and those who were far away was the same. It was the message of peace. "These things I have spoken to you, that in Me you may have peace. In the world you will have tribulation; but be of good cheer, I have overcome the world" (John 16:33).

Today, the Gospel of peace is still being preached! People all over the world, Jews and Gentiles, are responding to the Gospel and gaining access to God through the blood of Christ and the power of the Spirit. We gain "access … to the Father" not because of our rank or religion or race but because of Jesus Christ.

Now I want you to carefully read this important paragraph about what it means to have access to the Father:

> [The word "access"] is used only three times in the New Testament, in each case referring to the believer's access to God …. In ancient times a related word was used to describe the court official who introduced persons to the king. They gave access to the monarch. The term itself carries the idea not of possessing access in our own right but of being granted the right to come to God with boldness, knowing we will be welcomed.[8]

John R. W. Stott wrote, "The highest and fullest achievement of our peacemaking, reconciling Christ is the Trinitarian access of the people of God, as through him by the one Spirit we come boldly to our Father."[9]

Several passages of Scripture remind us of our accepted state as members of God's Kingdom, including these:

- "For you did not receive the spirit of bondage again to fear, but you received the Spirit of adoption by whom we cry out, 'Abba, Father'" (Romans 8:15).

- "And because you are sons, God has sent forth the Spirit of His Son into your hearts, crying out, 'Abba, Father!'" (Galatians 4:6)

- "Let us therefore come boldly to the throne of grace,
  that we may obtain mercy and find grace to help in
  time of need" (Hebrews 4:16).

I love this little illustration about boldly coming before the throne of grace: "Prayer pulls the rope below and the great bell rings above in the ears of God. Some scarcely stir the bell, for they pray so languidly. Others give but an occasional pluck at the rope. But the person who wins with heaven is the one who grasps the rope boldly and pulls continuously, with all his might."[10]

Once We Were Strangers, Now We Are the Church

"Now, therefore, you are no longer strangers and foreigners, but fellow citizens with the saints and members of the household of God, having been built on the foundation of the apostles and prophets, Jesus Christ Himself being the chief cornerstone, in whom the whole building, being fitted together, grows into a holy temple in the Lord, in whom you also are being built together for a dwelling place of God in the Spirit" (Ephesians 2:19-22).

In the final four verses of Ephesians 2, Paul uses three pictures to describe the privileges believing Gentiles now have in Christ. In the process, he also gave us three wonderful pictures of the Church.

The first picture is that of a city, emphasizing the Church as a community. He informed the Gentiles in Ephesus that they were "no longer strangers and foreigners, but fellow citizens."

The Greek word translated "fellow citizens" is a term connected to our English word *politics*. It is connected with the elements that make a society. Paul was saying that these Jews and Gentiles had come together as believers in Christ, which made them a whole new society. The Gentiles—and remember that most Christians today would qualify as Gentiles—were no longer on the outside looking in.

Here's another way of thinking about this: The Church is important because it supersedes our national identities—and yes, even our different racial backgrounds. When you choose to follow Christ, it doesn't matter if you are American or Russian or Korean or European or African or any other differentiator we tend to focus on today. No matter your background, you become part of the Church. You are given access to the fellowship of this new society.

The second picture is even more intimate: a family. This emphasizes the unity of the Church. Paul wrote at the end of Ephesians 2:19 that Gentile believers are now "members of the household of God." In other words, all followers of Christ are part of God's family.

What does this mean on a practical level? It means all followers of Christ should be—and can be—unified. In the same way that pianos attuned to the same fork will play in tune with one another, believers who are following Christ within the family of God can experience tremendous unity.

Dr. Paul Brand was a surgeon who wrote a wonderful book called *Fearfully and Wonderfully Made*, which uses a lot of pictures from the human body to illustrate spiritual truth. Here is how Dr. Brand explained the unity that we have in Christ as members of His family:

Just as the complete identity code, the DNA, of my body is found in each individual cell, so also the reality of God permeates every cell in Christ's body, the church, linking us members with a true organic bond. And I sense that bond when I meet strangers in India, Africa, or California who share my loyalty to the Head. Instantly, we become brothers and sisters, fellow cells in Christ's body. I share the ecstasy of community in a universal body that includes every man and woman in whom God resides.[11]

Let me tell you, this reality creates a lot of joy for someone like me who has the privilege of traveling often. I meet flight attendants who are a part of the family. I meet pilots who are part of the family. I meet hotel workers who are part of the family. And because I'm on the radio and I've written books, I've found that my brothers and sisters come out of the woodwork to tell me, "Hey, I'm in the family!"

As Christians, we are never very far away from our family because the family of God is everywhere.

The third picture Paul used to describe the importance of the Church is the picture of a building. It's a picture of stability, and Paul illustrated that idea through the image of a foundation: "Having been built on the foundation of the apostles and prophets, Jesus Christ Himself being the chief cornerstone" (Ephesians 2:20).

Now, when Paul mentioned the "apostles and prophets," he was referring to their role in recording Scripture. The prophets were men like Moses and Isaiah and Daniel who recorded most of the Old Testament. And the apostles were men like Matthew and John and Peter who recorded the majority of the New Testament.

But really, the foundation of the Church is Jesus Christ. In Paul's words, He is the "chief cornerstone."

We have had several building projects at Shadow Mountain Community Church, and I've noticed with each of those projects that the construction crews spend what seems to me like a lot of time digging around in the ground. They measure, they bring in huge pieces of equipment, they dig holes, they pour cement, and on it goes. And then, finally, that crew leaves the property once the foundation has been laid, and then the framers and carpenters can come in and do the actual work of constructing the building.

Looking at Paul's picture, the apostles and prophets were tasked with laying the foundation for the Church. Those apostles and prophets have left the scene—they have moved on. But Jesus remains. Jesus is the chief Cornerstone, "in whom the whole building, being fitted together, grows into a holy temple in the Lord, in whom you also are being built together for a dwelling place of God in the Spirit" (Ephesians 2:21-22).

Just as God used to dwell in a temple in Jerusalem made with stones, so He dwells today in a temple made with living stones— believers in Jesus. We, the Church, are the temple of God. And when we gather collectively, God dwells in us.

If you are Christian, you are a living stone that God wants to fit together with all other living stones to build His Church. You can't be fit together to form His building if you don't show up. The Church is weak today to the extent that living stones are absent and not being fit together.

Think about what would happen if no one showed up—then think what would happen if everyone did!

Pastors come and go. Buildings come and go. Congregations come and go. Nations come and go. Societies morph and change, sometimes so quickly that it feels frightening. But the Church has remained, and the Church will remain throughout eternity. Why? Because the Church is founded on Christ.

The Church Will Bless You

Clarence Macartney once told of a man who dreamed of a city filled with splendid and notable buildings: great granite temple of finance and commerce where business was transacted, marble halls where university classes met, and ornate homes for the people of that city. Along the roadside was a humble structure into which men and women kept going.

A hundred years passed in his dream, and the man found himself in the same city but the buildings had been torn down and rebuilt. They were even taller and more impressive. Yet in the middle of them was the same small white structure into which people were coming and going with joy on their faces.

A thousand years passed in the man's dream, and again he saw the same city. It was a complete transformation, for the old buildings had vanished and new buildings with new architecture and new grandeur had taken their places—all except that little frame building along the road into which men, women, and children were coming and going with joy and satisfaction on their faces.

"What is that building?" he asked a stranger in his dream.

"That building?" said the stranger. "That represents the church, the house of God. Cities and societies rise and fall, but the church remains steadfast through the ages to assist God's people along the road of life."[12]

Don't neglect your roadside assistance. Don't forsake the assembling of yourselves together. Go to church and discover the worship, fellowship, and partnership of being a part of a group that says, "I was glad when they said to me, 'Let us go into the house of the Lord'" (Psalm 122:1).

In his book *Love One Another: Becoming the Church Jesus Longs For*, Gerald Sittser told the story of his daughter, Catherine, visiting Quito, Ecuador, on a mission trip. During one weekend a number of volunteers and staff members rented a bus and traveled to the coast to spend a couple of days relaxing on the beach.

The beach was packed with people, so Catherine decided to go for a swim to escape the crowds. Swimming in deep water far from shore, she noticed a boat fast approaching her. She yelled and waved as best she could, but to no avail. The boat continued on its course. She finally decided to dive head first to get out of the way—but the propellor caught her on her lower back.

As it turned out, two young Ecuadorians witnessed the accident from shore and frantically swam to her, reaching her in just enough time. Once on shore, an EMT stopped the bleeding, cleaned out the gaping wounds, stitched her up, and then transported her to a missionary hospital back in Quito.

"Over the next week, Catherine discovered what it means to belong to the worldwide Church. As word spread, people in the

U.S. contacted Christian friends in Quito who began to visit and help her. A retired missionary doctor ... stopped in to see her every day and took personal responsibility for her care. People sent letters, emails, flowers, and gifts."

"I just can't believe it," Catherine told her dad. "These people loved me for no other reason than that I needed to be loved."

To which Gerald responded, "It's the church. When the church is functioning at its best, there is simply no community on earth that can rival it."[13]

Amen to that!

CHAPTER 6

Unity

EPHESIANS 3:1-13

I once heard about a man who was rescued from a desert island where he had survived for fifteen years all by himself. No other people for hundreds of miles. When this man was rescued, he took his rescuers on a little tour of the island. "That was my house," he said, "and that was my store, and this was a cabana I used, and that one over there is where I go to church."

One of the rescuers gestured and asked, "What about that building next to your church? What is that?"

"Oh," said the man with an exaggerated roll of his eyes. "That's where I used to go to church before the split."

In the *World Christian Encyclopedia*, David Barrett claimed that there are more than 33,000 Christian denominations in the world, all of which owe their origin to a church split at some point in their history.[1] Yet it was Jesus Christ who prayed for His followers that they might all live as one (John 17).

The passage we are going to study in this chapter is Paul's reminder to the Ephesians (and to us) about the importance of maintaining unity in the Church. This was obviously a timely topic for Paul, as we have already noted, because of the cultural (and other) barriers that existed between Gentiles and Jews who were coming together to form the first churches all over the Mediterranean world.

This passage asks and answers the question, "What do you do when you have two cultural groups but there is only one Church?" Given the number of cultures to which Christianity has spread over the last two thousand years and the number of groups into which Christians have divided, this remains an important question for today.

Now when we talk about unity, we're not talking about *union*. You can tie the tails of two cats together and throw them over a back fence, and they will be in union—they will be connected. But I promise you, they are not in unity. There is a difference between union and unity.

Unity is also not *uniformity*. Uniformity is everybody being exactly the same. You get the idea from uniforms.

Finally, unity is not *unanimity*. Unanimity is everybody agreeing about everything. Paul's call for unity in the Church is not the call to put aside all doctrinal differences and pretend they don't matter at all.

Instead, unity comes when you have a shared center, and that center is Jesus Christ. Somebody told me something a long time ago that I've never forgotten. It goes like this:

If you concentrate on WHAT you know, you will tend toward disunity.

But if you concentrate on WHOM you know, it will lead you toward unity.

Isn't that a good thought? I'm glad I know what I know, and I try to learn as much as I can. But it's easy, especially if you're a teacher, to focus on what you know and forget about Whom you know. But when you concentrate on Whom you know, you continue to preserve the unity of the Church.

Ephesians 3:1-13 is an interesting passage because the first verse is the beginning of a prayer—but that prayer doesn't actually get going until verse 14. You'll notice verse 1 says, "For this reason I, Paul, the prisoner of Christ Jesus for you Gentiles." And then there is a hyphen in most translations. What happens next is that Paul digresses away from that prayer for several paragraphs, and then picks it up again in verse 14: "For this reason I bow my knees to the Father of our Lord Jesus Christ."

In between verses 1 and 14, what we find is a quick recap or reemphasis of some of the themes Paul had already covered back in Ephesians 2. But the overall emphasis of those verses is a desire for the Church to be unified.

The Mystery of the Church

Paul mentioned the "mystery of [God's] will" in Ephesians 1:9, but he writes about that idea three times (verses 3, 4, 9) with reference to the Church in chapter 3.

The mystery of the Church is simple: It was an unknown concept. In the Old Testament it's never even mentioned. It is a new entity made up of Jewish and Gentile believers in Jesus Christ. Some say that Israel was the Church in the Old Testament, but that is incorrect. The Church was unknown in the Old Testament, which is why Paul calls it a mystery. In fact, the Church doesn't begin until Acts 2 when the Holy Spirit is given. The Church wasn't revealed until Christ commissioned Paul to be the apostle to the Gentiles and explain the concept of the Church to Jews and Gentiles alike.

The Mystery Received

"For this reason I, Paul, the prisoner of Christ Jesus for you Gentiles—if indeed you have heard of the dispensation of the grace of God which was given to me for you" (Ephesians 3:1-2).

Paul identifies himself as one who has received a "dispensation of the grace of God" (verse 2). The words identify Paul as a steward, a person who has been given the responsibility to take care of matters for someone else.

Paul wrote to the Ephesians during his three-year imprisonment in Rome before which he had been imprisoned in Caesarea for two years. Do you know why he was imprisoned? Ultimately, for preaching the mystery of the Church. It started when he was arrested in Jerusalem for preaching the Gospel and allegedly bringing a Gentile (a Greek) onto the temple grounds. This angered the Jewish leaders so much they nearly started a riot, causing the Romans to arrest Paul (Acts 21:27-29).

The Mystery Revealed

How did Paul gain knowledge of the mystery of the Church? By divine revelation: "How that by revelation He made known to me the mystery (as I have briefly written already, by which, when you read, you may understand my knowledge in the mystery of Christ)" (Ephesians 3:3-4).

He didn't read about it in the Old Testament because it's not there. This is a case of "truth being stranger than fiction"—that is, no one, Jew or Gentile, would ever have thought of this. It could have only come from heaven.

Perhaps God revealed these truths to Paul shortly after his conversion when he seemed to have been out of public view (Acts 9:30; Galatians 1:17). It is clear from Christ's commission to Paul that he was to be an apostle to the Gentiles, which presupposes the revelation of this mystery to him (Acts 9:15-16; 22:21; 26:15-18).

In verse 5, Paul confirmed the origins of this mystery, saying, "Which in other ages was not made known to the sons of men, as it has now been revealed by the Spirit to His holy apostles and prophets."

There were a few hints in the Old Testament but no direct prophecies. Isaiah in particular has a number of references to the Servant of the Lord being a light to the Gentiles (42:6; 49:6), showing that the Gentiles have always been in God's plan of redemption. But no one could have known that the Gentiles would become fellow heirs of the promises of God with Israel if it had not been revealed "to His holy apostles and prophets."

The prophets often wrote things down that they didn't fully understand, and references to Gentile salvation remained in that category. So the salvation of the Gentiles was pictured in the Old Testament but only dimly.

The Mystery Restated

To drive the point home again, Paul restates the mystery in three points: "That the Gentiles should be fellow heirs, of the same body, and partakers of His promise in Christ through the gospel" (Ephesians 3:6).

The Gentiles are fellow heirs. Throughout the Old Testament, the Jews lived with the anticipation of being the inheritors of the promises God made to Abraham, Isaac, and Jacob. These were the blessings they expected to experience as God's chosen people. Now the Gentiles have been made fellow heirs (fellow inheritors). They get the blessings too—all the same blessings Israel was promised.

The Gentiles are fellow members. Up to the time of Christ and the giving of the Holy Spirit (the birth of the Church), to become a child of God, a member of God's household, you had to be or become a Jew. No longer! Now Gentiles could become children of God as well, fellow members "of the same body" (God's family).

The Gentiles are fellow partakers. The Gentiles, according to Paul, are now fellow partakers of the promises in Christ through the Gospel. Everything that is associated with the Gospel of Christ is now not only the full possession of every Jew who believes but also of every Gentile who believes as well.

This was a revolutionary moment within the Church and the human race. The Jews, who absolutely despised Gentiles, were now being told they must move over and allow the Gentiles to become co-participants with them in the blessings of God. What a change! And what an opportunity to live out God's grace.

Oh, that we would live out that same opportunity! We have far too many divisions and separations and tensions in our churches between different groups, and this simply should not be. What a testimony we could be to the world of the loving acceptance of God if we would but model the idea of fellow heirs, fellow members, and fellow partakers.

The Minister to the Church

Paul probably could imagine some in Ephesus asking, "Well, who are you to be telling us we are now equal? Who gave you that authority?" So Paul took a moment to document his role as minister to the Gentiles as appointed by God.

That role can be summarized in three important words from Ephesians 3: appointed, anointed, and amazed.

Appointed

"Of which I became a minister according to the gift of the grace of God given to me by the effective working of His power" (Ephesians 3:7).

Paul became the apostle to the Gentiles by the grace of God. Paul didn't volunteer for the ministry; he was drafted by Almighty God—an experience which marked him and changed him for life. Being in the ministry at the direction of God is the only reason anyone ought ever to be made a minister.

Prior to that calling, Paul knew about the grace of God. He had been the persecutor of the church in Jerusalem before becoming a Christian. He was actually converted to Christ while on his way to Damascus to throw Christians in jail!

He said in 2 Timothy 1:11 that he was "appointed a preacher, an apostle, and a teacher of the Gentiles." In Colossians 1:25-27, he confirmed again his appointment to his ministry to the Gentiles according to a stewardship given him by God.

In short, Paul's credentials to be the revealer of the mystery of the Church came straight from heaven.

Anointed

"Of which I became a minister according to the gift of the grace of God given to me by the effective working of His power" (Ephesians 3:7).

Paul not only had the message of the Church, but he also had the power to deliver it. He was not only appointed but also anointed. God's power was at work in Paul to equip him to deliver the message of the mystery of the Church all over the Roman Empire. People heard him and responded to the Gospel because of the power of God (the grace of God) at work in and through him.

Paul was the kind of person who was believable because of the power of God at work in him. He made an impact for Christ even though he considered himself the least of the apostles (1 Corinthians 15:9). Despite his history, he was confident of his calling and the grace that was at work in him: "But by the grace of God I am what I am, and His grace toward me was not in vain; but I labored more abundantly than they all, yet not I, but the grace of God which was with me" (1 Corinthians 15:10).

Amazed

"To me, who am less than the least of all the saints, this grace was given, that I should preach among the Gentiles the unsearchable riches of Christ" (Ephesians 3:8).

I don't think Paul ever got over the fact that he was called by God's grace to be a minister of the Gospel. It wasn't false humility on Paul's part. It was just honesty—he couldn't believe God had extended His grace toward him and called him to minister that grace through preaching the Gospel.

You may not think you are worthy to serve the Lord, and that's true—none of us are worthy. But the grace of God can make us worthy in that we are appointed and anointed to do something for Him. It's amazing that God uses times when we think we've failed miserably to show us His grace was at work.

Thirty-three years after I had spoken to a college group early in my ministry—an occasion at which I thought I had completely blown it—a man introduced himself to me and told me he had been in the crowd of college students that night and given his heart to Christ. He had gone on to Bible school and had been in the ministry ever since.

Wow! Even when we think we are the chief of failures, God is at work by His grace to do something eternal.

Specifically, Paul was amazed God had called him to preach "the unsearchable riches of Christ"—literally meaning "riches that can't be tracked." It is such a rich concept that translators have used many different words to try and explain it. Words such as *inexplorable*, *unfathomable*, *inexhaustible*, *inscrutable*, and *incalculable*.

In other words, they are infinite riches—riches that cover every aspect of our life from eternity past into eternity future!

Please note: Paul's message to us is that Christ always enriches our life. He doesn't deplete or exhaust us because His blessings can't be depleted or exhausted. He doesn't rob us—He enriches us. That's amazing!

The Mission of the Church

Paul continued his parenthetical digression by focusing on the mission of the Church—why God has united all believers in one new Body by His grace. That mission is to declare the truth of God on earth and in heavenly places.

Let's quickly take a deeper look at each of those elements.

To Declare the Truth to Men

"And to make all see what is the fellowship of the mystery, which from the beginning of the ages has been hidden in God who created all things through Jesus Christ" (Ephesians 3:9).

The Church is to be a living testimony of the work of God in humanity, a place where mercy and grace flow freely for all to see. Instead of acting like we've got it all together, we should acknowledge that we are nothing without the grace of God—that we are just pilgrims on our way, stumbling occasionally as we go. Based on that reality, we can invite those in the world to join us.

After all, how will they believe God can work in their broken lives if they don't see Him working in ours?

The Church is to be God's primary visual aid to the world by which they discover that the door to the riches of God's mercy is standing wide open by His grace.

To Display the Truth to Angels

"To the intent that now the manifold wisdom of God might be made known by the church to the principalities and powers in the heavenly places, according to the eternal purpose which He accomplished in Christ Jesus our Lord" (Ephesians 3:10-11).

It is not only people who need to have the wisdom of God preached to them—it is the heavenly hosts as well. The angels of heaven ("principalities and powers") are constantly observing the work of God on planet Earth, and Paul says that part of the Church's mission is to make God's wisdom known to them. When Gentiles and Jews join together in unity, overcoming barriers that used to divide, I believe the angels must marvel at how the grace of God has joined us into one new Body of believers.

The Bible says angels "desire to look into" the Gospel and salvation (1 Peter 1:12). Why? Because they have not experienced salvation. The Church offers them a picture of God's work in our world. When someone falls on their knees, repents of their sin, and receives salvation, the angels get to see a picture of God's grace. When we sacrifice our own resources and time to serve one another, the angels get to see a picture of God's goodness reflected through us. When we stand up for truth and confront the dangers of sin in our culture, the angels get to see a reflection of God's zeal and passion.

As the Church, we are witnesses and testimonies not just to the world but also to "the principalities and powers in the heavenly places." What a privilege! What a blessing to be part of this institution we call the Church.

The Ministry of the Church

Paul completed his teaching on the unity of the Church in this section of his letter by highlighting the prayer ministry of the Church. "In whom we have boldness and access with confidence through faith in Him. Therefore I ask that you do not lose heart at my tribulations for you, which is your glory" (Ephesians 3:12-13).

The ministry of the Church in prayer is now one of "boldness and access with confidence through faith in" Christ. Jews and Gentiles together, as co-heirs of the privileges of God, can enter into the presence of God with confidence.

This type of access to God was in stark contrast to the old system—to the one day a year when the high priest, and only the high priest, could enter the holy of holies in the temple to stand in the presence of God. One person, one day per year. Anyone else who went into the holy of holies would be struck dead. And if the high priest did anything wrong while he was in the Lord's presence, he would die as well.

But now, anybody who has trusted in Christ can enter the presence of God boldly and confidently any day of the year. The writer of the letter to the Hebrews says, "Let us therefore come boldly to the throne of grace, that we may obtain mercy and find grace to help in time of need" (Hebrews 4:16).

Three Questions to Consider

As we move toward the end of this chapter, allow me to pose three questions based on what we've studied in these thirteen verses. I'll give you my thoughts on those questions, but I'd like you to answer them honestly for yourself as well.

Do We Long for the Unity of Believers?

In John 17:21, we have Jesus' request to the Father that His disciples "may be one, as You, Father, are in Me, and I in You; that they also may be one in Us, that the world may believe that You sent Me."

When my young family lived in Fort Wayne, Indiana, many years ago, I used to work out at the YMCA during lunch. To get there, I'd walk through an archway inscribed with these words from John 17: "That they all may be one." Then I'd go down into the pit, as they called the basketball court, where we fought like cats and dogs for a whole hour and just about killed each other. Then we'd walk back out through the arch that said, "That they all may be one."

I'm afraid my workout in those days may have been a picture of the modern Church.

Someone compared Christians to a group of porcupines on a cold winter's night. They need to stay close to one another to keep warm, but when they get too close, they prick each other with their quills and have to move apart again.

In John 17, Jesus was concerned that His people experience a spiritual unity akin to His relationship with the Father. He was praying that we will love and honor one another like Jesus and the Father love and honor each other. He wasn't simply praying that we'll get along but that we will have deep, life-giving relationships with one another—with our spouse and parents, sons and daughters, friends and neighbors.

Experiencing the oneness of the Holy Spirit is impossible apart from Jesus Christ and His longing for us and His prayers on our behalf. By nature, we're selfish, prideful, and closed-hearted. But Jesus desires unity in our marriages, homes, families, churches, and friendships. Perhaps it will spur you onward to realize how deeply He prays for these things.

The Bible says, "How good and pleasant it is when God's people live together in unity!" (Psalm 133:1, NIV)

How do you think 33,000 denominations look to the world? Do you think they see us as one?

Do We Love All the Members of God's Family?

During His public ministry, Jesus gave us a new commandment that we "love one another; as I have loved you …. By this all will know that you are My disciples, if you have love for one another" (John 13:34-35).

Lee Iacocca once asked legendary football coach Vince Lombardi what it took to make a winning team. Here was Lombardi's answer:

> There have been a lot of coaches with good ball clubs who know the fundamentals and have plenty of discipline but still don't win the game. Then you come to the third ingredient: if you're going to play together as a team, you've got to care for one another. You've got to *love* each other. Each player has to be thinking about the next guy and saying to himself: "If I don't block that man, Paul is going to get his legs broken. I have to do my job well in order that he can do his."

"The difference between mediocrity and greatness," Lombardi said, "is the feeling these guys have for each other. Most people call it team spirit. When the players are imbued with that special feeling, you know you've got yourself a winning team."[2]

Dorothy Day made this statement: "I really only love God as much as I love the person I love the least."

Is there anyone in God's family whom you love less than you should for any reason?

Do We Look for Ways to Reach Out to Those Who Might Not Feel Included?

Every Christian who is a member of your church is your brother or sister in the Lord. They are fellow members of Christ's Body. Is there anyone in the family who is feeling left out—someone you could put your arms around and make sure they are affirmed in their standing as a fellow member of the Body?

If so, then I trust you know what to do.

I recently read about a special concert performed in the city of Philadelphia. The music was arranged by a famous composer named David Lang, and the performers included students, amateurs, and professionals. There was a 9-year-old cellist and an 81-year-old oboist. A writer from the *New York Times* described it as "the most diverse orchestra in America."

But the most interesting aspect of this particular performance was the instruments. Each one was damaged in some way. Many were barely playable. There was a trumpet held together by blue painter's tape, for example. And a French horn without a mouthpiece. And a violin reduced to little more than a silhouette. Yet under the direction of Mr. Lang, each performer was able to contribute to the music through whatever sounds his or her instrument could produce.

They called it "A Symphony for a Broken Orchestra." The goal of the concert was to raise awareness and funds to repair more than a thousand broken instruments in the Philadelphia school system—which Mr. Lang referred to as "1,000 missed opportunities."

The night in December 2017 was a complete success. Musicians came together and made something beautiful out of hundreds of imperfect instruments. By the time the concert was over, the Philadelphia School District had enough money to repair all of the instruments.[3]

I like that picture: A collection of broken instruments joined together to produce something lovely and make an impact on the community.

It reminds me of the Church.

As followers of Jesus, we are joined together as a broken orchestra. None of us are functioning as we were designed to function. None of us have everything figured out, and all of us make mistakes. We experience division and dissension and fractures and frustrations. Yet under the direction of God's loving hand, we can still produce beautiful music for His Kingdom.

CHAPTER 7

A Prayer for Inner Strength

EPHESIANS 3:14-21

Dean Karnazes stumbled as he reached the front porch of his San Francisco-area home. He'd just spent the evening of his thirtieth birthday at a local bar, and he was drunk. He was also miserable. He had a successful job in corporate America, but personally he knew his life was off track.

Glancing down, Karnazes saw a pair of old sneakers on the porch. Slipping them on, he decided to go for a run—and kept running for thirty miles.

Yes, thirty miles!

"I started sobering up around Daly City," Karnazes remembers. By that point, he was having too much fun to stop. "I was on this rural country road and it was kind of misty. The eucalyptus had those drips coming from them. It was real pungent, and I just felt so alive …. That night changed the course of my life."

In many ways, Karnazes hasn't stopped running more than two decades later. As one of the earliest stars in the sport of ultramarathons, his feats of strength and endurance are legendary.

Incredibly, Karnazes once ran fifty marathons in fifty different states on fifty consecutive days. That's 1,330 miles. No other person in history has matched that accomplishment. Perhaps even more impressive, Karnazes once ran for almost 81 hours straight without sleep—more than 3 full days. He covered 350 miles in that time span, and he did so without stopping. He estimates he has run more than 100,000 miles over the course of his life, which would mean running around the diameter of our planet four separate times.[1]

As you might expect, all that running has given Dean Karnazes a lot of time to think. And one of the things he believes most strongly is that people tend to place limits on themselves and on their bodies that are unnecessary and unhelpful.

"Your legs can only carry you so far," Karnazes wrote in one of his bestselling books. "Running great distances is mostly done with your head … and your heart. The human body is capable of amazing physical deeds. If we could just free ourselves from our perceived limitations and tap into our internal fire, the possibilities are endless."[2]

I like that image of an "internal fire." More than perhaps any person in history, Dean Karnazes has tested the limits of physical strength. But as he and many others have learned, physical strength can only carry us so far. We need something more substantial if we want to thrive in this world and hold fast to both the promises and the responsibilities that come with following Christ.

We need inner strength.

As we move to the second half of Ephesians 3, we have the privilege of listening to another prayer from that great saint, the apostle Paul. We already reviewed one of Paul's prayers from the first half of Ephesians 1. But in my estimation, Ephesians 3:14-21 is the most glorious prayer in the New Testament, apart from the prayers of our Lord Himself. We are about to explore a wonderful prayer that I hope will be realized in your life and in mine as we study it together. And it is a prayer for inner strength.

That focus on inner strength was not new for Paul. He wrote in another epistle, "Therefore we do not lose heart. Even though our outward man is perishing, yet the inward man is being renewed day by day" (2 Corinthians 4:16). In other words, inner strength is necessary because physical strength—what Paul referred to as the "outward man"—is fragile. I get more in tune with that truth the older I get, let me tell you.

We all need inner strength—that "internal fire" described by Dean Karnazes. In fact, inner strength is so critical to our spiritual survival that when Paul introduced his prayer to the Ephesians, he marshalled all three members of the Trinity: "For this reason I bow my knees to the Father of our Lord Jesus Christ, from whom the whole family in heaven and earth is named, that He would grant you, according to the riches of His glory, to be strengthened with might through His Spirit in the inner man" (verses 14-16).

We're going to explore the full prayer together in this chapter. As we do, I want to highlight three extraordinary elements involved with that prayer that will help us see everything Paul was communicating to the Ephesians and to us. Specifically, we will look at the posture for that prayer, the petitions of that prayer, and the potential for that prayer.

The Posture of Paul's Prayer

The first thing we notice in verse 14 is that Paul specifically called out the posture of his prayer: "For this reason I bow my knees to the Father of our Lord Jesus Christ."

Now, that probably doesn't sound strange to you. Lots of people bow their knees in prayer. It's a common habit among believers today, and it's a common expression throughout the history of the Church. When we pray, we bow our heads and often bow our knees.

This is where it's helpful to have a little context because it wasn't common for the ancient Jewish people to bow their knees in prayer—especially for public prayer. Most Jews stood upright while praying, usually with their hands uplifted toward the heavens.

Remember Jesus' parable of the Pharisee and the tax collector? Here's what He said: "The Pharisee stood and prayed thus with himself, 'God, I thank You that I am not like other men—extortioners, unjust, adulterers, or even as this tax collector'" (Luke 18:11). The Pharisee stood to pray, as was the custom. Even the tax collector was "standing afar off" (verse 13). Most Jewish people stood while they prayed.

But Paul specifically told the Ephesians that he was kneeling in his prayer for them. Why? Because he wanted to highlight the intensity of that moment—the intensity of his prayer. This was serious business. It was the kind of prayer that brought him to his knees.

Paul wasn't alone in adopting this posture toward God. In fact, as we look through Scripture, we see that he was in pretty good company:

"And [Jesus] was withdrawn from them about a stone's throw, and He knelt down and prayed" (Luke 22:41).

"Then [Stephen] knelt down and cried out with a loud voice, 'Lord, do not charge them with this sin.' And when he had said this, he fell asleep" (Acts 7:60).

"Peter put them all out, and knelt down and prayed" (Acts 9:40).

And of course we all know this famous promise from Philippians: "That at the name of Jesus every knee should bow ... and that every tongue should confess that Jesus Christ is Lord" (2:10-11).

What does this mean for us as believers today? What's the significance of these ponderings on posture? What we can learn is that when we are serious about prayer, we may not always kneel physically, but we had better be kneeling inwardly—because the act of kneeling displays our submission to the will of Almighty God.

Back when I was a student in seminary, I remember the first time I attended the First Baptist Church of Dallas, where Dr. W. A. Criswell was the pastor. When I walked into the sanctuary, I was surprised to see they had kneeling benches connected to all the pews. That was common in the more liturgical churches of that time period, but it was strange to find kneeling benches in a Baptist church.

Pretty quickly, however, I realized it wasn't strange at all. In fact, there was something special about the entire congregation getting on their knees every Sunday before God. You could feel it in the room—that intensity. You felt that physical reminder that you were part of something much larger than yourself.

In a similar way, there is something special about our experiences with prayer when we kneel before God today. Doing so says outwardly what should be true inwardly: that we are submitting to God and subjecting ourselves to His will.

The Petitions of Paul's Prayer

Of course, there is much more to glean from Paul's prayer for the Ephesians beyond his physical posture. So let's take a look at the petitions of that prayer.

We can find them in verses 16-19:

That He would grant you, according to the riches of His glory, to be strengthened with might through His Spirit in the inner man, that Christ may dwell in your hearts through faith; that you, being rooted and grounded in love, may be able to comprehend with all the saints what is the width and length and depth and height—to know the love of Christ which passes knowledge; that you may be filled with all the fullness of God.

A Prayer for Inward Power

First, Paul was asking God to fill the Ephesians with inward power—with inner strength. Notice all the strong words in those two verses: "riches," "glory," "strengthened," and "might."

How desperately we need inner strength in our day. We are living in a fragile world. We never know what a new day will bring forth. We wake in the morning, and everything is all right. But before the day is over, our lives can be upside down. As I'm sure you've already realized, that is true for Christians and non-Christians alike.

The old hymn said followers of Jesus are "safe and secure from all alarms," but that's not always the case. Not when it comes to this world. Sometimes following Christ sends us straight into the alarms! But if we have inner strength—if we have determined that we are going to be strong where it counts—we can face anything that may come our way. Yes, trials may jolt us. Pain and suffering may cause us to take a step back. But we find a kind of resilience and stamina in our walk with the Lord that carries us through.

Remember Paul's words from a different epistle: "God has not given us a spirit of fear, but of power and of love and of a sound mind" (2 Timothy 1:7).

Sadly, many of God's people wait until the crisis comes to worry about inner strength. They get to a place where they need that internal fire, but it's not there. It hasn't been developed. Let me encourage you: You need to be making strong investments in your spirit so that when the time comes to draw on that reservoir, you won't find the needle pointing to empty.

That raises an important question: How do we get inner strength? How do we develop it? Build it? Cause it to grow?

The answer is Christ. Specifically, Christ's presence and power within us—within our hearts. That's why Paul prayed that God would "grant" the Ephesian believers "to be strengthened with might through His Spirit."

Remember what Jesus said in John 15: "I am the vine, you are the branches. He who abides in Me, and I in him, bears much fruit; for without Me you can do nothing" (verse 5). I always tell people that "nothing" is a zero with the edges rubbed out. You and I can accomplish nothing without Christ. Without His strength.

In Luke 1, Scripture says this about the early years of John the Baptist: "So the child grew and became strong in spirit" (verse 80). Then, in the very next chapter, Luke used the same expression to describe Jesus: "And the Child grew and became strong in spirit" (2:40).

That's what I want. I want to be strong in my spirit. I want to be able to have the resilience and the strength and the stamina to face any challenges that come my way, no matter what they may be. Not because I'm strong but because there is a strength in me that is greater than I am.

A Prayer for Inward Presence

The next petition in Paul's prayer was a request for Christ's inward presence among the Ephesian believers. Specifically, he prayed "that Christ may dwell in your hearts through faith" (Ephesians 3:17).

But wait a minute. As I just mentioned, Paul wrote this epistle to the believers in Ephesus—to Christians. So why would the apostle include in his petition that Christ "dwell" in their hearts through faith? If they were disciples of Jesus, didn't that mean Christ was already dwelling in their hearts through His Spirit? What was going on?

The answer can be found in that word "dwell." In ancient Greek, which is the language of the New Testament, that is a unique term that refers to more than simply "being" somewhere or even "living" somewhere. To dwell in that context meant "to move in." To take up residence. To be at home.

Paul prayed that Christ would take up permanent residence in the hearts of the Ephesians and be at home there. That may sound simple and obvious based on our understanding of salvation, but in practice it is a little more complicated than we may understand.

So let me ask you this question: Is Jesus an unwelcome guest in the home of your heart? Do you resent His presence? Or have you submitted to His indwelling and given over control to Him?

Jesus said to His disciples in John 14:23, "If anyone loves Me, he will keep My word; and My Father will love him, and We will come to him and make Our home with him." That's what Almighty God wants. And that's what Paul was praying for the believers in Ephesus to experience. That God would not just be a resident in their hearts, but that He would be President of their hearts—that He would make Himself at home.

May the same be true of you and me!

A Prayer for Inward Perception

Look at Paul's next petition: "That you, being rooted and grounded in love, may be able to comprehend with all the saints what is the width and length and depth and height—to know the love of Christ which passes knowledge" (Ephesians 3:17-19).

Paul's third request was that believers would be able to perceive God's love.

Interestingly, Paul includes four dimensions when talking about God's love—"width and length and depth and height." Those words have caused a great many preachers to come up with a great many explanations for why Paul chose that specific language to describe God's love. I don't have space to go into each of those here, but there is one that has caught my attention over the years.

Look at John 3:16 in light of those four dimensions:

"For God so loved the world." That describes the width of God's love, as wide as the world and more.

"That He gave His only begotten Son." That's the length to which God went for us to receive His love.

"That whosoever believes in Him should not perish." That's the depth of God's love.

"But have everlasting life." That's the height; God's love reaches up to eternity.

Do you really understand God's love? Do you recognize it? Can you perceive it?

I think if you could see your own soul the way God sees it, you would understand His love on a whole new level. You would see the filth and the mire of your sin, yes. But you would also see the incredible depth of His care for you—a feeling so powerful that God Himself died on the cross through Christ so that your relationship with Him could be restored.

Many atrocities were committed during the period of history known as the Spanish Inquisition. I once heard a story about a Spanish prisoner whose bones were discovered when soldiers opened one of the underground dungeons used by the leaders of the inquisition. Flesh and clothing had long since dissolved, but the soldiers found the remnants of bones chained to a wall.

But that wasn't all they found.

On the wall of that prison, cut into the rock with a sharp piece of metal, was a cross. Above the cross in Spanish, the word "height" had been carved. Below the cross was the word "depth." On one arm was "length," and on the other arm was "breadth."

Try to imagine that for a moment. Even as that prisoner was starving to death, unable to free himself from the chains that bound him, he was contemplating God's grace. He was pondering and perceiving the reality of God's love.

You and I have the same opportunity. Whenever we see the cross, we see the symbol of God's love for humanity—love that reaches up to the heights, reaches down to the depths, and stretches out in length and breadth to touch all of us. Paul said if we could just perceive that, if we could just comprehend the love of God, it would do amazing things for our life.

Remember, Paul was praying this prayer right after his long discourse about the importance of Jews and Gentiles accepting one another in the same Body of believers. What can make such radical acceptance happen? The love of God. What allows us to reach out to those who may have hurt us and embrace them in forgiveness? The love of God. What inspires us go down into the worst parts of town and minister to the down-and-outers even when their lifestyles feel offensive to us? We can't do that in our own love, but we can relish those opportunities through the overwhelming love of God.

A Prayer for Inward Provision

We've seen how Paul asked God to help the Ephesians receive inward power, enjoy the reality of God's inward presence, and be blessed through the inward perception of His love.

Finally, Paul prayed for inward provision on behalf of those who believe. "That you may be filled with all the fullness of God" (Ephesians 3:19).

Notice the progression of these petitions. The inner strength of the Holy Spirit leads us to the indwelling of Christ. The indwelling of Christ leads us to the knowledge of His abundant love. And now, His abundant love leads us to experience the fullness of God's presence within us.

Now, this idea of being "filled" has caused some confusion within the Church over the centuries. I remember as a boy growing up, I would read that verse and think, *Well, some people are filled with God up to their waist, others are up to their shoulders, and some really spiritual folks get filled all the way up to their nose.*

But the Greek word translated "filled" doesn't mean "to be physically packed with" as much as "to be controlled by."

Look at the illustration Paul used later in the book of Ephesians: "And do not be drunk with wine, in which is dissipation; but be filled with the Spirit" (5:18). Paul wasn't talking about people who are so drunk that they are physically filled up with wine. No, he wanted believers to stop being controlled by wine and other outside factors. Instead, he wanted them to be filled with the Spirit—to be controlled by the Spirit.

That's the same idea Paul expressed when he prayed that the Ephesians would be "filled with the fullness of God." He wanted their lives, and our lives as modern believers, to be controlled by God.

Let's pause here for a moment and take stock. Are you "filled with the fullness of God"? To use a military term, does He have *command and control* of your mind and heart? As you go about your day and especially as you encounter difficulties or unexpected opportunities, do you respond to those moments based on what you want or what God wants? Do you act based on God's will or your own will?

I know those are complicated questions, not to mention uncomfortable ones. But they're important. They are worth reflection and contemplation.

If you are more controlled by your own will and your own plan than God's will and God's plan, that needs to be corrected. I don't mention that to shame you. In fact, if you have drifted into a way of life that is self-controlled rather than God-controlled, you're in good company. Certainly I drift into seasons where I rebelliously attempt to reassert control over my life. The same is true for all Christians, including the apostle Paul.

After all, it was Paul who wrote, "For what I am doing, I do not understand. For what I will to do, that I do not practice; but what I hate, that I do" (Romans 7:15). He added later, "I find then a law, that evil is present with me, the one who wills to do good. For I delight in the law of God according to the inward man. But I see another law in my members, warring against the law of my mind, and bringing me into captivity to the law of sin which is in my members" (Romans 7:21-23).

Don't be discouraged if you drift into seasons where you are controlling you, rather than being filled with the fullness of God. But don't stay in those seasons. Choose to submit yourself once more to God's plan and purpose.

Here's one more principle to keep in mind: God can only fill up a space that is empty. He won't come into our lives when we are filled up with ourselves—with our own importance and our own ego and our own values and our own priorities. That's why we need to empty ourselves. We need to let go of who we used to be so that we can be filled with everything God desires for us, beginning with Himself.

The Potential of Paul's Prayer

So far in this chapter we've seen the posture of Paul's prayer, which found the apostle on his knees in submission before God. We've also seen the four petitions of Paul's prayer: that believers in Christ would experience inward power, the reality of His inward presence, the inward perception of His love, and the inward provision of His Spirit.

As we bring this chapter, and Ephesians 3, to a close, I want to highlight the potential of Paul's prayer, which we can find in verses 20-21: "Now to Him who is able to do exceedingly abundantly above all that we ask or think, according to the power that works in us, to Him be glory in the church by Christ Jesus to all generations, forever and ever. Amen."

Haven't you found that some passages of Scripture seem too good to be true? We read about the incredible promises and the provisions contained in God's Word, and we wonder, *Could that really be for me? Could God really make that happen in my life?*

If you're wondering that very thing right now—*can God really fill me with inner strength and a deep perception of His love?*—then I'm pleased to say that Paul not only anticipated those questions, but he also answered them definitively.

Look at the first six words in verse 20: "Now to Him who is able."

I hope you'll say that out loud right now, and I hope you'll say it with conviction. "God is able!"

Can God fill you with strength in the inner man? Yes. Can He set up a home in your heart? Yes. Can He enable you to experience the depths of His love? Yes. Can He fill you so completely that He is the controlling factor in your life? Yes. Because He is able. God can do exceedingly abundantly above all that you ask or think.

That is the potential of Paul's prayer. That is the application of his prayer in your life. Right now. Today. If you will put your life in His hands, He can do everything He promised and more.

My friend Rob Morgan wrote about former United States President Grover Cleveland, who is the only chief executive that has served two non-consecutive terms. He was the twenty-second and twenty-fourth resident of the Oval Office. He was also the President who dedicated the Statue of Liberty in New York Harbor.

The son of a Presbyterian preacher, Cleveland was serious about his faith and thoroughly trained in Christian doctrine. That training stood him well as he grappled with many serious crises—both national and personal—during his time in office. In the middle of a nationwide financial panic, Cleveland was diagnosed with cancer and had to endure top-secret emergency surgery aboard a friend's yacht. The public didn't learn of those events for years!

My favorite piece of information about President Cleveland is that he framed his favorite Scripture verse and kept it within eyesight as much as possible throughout his life. That verse was Deuteronomy 33:25 in the King James Version: "As thy days, so shall thy strength be." Cleveland hung that promise in his law office. Then, after being elected President both times, he hung it over his bed at the White House so that he would see it each morning upon waking and each evening before bed.

"He awoke every morning with the firm conviction God would give him the strength required for the work assigned. He believed God would give him sufficient strength for each day's tasks as long as he lived."[3] May the same be true of us each day!

CHAPTER 8

The "Oneness" of Our Faith

EPHESIANS 4:1-6

In the fall of 2020, Burger King posted a message on its social media account with this surprising header: "Order From McDonald's." As you know, Burger King and McDonald's are corporate rivals on a grand scale—right up there with Coke vs. Pepsi, Ford vs. Chevy, and Amazon vs. Walmart. So what gives?

Well, the pandemic was especially difficult for the many restaurant workers and employees of service industries who often needed to go to work to maintain their paychecks, yet worked in industries that were hit especially hard by lockdowns and people feeling afraid to venture out. So Burger King was recommending that their customers step up by supporting local restaurants and their employees—even those at McDonald's.

"We never thought we'd be asking you to do this," read the statement, "but restaurants employing thousands of staff really need your support at the moment. So, if you want to help, keep treating yourself to tasty meals through home delivery, takeaway, or drive thru. Getting a Whopper is always best, but ordering a Big Mac is also not such a bad thing."[1]

Now, if Burger King and McDonald's can work together, I'd say there is hope for all of us!

It is a sad commentary on modern Christianity that we are often known more for our disagreements and division than for our unity. We seem to have a hard time getting along with each other, don't we?

That problem is not new. Even our Lord's disciples disagreed and argued with one another with the Lord right there among them. Paul and Barnabas had a falling out over John Mark. And most of the New Testament churches were riddled with disputes and divisions.

In his book on Church unity, Paul Billheimer said:

The most important, momentous, crucial, but the most ignored, neglected, and unsolved problem that has faced the Church from its infancy to the present throbbing moment is the problem of disunity. The continuous and widespread fragmentation of the Church has been the scandal of the ages. It has been Satan's master strategy. The sin of disunity probably has caused more souls to be lost than all other sins combined. Possibly more than anything else, it is the one thing that binds the hands of the Holy Spirit and thwarts His work of convincing of sin, righteousness and judgment.[2]

What a picture of the Church of Jesus Christ! Understanding that picture helps us to know why our Lord prayed the way He did. Jesus knew that disunity would be one of the great problems the Church would face in the future, and so on the evening before His crucifixion He prayed: "That they all may be one, as You, Father, are in Me, and I in You .... That they may be made perfect in one, and that the world may know that You have sent Me, and have loved them as You have loved Me" (John 17:21, 23).

Paul longed for the Church to experience the kind of oneness Jesus prayed for and died for. He preached it, taught it, and fought for it in nearly every letter he wrote. But his great discussion on the unity of believers is found in Ephesians 4. Here, in my estimation, is the best commentary on unity in the entire Bible.

The Plea for Unity

Notice what Paul wrote in verse 1: "I, therefore, the prisoner of the Lord, beseech you to walk worthy of the calling with which you were called."

As I mentioned earlier, the book of Ephesians is one of the prison epistles. That simply means Paul wrote this letter while he was a prisoner in Rome. But look at the language Paul used in verse 1. He didn't say he was a prisoner of Nero or a prisoner of Rome. No, he labeled himself as "the prisoner of the Lord."

Why refer to himself that way? I believe Paul wanted to impress his readers regarding the importance of what he was about to say. He wanted to help the early believers understand and apply the concept of Christian unity, so he used his own chains to underscore what was at stake.

Then came the plea itself: "I … beseech you to walk worthy of the calling with which you were called." Paul was pleading with his readers. He was begging them to hear what he had to say: Walk worthy of your calling.

What, then, is our calling? Well, that's just another way to talk about how we have been called as children of God. We're Christians. Paul wrote in Philippians 3:14 that we have an "upward call." In 2 Timothy 1:9 he described it as a "holy calling." He also described our calling as humble in 1 Corinthians 1:26 because that calling has come not to the rich and powerful but to ordinary folks like you and me. Finally, the book of Hebrews refers to our "heavenly calling" (3:1) because, ultimately, all of us who are saved will end up in heaven one day with our Lord.

That's our calling as followers of Jesus. And Paul wrote to the early Christians, and to us, to plead that they walk in a way that is worthy of that calling.

When I was growing up, I used to attend one or two camps during the year. Mostly they were summer camps. And I remember that right before we left, my mother would sit me down and say something like this: "Now son, you're going to camp. While you're there, I want you to remember who you are."

Of course, I never understood exactly what she meant by that. But I assumed she was saying, "You are a Christian, so behave like one." Or, she may have been saying, "Your dad is a pastor, so you'd better behave." (In hindsight, the second option might be the most likely.)

But essentially my mom was reminding me that my actions didn't affect only me. I was a representative of Christ,

I was a representative of the Jeremiah family, and yes, I was a representative of my father's church. Therefore, I needed to remember those associations—I needed to walk in a way that was worthy of those associations—when I was outside my mother's supervision.

That's essentially the same thing Paul was communicating to the Ephesians in verse 1. He wanted them to live worthy of their calling, so he pleaded with them to remain unified as followers of Christ.

The Points of Unity

Verse 1 is Paul's plea for unity. Now let's skip down to verses 4-6, which show us the different points of unity Paul highlighted within the Church. As you read these verses, pay attention to the word "one": "There is one body and one Spirit, just as you were called in one hope of your calling; one Lord, one faith, one baptism; one God and Father of all, who is above all, and through all, and in you all."

Paul used "one" seven times in those three verses, which shows us what he wanted to emphasize after his plea. He wanted the Church to be "one," to be unified. And he revealed to his readers seven specific ways we can walk worthy of our calling by living out our unity as followers of Christ.

Let's explore each of those seven points of emphasis together.

One Body

First of all, those of us in the Church make up "one body." Paul was talking about the family of God—the Body of Christ.

The Bible says any person who accepts God's free offer of salvation by grace through faith becomes part of that Body. It doesn't matter what our skin tone might be, what our background is, what country we're from, or even what we did or didn't do before that moment of salvation. The fundamental truth of Scripture is that each and every person who has trusted Jesus as their personal Savior is part of the Body of Christ.

I don't want to belabor this point, but I do think it's important to emphasize that there is one Body, and only one Body. There is no Presbyterian body, no Baptist body, no Charismatic body, and so on. As Paul wrote later in Ephesians, we are all "members of His body, of His flesh and of His bones" (5:30).

That means we have the potential to live in unity because we're all part of the same family. We're all part of the Body of Christ.

One Spirit

Secondly, Paul said there's not just one Body, but also "one Spirit."

Did you know there are not multiple versions of the Holy Spirit? There's not a Holy Spirit for America and a Holy Spirit for Asia and a Holy Spirit for Africa, and so on. There's not a Holy Spirit for each denomination of the Church or even one for Protestants and another for Catholics.

There is "one Spirit." As Paul wrote in another epistle, "By one Spirit we were all baptized into one body—whether Jews or Greeks, whether slaves or free—and have all been made to drink into one Spirit. For in fact the body is not one member but many" (1 Corinthians 12:13-14).

The reason that's important is because the Holy Spirit resides in every disciple of Jesus. He is part of each one of us, speaking to us and guiding us and leading us as we seek to follow Christ. For that reason, we can experience unity in the Church when we are all being led by and convicted by that same Spirit.

One Hope

Third, Paul says we as followers of Jesus have "one hope."

Now, the first two items on Paul's list are hard to argue with. It's easy to say we are one Body in the Church empowered by one Spirit. But I can see some readers arguing with me on this point. Why? Because the idea of hope points to the future, and different groups of Christians have very different ideas about what we will experience in the future.

Dr. Jeremiah, how can you say all of us as Christians have one hope? You know as well as anyone that some believers are pre-tribulationists, some are mid-tribulationists, and others are post-tribulationists—so how can we all have the same hope?

If you've read any of my prophetic books, you know I believe Jesus is going to return before the Tribulation. I believe that with all my heart, and I have gone on record with that belief many times.

But listen to me: As much as I agree with that doctrine and choose to teach it when appropriate, that is not a topic that should divide us as followers of Christ. I know and am friends with and love many brothers and sisters in Christ who disagree with me about all manner of doctrinal issues that are not of primary importance—including eschatology.

So whether you are pre-trib or post-trib or mid-trib or something else completely, as followers of Jesus we all agree we're going to see Jesus one day. And that is our "one hope."

One Lord

Sometimes there are some interesting structural elements in Scripture that catch my attention, and one of them occurs in Ephesians 4:4-6. Remember how Paul listed seven ways we can be worthy of our calling as followers of Jesus? That means this fourth "one" statement is in the middle. There are three that precede it and three that follow after.

Well, it just so happens that the central point in Paul's plea for unity is the reality that we have "one Lord," Jesus Christ. Because really, that is the centerpiece of our faith. Every believer is following and worshiping the same Lord.

Do you know why the early Christians were persecuted by the Roman Empire? Some might say, "Because they were Christians." No. There wasn't any nation or empire that was more tolerant of other religions than the Roman Empire. In fact, when the Romans went and conquered a nation, it was their common practice to bring captives back, and they would also bring samplings from that nation's gods—their idols and religious myths. The Romans liked learning about new gods.

If you go to Rome today, one of the best-preserved buildings from the ruins of ancient Rome is what they call the Pantheon. Of course, *pantheon* is a word that means "all the gods." The Romans took the gods from foreign countries and put them on the shelves of the Pantheon as a kind of collection, which they admired. You could go in that building and find a god for just about any situation or circumstance you could ever dream of.

Now, when the Christians came along, the Romans wanted to put their God in the same category with the other gods—in the same building. But the Christians refused to let Jesus Christ be on a shelf with Jupiter and Juno. They said, "There's only one Lord, there's only one God, and we will not put Him on the same level with all these other deities." That's why the Romans took them to the Colosseum and fed them to the lions. Because they believed in one Lord.

Do you believe that today? There is one Lord. The Bible says, "For there is one God and one Mediator between God and men, the Man Christ Jesus" (1 Timothy 2:5). There is one way to heaven. Jesus said, "I am the way, the truth, and the life. No one comes to the Father except through Me" (John 14:6).

So there is one body, there is one Spirit, there is one hope, and there is one Lord.

One Faith

Next, Paul said there is "one faith."

Remember, of course, that Paul was writing to believers. He was writing to Christians. So he was not denying or rejecting the existence of other faiths in terms of other religions. As I just mentioned, the ancient world was packed to the brim with idol worship of all kinds.

Instead, Paul was teaching that believers in Jesus are united by one faith—we are united by one system of truth, which is contained in the Bible. The book of Jude says that faith was "once for all delivered to the saints" (verse 3).

Another way to say it is that Christians everywhere have only one textbook, which is the Word of God. We are united by one collection of truth that sets the boundaries for our faith.

You might ask, "If that's the case, why do Christians have so many different opinions about what the Bible says?" Good question. But we really have to chalk that up to the reality that we're all imperfect. God's Word is not imperfect, but we tend to understand it and apply it imperfectly.

One Baptism

Not only do we have one faith as followers of Jesus, but we have one baptism.

Again, you are probably already thinking about the different ways people experience the sacrament of baptism in different types of churches. Some get sprinkled. Some get dunked. Some even get dunked three times. So how can there be "one baptism"?

To answer that question, we need to remember what baptism represented—and what it was like in terms of the overall experience—for the earliest believers. For the people of Paul's day, in Ephesus and beyond, being baptized was much more than coming to a comfortable church, stepping into a heated pool, and having a pastor take you under the water in front of your friends.

No, in the ancient world, baptism meant finding a pool or a bath in the center of a city. It meant standing in a public area and giving testimony about your faith—including speaking in front of those who had the authority to punish or persecute you. It meant saying for all to hear, "I have trusted Jesus Christ as my Savior, and through this act of obedience, I declare my allegiance to Jesus Christ."

That's what baptism meant in the Early Church. And I believe that's what baptism should mean today. Because there is one baptism for all of us as believers in Jesus.

One God

Paul's final point of unity is that every disciple of Jesus worships "one God." Specifically, "one God and Father of all, who is above all, and through all, and in you all" (verse 6).

Paul started his seven points of unity within the Church by talking about the Body of Christ, and he ended his list by reinforcing the truth that there is one God. That is the God we worship as believers in Jesus Christ.

Have you noticed what's not in Paul's list? Worship styles. Or the type of chair we sit in on a Sunday morning. Or the ethnicity of the pastor who preaches. Or the age of the pastor. Or the size of the church building. Or the Bible translation.

In short, think of the silly stuff that divides us in the Church today, and you won't find any of it on Paul's list. Those issues and idiosyncrasies feel so foolish in light of the opportunity for absolute unity we have been given—the unity we can achieve through Christ.

The Practice of Unity

So far we've explored Paul's plea for unity, and we've seen the seven points of agreement that unite us as the Body of Christ. Now I want to jump back again to verse 2, which highlights the practice of unity in the Church—how to make it happen.

How can we be unified as believers in Jesus? Paul tells us: "I, therefore, the prisoner of the Lord, beseech you to walk worthy of the calling with which you were called, *with all lowliness and gentleness, with longsuffering, bearing with one another in love, endeavoring to keep the unity of the Spirit in the bond of peace"* (verses 1-2, emphasis added).

Notice in verse 3 that we are called "to keep the unity of the Spirit in the bond of peace." That's important because we need to recognize that unity does not originate with humanity. For those of us in the Church, we do not create unity within that Body. God creates it. God is the source of our unity, but He has called us to "keep" it. To maintain it.

Humility

We do that by living as Paul described in verse 2. Specifically, Paul gave four characteristics that are necessary for keeping the unity God has given to us, starting with this concept of "lowliness," which means humility.

The first thing we need to do to retain unity in the Church is humble ourselves. That applies to each of us and all of us in the Body of Christ. We can't be filled with ourselves and maintain unity. We can't be puffed up. We can't think of ourselves as better than others without causing separation and discord.

Remember what Paul wrote about Jesus: "Let this mind be in you which was also in Christ Jesus, who, being in the form of God, did not consider it robbery to be equal with God, but made Himself of no reputation, taking the form of a bondservant, and coming in the likeness of men. And being found in appearance as a man, He humbled Himself and became obedient to the point of death, even the death of the cross" (Philippians 2:5-8).

Humility is necessary for unity in the Church.

Meekness

Next, out of humility grows the spirit of "gentleness," which is often translated as meekness. Have you noticed that humble people tend to be gentle? It's true. When a person grows in humility, they become gentler. They become meeker.

Now, it's important to remember that meekness is not weakness. Instead, meekness means having power that is under control. Horses are an example of what I mean. Have you ever been up close to a horse? Have you seen its size? The muscles bulging and rippling through its chest? Horses are powerful! Yet when we place a saddle on a horse's back and ride, we experience that power under control.

Here's another illustration of gentleness. Remember when Jesus was being arrested in the Garden of Gethsemane, and one of His disciples tried to fight back by slicing the ear off one of the arresting authorities with his sword? Here's how Jesus responded: "Put your sword in its place, for all who take the sword will perish by the sword. Or do you think that I cannot now pray to My Father, and He will provide Me with more than twelve legions of angels? How then could the Scriptures be fulfilled, that it must happen thus?" (Matthew 26:52-54)

That's gentleness. That is strength under control. Jesus had the power to destroy His enemies, yet He chose to set aside that power for the greater good.

We can keep unity in the Body of Christ when we demonstrate that kind of gentleness.

Patience

Third, Paul said we also need "longsuffering," which is another way of saying patience. The Greek word Paul used is *macrothumia*, which has a prefix that we recognize today. *Macro* means "big or large." And *thumia* means "temper." So Paul said we need to have large or long tempers in order to maintain unity in the Church—which is the opposite of having a short temper.

If you've been part of a church for any length of time, you already know that's true. That's because churches are filled with people, and people are often filled with strife and stress. Most of the time we don't mean to cause offense or try the patience of others, but it happens. Especially in a large body—a large family. But just because somebody irritates or offends you doesn't mean you have to respond in kind.

We need to be patient to maintain our unity in the Church.

Forbearance

Finally, we need to act in a way that is "bearing with one another in love." I call that forbearance. What does that mean, or what does that look like on a practical level? Well, it's simply putting up with people.

That's what we do in the Body of Christ, isn't it? We put up with one another. We forbear the slights and misunderstandings and offenses we receive from one another, and we do so in love.

What that also means is that we refuse to get bent out of shape when somebody does something in a different way than we would do it. I've already mentioned worship and prayer and preaching styles and types of church governance and so on. These are all opportunities for forbearance because these are all practices that can be performed in different ways.

God has given us the opportunity for unity in the Church—it starts with Him, but we can keep it. We can maintain it. And we do that by choosing to demonstrate humility, gentleness, patience, and forbearance within the Body of Christ.

The Price of Unity

As we get ready to wrap up this chapter, I want to look once more at Ephesians 4:3, where Paul pleads for us to walk worthy of our calling by "endeavoring to keep the unity of the Spirit in the bond of peace."

We've already focused on that word "keep," which is important. God is the source of our unity in the Church, but we can choose to behave in ways that will keep it—that will maintain it.

But now I want to focus on the word "endeavoring." Did you know unity is hard to maintain? It requires effort. It requires work on our part. In other words, keeping our unity requires us to pay a price, and that price is our "endeavoring." We keep unity in the Body of Christ through diligent, hard work.

Recently I read a great book entitled *Boys in the Boat*. Author Daniel James Brown recounts the fascinating tale of the University of Washington's crew team. Against all odds, this unlikely team of young men rose to the occasion and took home the gold medal at the 1936 Berlin Olympics. The team's success was largely attributed to their diverse backgrounds—hailing from farming communities, logging towns, and shipyards—which they molded into a cohesive unit. By overcoming their differences and working together, the team managed to beat their Californian and Ivy League rivals on their way to securing Olympic glory. Brown's account reveals how the team's commitment to unity played a key role in their triumph:

[Races] are won by crews, and great crews are carefully balanced blends of both physical abilities and personality types .... A crew composed entirely of eight amped-up, overtly aggressive oarsmen will often degenerate into a dysfunctional brawl in a boat or exhaust itself in the first leg of a long race. Similarly, a boatload of quiet but strong introverts may never find the common core of fiery resolve that causes the boat to explode past its competitors when all seems lost. Good crews are good blends of personalities: someone to lead the charge, someone to hold something in reserve; someone to pick a fight, someone to make peace; someone to think things through, someone to charge ahead without thinking. Somehow all this must mesh. That's the steepest challenge .... It is an exquisite thing when it all comes together in just the right way.[3]

That is a good illustration of biblical unity—different individuals with different ideas and different behaviors all coming together around a shared center, which is Jesus Christ. That is the unity we have been given in the Church. And Paul has told us, in effect, "Brothers and sisters, endeavor to keep that unity. Work to maintain it."

Please hear me on this: Endeavoring to maintain unity in the Church is hard work! Yet all of it is incredibly worthwhile, which makes unity an incredible calling for all followers of Christ. Why? Because Almighty God is honored when His Church is united.

CHAPTER 9

The Diversity of Unity

The first time it happened, Domenic Italiano was annoyed. One of his regular customers got in touch to say the gift card Italiano had given him wasn't working. It had a balance of zero dollars.

But then it happened again. And again. And again!

Italiano had purchased several gift cards from a local Petro Canada station. As the owner of an auto business, he gave them to regular clients to show his appreciation for their patronage. Finding out the gift cards were not working took Italiano from annoyed to frustrated to outright angry.

"I have a stack of worthless gift cards here and these are for $800," he told a local news station. "And these are just the ones that I know of."

Apparently, Italiano had purchased the cards from a store hit by a group of technologically sophisticated thieves. Billions of dollars in gift cards are sold to consumers every year, which makes them a valuable asset for many businesses. But scammers have developed ways to access or drain the account balances of those gift cards without even opening the packaging around them. They can access the funds and leave the gift cards still on the rack.

Too often, customers like Domenic Italiano are the ones left holding the bag.[1]

How frustrating to buy a worthless gift. And how frustrating to receive one!

Thankfully, our Heavenly Father is history's greatest Gift-Giver. As we've seen throughout the first half of this book, the gifts God gives to His children are never wasted. They are always fully funded and completely secure. And as we'll see in this chapter, that includes God's spiritual gifts given both to individual believers and to the Church.

While your actual existence is a gift from God and if you are a Christian, you have been given a special gift of service, you may be totally unaware of just how gifted you are. Not all of God's children are passionate to discover their special gift, and not all of God's children who know what their gift is are passionately pursuing the development and implementation of that gift.

As we continue our study of Ephesians 4, we're going to see how God has equipped each person in the Body of Christ with special, one-of-a-kind gifts—gifts that are essential to the health and growth of the Church.

The Provision of God's Gifts

Notice the transition present in Ephesians 4:7, which says: "But to each one of us grace was given according to the measure of Christ's gift." The word "but" sets up a contrast with what preceded. The contrast is between the unity of the Church in verses 1-6 and the diversity of its members in verses 7-12. In the Church, no two members are alike, and no two members have exactly the same gifts or function.

The great Bible scholar F. F. Bruce wrote, "Diversity, not uniformity, is the mark of God's handiwork. It is so in nature; it is equally so in grace, and nowhere more so than in the Christian community. Here are many men and women with the most diverse kinds of parentage, environment, temperament and capacity. Not only so, but since they became Christians they have been endowed by God with a great variety of spiritual gifts as well. Yet because and by means of that diversity, all can co-operate for the good of the whole."[2]

Paul said it this way, "There are diversities of gifts, but the same Spirit. There are differences of ministries, but the same Lord. And there are diversities of activities, but it is the same God who works all in all" (1 Corinthians 12:4-6).

The Bible teaches that Jesus has given a spiritual gift to every one of His children. In Paul's words, "Each one of us" receives at least one of those gifts.

A spiritual gift is a divine ability God gives to an individual for the purpose of glorifying God and serving others. Spiritual gifts are not necessarily the same as what we might call talents or natural abilities. We don't receive them at birth but at conversion, our second birth. All of us have natural abilities, but when we become Christians, God gives us a special ability of ministry. Often that ability goes with our natural ability, but I have seen it happen where a person gets a gift from God at his conversion that is totally different than you would ever imagine them to get.

We will not go through all of the individual gifts of the Spirit in this chapter, but they are mentioned in three main passages in the New Testament: Romans 12, 1 Corinthians 12, and here in Ephesians 4. There are about nineteen different gifts when you compile all the ones mentioned in these chapters.

One thing we know for certain is that every Christian has at least one spiritual gift. Peter said, "As each one has received a gift, minister it to one another, as good stewards of the manifold grace of God" (1 Peter 4:10).

Some believers have more than one gift, but every follower of Jesus has at least one. That includes you. That may sound strange, or you may have a hard time believing it, but it's true. You have been given at least one spiritual gift through the grace of God. You are uniquely equipped as part of the Body of Christ to do something nobody else can do.

Here's another truth. The Bible says that when God gives us gifts, He always gives us grace to go along with those gifts. In fact, in Ephesians 4, it says the grace of God is sufficient for the gift we have received. In other words, the more gifted you are, the more grace you need. The more gifted God has created you to serve Him, the more grace you need to exhibit those gifts in the spirit of humility.

We need to remember that because God has promised to lift up the lowly and bring down those who are proud. It's a terrible thing to see gifts being used without grace, which leads people to become harsh and presumptuous and arrogant.

So thank God for His gifts to you, yes. But also thank Him for the grace to remain humble as you use those gifts.

The Price of God's Gifts

In verse 7, Paul highlighted Christ as the Giver of spiritual gifts. Now, in verses 8-10, he pauses to reflect on why this Giver has the right to give gifts to Christians: "Therefore He says: 'When He ascended on high, He led captivity captive, and gave gifts to men.' (Now this, 'He ascended'—what does it mean but that He also first descended into the lower parts of the earth? He who descended is also the One who ascended far above all the heavens, that He might fill all things.)."

Verse 8 has baffled believers for centuries. It can be difficult to follow Paul's argument if you don't understand what he was doing. So let's dig in a little deeper.

The Old Testament Promise

Paul, the master teacher, quotes a difficult passage from the Old Testament to make his point: "You have ascended on high, you have led captivity captive; you have received gifts among men, even from the rebellious, that the Lord God might dwell there" (Psalm 68:18).

Paul's words are not a direct quote of Psalm 68:18, but he uses it as an analogy. Psalm 68 was written by David, the great poet, after a military victory. It was a song of celebration. What we need to know is that in the ancient world when an army conquered a city, the commander of that army would enter the city and gather up all the spoil. Then he would gather up all the captured soldiers and other people who lived in that city. Lastly, he would rescue and set free any of his own soldiers that had been captured by the enemy.

At that point, the commander would return to his own city and lead a sort of parade. The army would march through their city to display the results of their victory—the spoil, the captives who had been taken in the battle, and their own captives who had now been freed. That's what Scripture means when it says, "He led captivity captive."

Paul uses this well-known motif to illustrate what Christ did. He came to earth and defeated our enemies: sin, Satan, and death. He was victorious over them all, then returned back to heaven as the conquering King and paraded before all the hosts of heaven with the spoils of war.

Colossians 2:15 says it this way: "Having disarmed principalities and powers, He made a public spectacle of them, triumphing over them in it."

The New Testament Proof

Next, Paul applies this Old Testament reference to Christ in the New Testament by asking a question: "Now this, 'He ascended'—what does it mean but that He also first descended into the lower parts of the earth? He who descended is also the One who ascended far above all the heavens, that He might fill all things." (Ephesians 4:9-10).

When Christ came into our world, He came down into Bethlehem and was born as a baby. Then, when He died, He descended even further. He went into the grave. And then after His death, He went into the bowels of the earth, and there He preached the Gospel.

That's what Peter was referring to in another difficult to understand passage: "For Christ also suffered once for sins, the just for the unjust, that He might bring us to God, being put to death in the flesh but made alive by the Spirit, by whom also He went and preached to the spirits in prison" (1 Peter 3:18-19).

According to Peter, Jesus was put to death in the flesh but made alive in the Spirit between His death and resurrection. During those three days, He announced His victory over the demons even while they tried to hold Him in death.

"Paul's point in Ephesians 4:8-10 is to explain that Jesus' paying the infinite price of coming to earth and suffering death on our behalf qualified Him to be exalted above all the heavens ... in order that He might rightfully have the authority to give gifts to His saints."[3]

So if somebody says, "Yeah, I have a spiritual gift, but it's not a big deal." Let me tell you something: It's a big deal! It's a big deal because Jesus Christ paid for that gift with His own blood. He's given us gifts with which we can serve Him and bring glory to His Name.

The Purpose of God's Gifts

We've talked about the provision of spiritual gifts and the price of those gifts. Now let's focus on the purpose. Why has God given spiritual gifts to His children?

Paul answered that question in Ephesians 4:11-13: "And He Himself gave some to be apostles, some prophets, some evangelists, and some pastors and teachers, for the equipping of the saints for the work of ministry, for the edifying of the body of Christ, till we all come to the unity of the faith and of the knowledge of the Son of God, to a perfect man, to the measure of the stature of the fullness of Christ."

Let's take a closer look at how our spiritual gifts contribute to the Church.

Gifts for the Foundation of the Church

The word "apostles" in verse 11 refers to men who were directly commissioned by Jesus to preach the Gospel and plant churches—people like the eleven original disciples, Matthias, and Paul (Mark 3:13; Acts 9:15). Those people had witnessed the Resurrection (Acts 1:22; 1 Corinthians 9:1) and had the ability to perform signs and wonders (2 Corinthians 12:12). Paul's witness of the resurrected Christ came at his conversion on the road to Damascus (Acts 9:15).

Prophets were spokespeople or mouthpieces of God. They had two ministries: forthtelling (speaking forth the word of God) and foretelling (knowing the future by supernatural revelation).

In the primary sense, we no longer have apostles and prophets. Their ministry ended when the New Testament canon was completed, which is when the foundation of the Church was laid. In Ephesians 2, Paul said that the Church was "built on the foundation of the apostles and prophets, Jesus Christ Himself being the chief cornerstone" (verse 20).

In other words, apostles and prophets were given to help the Church get started. They were foundational pieces for that moment and are not present in the Church today. Two thousand years later, we are not still working on the foundation.

Gifts for the Formation of the Church

Look again at Ephesians 4:11: "And He Himself gave some to be ... evangelists, and some pastors and teachers."

In the New Testament, evangelists went about preaching the Good News of the Gospel like Philip did in the book of Acts (8:12, 26-40). Evangelists are those who are divinely equipped to win the lost to Christ. They have a special ability to understand a sinner's condition, answer objections to the Christian faith, and encourage decisions for Christ.

Many scholars believe the phrase "pastors and teachers" refers to two aspects of the same office. Pastors guide and feed the flock. They lovingly counsel, correct, and encourage believers. Teachers are gifted to explain what the Bible says, interpret what it means, and apply it to the hearts of the saints.

Gifts for the Function of the Church

Next, Paul said that Christ gives spiritual gifts "for the equipping of the saints, for the work of the ministry, for the edifying of the body of Christ" (Ephesians 4:12).

Now, here's the way this verse normally looks in the minds of most people: "And He Himself gave some to be apostles, some prophets, some evangelists, and some pastors and teachers, *so that they* could equip the saints *and* do the work of the ministry *and* edify the body of Christ." Meaning, the pastors and teachers carry all the responsibility.

It's not just pastors who think that way. There are many in the Church who say, "Hey preacher, we pay your salary, so you do the work. We'll be here every Sunday, we'll put a little money in the plate, and then you do whatever needs to be done around here."

Please hear me: That kind of thinking leads to burnout. It will ruin a ministry and ruin a church because no human being can do all those things—let alone do all of them well.

Here is what Ephesians 4:11-12 really says if you diagram those verses and look at them grammatically: "And He Himself gave some to be apostles, some prophets, some evangelists, and some pastors and teachers, for the equipping of the saints so that they, *the saints*, can do the work of the ministry, for the edifying of the body of Christ."

It is the job of church members to carry out the work of the ministry. It's the pastor's job to teach and equip and prepare the congregation, but the congregation goes out and does the bulk of the work. Spiritual gifts are given for the formation of the Church so that it can continue to expand and grow.

We commissioned an audit one year at Shadow Mountain to see how many people it actually took to manage what we do on a typical Sunday. The answer was 1,800. There were 1,800 volunteer jobs, and that was several years ago. The number could be twice that today.

We all need to be employed in the work of the ministry. There's no such thing as an unemployed Christian in that sense. Because if we are not using the gifts we've been given, we are hurting the Body of Christ by not contributing what God intended us to contribute. Each of us has been given a gift so we can help build one another up as fellow members of the Body.

The Point of God's Gifts

We've seen in Ephesians 4:7-12 that God provides spiritual gifts to every individual follower of Christ. We've seen that He paid the ultimate price for those gifts, and we've seen that every individual gift has a specific purpose—they are given to benefit us as individuals and to help us accomplish "the work of the ministry."

Now, as we shift to verses 13-15, we'll see Paul take a deeper look at the way spiritual gifts impact the Church as a whole. Specifically, we'll see the reason for God's gifts to the Church and the reflection those gifts produce in the Church.

Here are those verses:

> Till we all come to the unity of the faith and of the knowledge of the Son of God, to a perfect man, to the measure of the stature of the fullness of Christ; that we should no longer be children, tossed to and fro and carried about with every wind of doctrine, by the trickery of men, in the cunning craftiness of deceitful plotting, but, speaking the truth in love, may grow up in all things into Him who is the head—Christ.

Unity

Notice the first part of verse 13: "Till we all come to the unity of the faith." The first reason God has poured His spiritual gifts into the Church is so that the Church will have unity.

Maybe you're thinking, *What is it with Paul and unity in the Church? He already talked about that a bunch in previous chapters in Ephesians, so why is he bringing it up again?*

Well, just look around. Look at how many different and distinct denominations are operating in the world today. Look at the number of disagreements plaguing the Church right now. Look at the division we experience as members of Christ's Body. Paul talked about unity so much because he understood the Church has a desperate need to be reminded about the importance of unity. We have to fight for it. God is the source of our unity, but we have to keep it.

When Paul wrote about "the unity of the faith," he wasn't describing faith in terms of belief and believing in Jesus. Rather, he was describing the body of truth we all accept as followers of Jesus. Our faith is what we believe—what the Bible teaches. Paul wrote that God gave the gift of apostles, prophets, evangelists, and pastor/teachers so that we could maintain unity in our faith.

Does that mean the Church can be perfectly united in this life, and that every doctrinal disagreement can be resolved and agreed upon? Probably not. We are still flawed human beings. But the Word of God is not flawed, and that is exactly Paul's point. When we join together to place Scripture as the center of our faith, we can find unity.

Intimacy

The second reason why God gives spiritual gifts to the Church is intimacy. Paul wrote, "Till we all come to the unity of the faith *and of the knowledge of the Son of God*" (emphasis added).

That word "knowledge" here is important. It means not just being acquainted with someone but having a deep, ongoing knowledge of that person. The Bible says we as Christians are to give ourselves with intensity to knowing Jesus Christ. Not just knowing about Him, not just knowing who He is, but knowing Him in a really personal relationship.

How do you get to know Him? You do it primarily through the study of the Word of God and through prayer. Also, I happen to believe that pain and suffering are tools God uses to help us get to know Him, and I'm sure you have some experience in that regard.

Maturity

Unity, intimacy, and then the third reason is maturity. Paul concluded verse 13 by reminding us that we are reaching "to a perfect man, to the measure of the stature of the fullness of Christ." In short, Almighty God wants you and me to grow up. He wants us to be in a place where we can look back over our shoulders and see some progress in our spiritual walk.

Notice it says, "To a perfect man." That means "a complete man." We are to measure ourselves spiritually by "the measure of the stature of Christ." What is our goal in our spiritual lives? To be like Christ. Nothing less will do. True, we will never achieve that goal on this side of eternity, but we should strive for it. It should be our mission that wherever we go and whatever we do, we bring the presence of Christ into that situation.

The Bible tells us that as followers of Jesus, we are to walk just as He walked (1 John 2:6). We're to follow Christ. We're to be mature. Paul's great goal as a teacher was the maturity of his followers, and you and I should carry that same goal as members of Christ's Body and leaders in the Church.

Stability

The next reason for spiritual gifts in the Church is stability. Look at verse 14: "That we should no longer be children, tossed to and fro and carried about with every wind of doctrine, by the trickery of men, in the cunning craftiness of deceitful plotting."

I think God must be in pain when He looks down upon His Church today and sees what's going on. I know He sees all the things dragging people away from the truth—the cults and the "isms" and the "new" versions of the gospel. God must look at that and say, "Where are the stable, mature people in the Church?" Almighty God wants a mature Church made up of believers who will not get sucked into every new thing that comes down the road.

Paul urged "that we should no longer be children." The word "children" literally means "too young to be able to speak." It's a word for infants. The Bible says it's possible to be a Christian, to be fifteen or even fifty years old chronologically in the faith, yet still be a baby in terms of our walk with the Lord. God gave us spiritual gifts so that the members of His Church would be stable and mature.

Notice also the word "trickery" in verse 14. The Greek term used there is *kubia*, from which we get our English word *cube*. That term described the loaded dice gamblers used in Paul's day (and still use in our day) to cheat people—to trick and deceive. In other words, Paul was telling us that there are people out there using loaded dice in a spiritual sense. They are seeking to snare people and drag them away from their faith in Christ through "cunning craftiness" and "deceitful plotting."

This is a reminder that Satan has a strategy for each of us. The enemy of our soul does not want us to believe the Bible word for word. He wants us to discount or distort what Scripture says—because if he can undermine the truth of God's Word, he can undercut the foundation of the Christian faith.

We need stable leaders and stable members in the local church to resist those efforts.

Authenticity

To recap, God has poured out spiritual gifts on the Church so that we can experience unity, intimacy, maturity, stability—and the final reason is authenticity. Paul wrote in Ephesians 4:15, "But, speaking the truth in love, may grow up in all things into Him who is the head—Christ."

What is authenticity? It is speaking the truth in love. While our enemies and the deceivers around us use trickery and craftiness, we are called to be authentic. We are called to speak the truth in love.

Someone has said, "Truth without love is brutality, and love without truth is hypocrisy."

Notice, we need both truth and love in balance. Previous generations in the Church had a tendency to emphasize truth but be meager in the love department. Have you been around such people? "I've got the truth from God's Word, and I don't care how much it cuts you. I'm here as a prophet of Almighty God to give you the truth." The reality is that truth without love ultimately becomes destructive.

But I think in recent generations the greatest danger has been emphasizing love without truth. That's what we see in our culture today, and it's true even in many areas of the Church. We live in a culture defined by tolerance toward everything *except* the truth. We live in a world that wants everyone to have fuzzy feelings and everyone to accept everything and just love each other. But in order to do that we have to focus on "your truth" or "my truth"—and ultimately we have to reject *the truth*. God's truth.

Here's the reality: The Bible is the standard for absolute truth. And God has poured out His gifts on the Church so that we can speak the truth in love.

The Potential of God's Gifts

All of this leads to the potential of God's gifts. As we live into our gifts, the Church will "grow up in all things into Him who is the head—Christ—from whom the whole body, joined and knit together by what every joint supplies, according to the effective working by which every part does its share, causes growth of the body for the edifying of itself in love" (Ephesians 4:15).

How does a local church grow? From the inside. The church grows as the people within the church do two things: They grow up as believers, and through growing up as believers, they exercise their gifts in building up others.

Notice the words "growth" and "edifying" are both in verse 16. When we grow, it's not just growth in numbers, growth in the amount of baptisms, or growth in people that are coming to Christ. It's also growth inwardly, in our own spiritual lives as we walk with the Lord. Because if you are a believer and you're growing in Christ, you cannot help but have an impact on somebody else in the church who may be coming along behind you or walking alongside of you.

So the question we have to ask is: Where do I fit? What is my part? God, how have You equipped me? My friend, I don't know what your gift is, but I know you have a gift. And I know you won't be happy if you aren't using it to help advance the Body of Christ.

I once heard a story about D. L. Moody that made me laugh. As many know, Moody was a powerful evangelist, but he was not the world's best grammarian. He didn't say things in a way that was technically correct all the time.

Well, one time after D. L. Moody preached, a man came up to him and said, "Mr. Moody, I listened while you were speaking, and you made seventeen grammatical errors in your sermon." And then this man held out a piece of paper. He had made a list of Moody's mistakes!

D. L. Moody just said this in response: "I'm doing my best with what God has given me. Are you?"

That's a good question. In fact, that's a question we all need to wrestle through. God is the great Giver of gifts. What are you and I doing with everything we have received?

THAT YOU PUT OFF
CONCERNING YOUR
FORMER CONDUCT,
THE OLD MAN . . . AND
BE RENEWED IN THE
SPIRIT OF YOUR MIND,
AND THAT YOU PUT
ON THE NEW MAN.

EPHESIANS 4:22-24

CHAPTER 10

The New and the Old

EPHESIANS 4:17-24

If you've ever tried to break a bad habit, James Clear can help. Clear is one of the world's best-known writers and speakers on the topic of how to develop good habits. His book on the subject has sold more than ten million copies, and his weekly newsletter is read by more than two million people.

For Clear, bad habits aren't to be resisted but replaced. He says, "Because bad habits provide some type of benefit in your life, it's very difficult to simply eliminate them .... Instead, you need to replace a bad habit with a new habit that provides a similar benefit."[1]

One author calls this approach "habit switching. It's breaking a bad habit by replacing it with a good habit. You need a *yes* that is bigger and better than the *no*! You need a vision that is bigger and better than the obstacle you're trying to overcome. That's where habit switching enters the equation."[2]

The process of replacing bad habits with good ones goes by many names, but I like to call it "the power of positive replacement." That concept reminds me of a spiritual principle that appears often in the New Testament—"The Put Off and Put On Principle."

Here are some examples of that principle in action:

"Let us cast off the works of darkness, and let us put on the armor of light" (Romans 13:12).

"Do not lie to one another, since you have put off the old man with his deeds, and have put on the new man who is renewed in knowledge according to the image of Him who created him" (Colossians 3:9-10).

"Let us lay aside every weight, and the sin which so easily ensnares us, and let us run with endurance the race that is set before us" (Hebrews 12:1).

But the most well-known example of this powerful principle is found in the passage we come to in Ephesians chapter 4: "Put off, concerning your former conduct, the old man which grows corrupt … and … put on the new man which was created according to God, in true righteousness and holiness" (verses 22, 24).

In the original Greek text, this section of Ephesians 4 contains two long sentences. In verses 17-19, Paul gives four characteristics of the walk of the old man; these are what we need to "put off." In verses 20-24, he describes four characteristics of the walk of the new man, which we need to "put on."

This section is so significant to the book of Ephesians that many commentators believe the rest of the letter is basically an application of these seven verses. That's one reason why Paul begins this section of his letter with a sense of great urgency and firmness: "This I say, therefore, and testify in the Lord" (Ephesians 4:17).

This sense of urgency is all about the importance of believers understanding that Christianity is a revolutionary change in the way a person lives. They can "no longer" live as they once lived.

Peter says something similar to the scattered believers who received his letter: "For we have spent enough of our past lifetime in doing the will of the Gentiles—when we walked in lewdness, lusts, drunkenness, revelries, drinking parties, and abominable idolatries. In regard to these, they think it strange that you do not run with them in the same flood of dissipation, speaking evil of you" (1 Peter 4:3-4).

To the Ephesian Christians—and to us—Paul is going to offer three imperatives in this section of his letter: expel the old man, embrace the new man, and empower the inner man.

As a reminder, the city of Ephesus was a place of deep spiritual darkness. It was one of the vilest cities of Asia Minor. The Temple of Diana with its one thousand religious prostitutes was the centerpiece of that city. But there was also a quarter of a mile around the temple that had been declared a safe zone for criminals. Anyone who committed any crime, if they could get to that quarter of a mile perimeter around the temple, could escape any kind of prosecution or punishment. So in the center of Ephesus was this wicked temple surrounded by a quarter of a mile radius populated by some of the most hardened criminals of the day.

The members of the Ephesian church, then, surrounded by all of this wickedness, were struggling to figure out how to live the Christian life in the midst of such darkness. So Paul, in this section, began to remind them of their experiences with Christ— of the ways they had been spiritually transformed.

Let's take a look at this first section of verses:

> This I say, therefore, and testify in the Lord, that you should no longer walk as the rest of the Gentiles walk, in the futility of their mind, having their understanding darkened, being alienated from the life of God, because of the ignorance that is in them, because of the blindness of their heart; who, being past feeling, have given themselves over to lewdness, to work all uncleanness with greediness. But you have not so learned Christ, if indeed you have heard Him and have been taught by Him, as the truth is in Jesus: that you put off, concerning your former conduct, the old man which grows corrupt according to the deceitful lusts, and be renewed in the spirit of your mind, and that you put on the new man which was created according to God, in true righteousness and holiness. (Ephesians 4:17-24)

Within those verses are three powerful commands Paul gave to the believers in Ephesus—and by extension, to you and me. The first was that they (and we) expel or get rid of their old way of life.

Expel the Old Man

To get started, let's skip down to verse 22 and notice Paul's instructions to the Ephesians about how to deal with their old way of life: "Put off, concerning your former conduct, the old man which grows corrupt according to the deceitful lusts."

C. I. Scofield, who is famous for his annotated Bible, said that when we speak of the old man, the best way to understand it is to refer to it as the "man of old," the man the Christian used to be. That man was born with a corrupt nature!

The verb phrase "put off" means "to strip off," as in the case of old filthy clothes. It is not a process word. It is an action word. It means to take a definitive action and put off the old man. Stop living according to the manner of life which was yours before Christ came into your heart.

The phrase "former conduct" translates a Greek word that means "manner of life." To put off the old man is to "refuse our former manner of conduct." Though our old man legally died at our conversion and though our sinful nature no longer has authority to enslave us, we can still choose to submit to its domination.

In other words, as followers of Jesus, two kinds of life are open to us: life in the flesh or life in the spirit. "I say then: Walk in the Spirit, and you shall not fulfill the lust of the flesh .... And those who are Christ's have crucified the flesh with its passions and desires" (Galatians 5:16, 24).

The believer is to put off his or her old manner of life because that manner of life only grows more corrupt as it is allowed to manifest itself.

Paul then makes his case for expelling the old man by giving us a picture of what he is like. The old man is ...

In Philosophical Despair

"You should no longer walk as the rest of the Gentiles walk, in the futility of their mind" (Ephesians 4:17).

Futility is a fitting description for the way men's minds work without God. This was the experience of Solomon that he described in the book of Ecclesiastes. He traced the way of man under the sun and found that all of it was vanity and chasing the wind. He tried possessions and position and prominence and power, and when it was all done, he said that without God it was all emptiness and aimlessness and without meaning.

I remember reading these chilling words from a college student in the midst of philosophical despair:

> To anyone in the world who cares: Who am I? Why am I living? Life has become stupid and purposeless. Nothing makes sense anymore. The questions I had when I came to college are still unanswered and now I am convinced there are no answers. There can only be pain and guilt and despair here in this world. My fear of death and the unknown is far less terrifying than the prospect of the unbearable frustration, futility, and hopelessness of continued existence.

The psalmist says it this way: "The Lord knows the thoughts of man, that they are futile" (Psalm 94:11).

In Mental Darkness

Paul continued by saying that the Gentiles also have "their understanding darkened" (Ephesians 4:18).

This idea of a darkened understanding was a common theme in Paul's epistles. For example, he told the Corinthians that those who do not know Christ are those "whose minds the god of this age has blinded, who do not believe, lest the light of the gospel of the glory of Christ, who is the image of God, should shine on them" (2 Corinthians 4:4).

He described the condition of men in the Last Days this way: "Always learning and never able to come to the knowledge of the truth" (2 Timothy 3:7).

In his letter to the Romans, Paul added this descriptive note: "Although they knew God, they did not glorify Him as God, nor were thankful, but became futile in their thoughts, and their foolish hearts were darkened. Professing to be wise, they became fools" (1:21-22).

One scholar has noted that "Paul's primary concern here is not with a list of specific sins, but with a distortion and disorientation of the mind .... [He] views sin as a malfunction of the mind .... [In other words,] sins are not the cause of the problem, but the result; the problem lies in the mind and in choices made against God."[3]

In Spiritual Disconnectedness

"Being alienated from the life of God, because of the ignorance that is in them, because of the blindness of their heart" (Ephesians 4:18).

Paul used two words in this verse that are very important in understanding the condition of man without Christ. The first is "ignorance." This is a word which simply means that they do not know; those who don't have Christ lack knowledge. But the second word, which is translated "blindness," is better translated "hardness." Not only are many people ignorant of God, but we can become hardened against God and refuse any attempt to offer us the knowledge we need.

Jesus said, "And this is the condemnation, that the light has come into the world, and men loved darkness rather than light, because their deeds were evil" (John 3:19).

Let me tell you a short story about a brilliant woman who had her hard heart transformed by the living God. Her name is Dr. Rosalind Picard, and she is credited with starting an entire branch of engineering science known as affective computing. But in high school Rosalind was a committed atheist, leading debates in favor of the case for evolution and dismissing those who didn't agree with her.

One night Rosalind babysat for a doctor and his wife. As they paid her at the end of the evening, they invited her to church. Rosalind begged off, but eventually she accepted their suggestion to read the Bible, specifically the book of Proverbs.

"To my surprise," she says. "Proverbs was full of wisdom. I had to pause while reading and *think*."

Rosalind read through the entire Bible, and it intrigued her more than she could have imagined. Reading through the Bible a second time, she was conflicted. "I didn't *want* to believe in God," she said, "but I still felt a peculiar sense of love and presence I couldn't ignore."

In college, a friend invited her to church, and she made Christ the Lord of her life. Listen to how she explains what happened to her: "My world changed dramatically, as if a flat, black-and-white existence suddenly turned full-color and three-dimensional .... I once thought I was too smart to believe in God. Now I know I was an arrogant fool who snubbed the greatest Mind in the cosmos—the Author of all science, mathematics, art, and everything else there is to know."[4]

In Moral Deterioration

Our old way of life before Christ—what Paul called the "old man"—is characterized by philosophical despair, mental darkness, spiritual disconnectedness, and moral deterioration.

The old man includes those "who, being past feeling, have given themselves over to lewdness, to work all uncleanness with greediness" (Ephesians 4:19).

The inevitable result of leaving God out of one's life is that life for that person begins to deteriorate. Listen to the way the psalmist puts this all together: "The fool has said in his heart, 'There is no God.' They are corrupt, they have done abominable works, there is none who does good" (Psalm 14:1).

The phrase "past feeling" is a Greek word that only occurs here in the New Testament. A person who is past feeling is someone who has lost their sense of pain. Leprosy is the ultimate result of losing the sense of physical pain. Lepers lose their limbs and are disfigured because their disease will not let them feel pain.

Those who are past feeling work hard at their evil pursuits. They do it out of greediness. Their motive is money. Their goal is gain! How could a person exploit children, print and distribute pornography, and sell enslaving drugs to teenagers and children? Why does the tobacco industry purposefully try to get children and young people hooked on cigarettes when they know that by doing so, they are systematically killing them? The reason, according to Paul, is that they are "without feeling."

The motive behind all that they do is "greediness." They do it for money.

Embrace the New Man

In Ephesians 4:24, Paul moves from the negative to the positive. It is not enough to expel the old way of life; we must embrace the new! So he writes, "Put on the new man which was created according to God, in true righteousness and holiness."

I like what one commentator wrote about this verse: "Here we must keep in mind that we do not put on the new man merely by putting off the old. We need to put on love, to put on peace, to put on joy, to put on patience …. For example, I may have lost my temper with my children, and I have repented and put it off. But I have not completed my responsibility unless I have also put on love and patience."[5]

The simplest illustration of this great truth is found in John 11, which describes the resurrection of Lazarus. Our Lord's friend, Lazarus, had been in the grave for four days when Jesus and His disciples arrived at Bethany, and even Martha admitted that by now the decaying body would smell. But Jesus spoke the word, and Lazarus came forth alive. Notice our Lord's next words: "Loose him, and let him go" (John 11:44).

In other words, "Take off the graveclothes!" Lazarus no longer belonged to the old dominion of death, for he was now alive. Why go about wearing grave clothes? Take off the old and put on the new.

Since the old man has been "put off," we are to embrace the new man. In the next four verses, Paul gives us three characteristics of the new man.

The new man is …

A New Connection

"But you have not so learned Christ" (Ephesians 4:20).

Instead of philosophical despair, the new man has a new connection with Jesus. When a person becomes a Christian, they take off despair and discouragement and put on Christ, who is the hope of glory.

In contrast to the alienation from God in the old life, Paul wrote of the connection with God through Christ in the new life. Note, he did not write, "You have not so learned Christianity." He wrote, "You have not so learned Christ." The walk of the new man is not an adherence to a religious system. The walk of the new man is a relationship with a personal Savior, the Lord Jesus Christ. Everything that is old and ugly about the first few verses of this passage is overcome by a personal relationship with Jesus Christ.

To be connected to Jesus means to be connected to hope! Hope for the future—that eternity will be better than we can imagine. Hope for today—that He is with us to guide us and encourage us. And hope for the past—that our sins are forgiven and our failures are forgotten.

Put off despair and put on Christ.

A New Conviction

"If indeed you have heard Him and have been taught by Him, as the truth is in Jesus" (Ephesians 4:21).

Instead of mental darkness, the believer has a new conviction. Note that these Ephesian believers had learned Christ, heard Christ, and been taught by Christ.

The new man recognizes Jesus as their Master Teacher. If you take a concordance and look up every time Jesus was addressed as "Teacher" or "Rabbi," you'll be surprised. More than 45 times Jesus is referred to in this role.

He also spoke of Himself in this way. In John 13:13, He told the disciples, "You call Me Teacher and Lord, and you say well, for so I am."

Just as Jesus is King of kings and Lord of lords, He is Teacher of teachers—the Supreme Educator of the ages. Sometimes He taught one or two or three people at a time; other times He spoke to thousands at once without amplification or electronic projection. Even now, He speaks across the ages, and His words reach the deepest foundations of our mind and heart. Whenever you open the Bible, you're sitting at His feet just like the disciples did.

The new way of living is a new way of thinking. We dedicate ourselves to the truth, and we set our minds on heavenly things: "If then you were raised with Christ, seek those things which are above, where Christ is, sitting at the right hand of God. Set your mind on things above, not on things on the earth. For you died, and your life is hidden with Christ in God" (Colossians 3:1-3).

Putting on the new man must be an experience as decisive as putting off the old. If we are living defeated lives, it is not because God's power is insufficient. The remedy for indecision is not more prayer and more Bible reading. It is decision. Power always follows purpose.

A New Creation

Next, instead of experiencing moral deterioration, the Christian is a new creation who is growing in godliness. Paul continued, "Put on the new man which was created according to God, in true righteousness and holiness" (Ephesians 4:24).

He wrote something similar to the Corinthians, phrasing it this way: "If anyone is in Christ, he is a new creation; old things have passed away; behold, all things have become new" (2 Corinthians 5:17).

The old man produces corruption. The new man creates righteousness and holiness. The creative power of the new man puts back together what sin has disintegrated.

John Stott summed it up: "As we are called to put off our corrupt nature as a ragged and filthy garment, so we are required to put on our new nature as a garment of light. And as the former was seen as decrepit, deformed, and tending to corruption, so the latter is seen as fresh, beautiful and vigorous, like God [that is, created in His image]."[6]

Each day, the new you is becoming more beautiful, more vigorous, and more alive. What a mystery! What a blessing!

Empower the Inner Man

Sandwiched between the putting off of the old self and the putting on of the new self is verse 23: "Be renewed in the spirit of your mind."

To the Corinthians, the apostle again said something similar: "Therefore we do not lose heart. Even though our outward man is perishing, yet the inward man is being renewed day by day" (2 Corinthians 4:16).

It is through the renewing of the mind that the old man is finally and completely put off, and the new man is finally and completely put on. All the things that we learned before Christ are replaced with an entirely new way of thinking. Each and every day, as we read God's Word and pray, we find that our minds are being purged of the old corrupt ways of thinking and we are being renewed in righteousness and holiness.

Satan tries with all of his might to keep us thinking the old way, and when we neglect the input of spiritual truth, we allow him to win that battle. But here we are given a principle that will always win the victory over the evil one. We can renew our mind with God's truth, and as His truth comes into our spirit, it purges the old thoughts out!

The best commentary on this truth is found in Romans 12: "I beseech you therefore, brethren, by the mercies of God, that you present your bodies a living sacrifice, holy, acceptable to God, which is your reasonable service [embracing the new man]. And do not be conformed to this world [expelling the old man], but be transformed by the renewing of your mind, that you may prove what is that good and acceptable and perfect will of God [empowering the inner man]" (verses 1-2).

Here is what it means to renew your mind:

> When the Bible says to renew your mind, it is talking about the complete renovation and replacement of what was formerly present with something better. When you renovate an apartment or building, you knock down and tear out all the old materials that [do] not fit into the new design and plan. If it does not fall within the plan, you throw it out and replace it with something that does. This is what happens when we have our minds renewed. We take all of the stuff that previously occupied our minds and replace it with what is in line with God's plan for our lives .... When we fill our minds with the Word of God, which contains the Mind of God, it helps us discover His Will for our lives.[7]

New Testament scholar Grant Osborne reminds us that "the mind is where spiritual growth occurs, and in the mind decisions are made that determine one's spiritual direction and destiny. In other words, the ongoing conduct of the believer is based on input from the world or from God. This will determine whether one lives the victorious Christian life or a life of spiritual defeat."[8]

General William K. Harrison was a highly decorated twentieth century soldier and statesman, renowned for his character and self-control. He was chosen by President Eisenhower to negotiate the end of the Korean War. Despite his busy schedule during war, he maintained a disciplined reading of the Bible—reading through the New Testament four times a year and the Old Testament once. By the end of his life, he had read through the Old Testament 70 times and the New Testament 280 times! Those who knew him best believe this was a crucial factor in his achievements.[9]

His inspiring story serves as a testament to the power of diligent training in God's Word and the incredible benefits it can bring to every aspect of our lives. Just as he did, each of us has the potential to cultivate this same transformation if we are willing to let go of old ways and embrace the new.

CHAPTER 11

A New Lifestyle

EPHESIANS 4:25-32

From the moment the first episode aired back in 1984, *Lifestyles of the Rich and Famous* became an instant hit. Every week the show's host, British-born American journalist Robin Leach, traveled the world to show off celebrity mansions, expensive cars, private jets, and all the other toys of prodigious materialism. You might even remember the show's catchphrase: "Champagne wishes and caviar dreams."

The show lasted another 75 episodes before being taken off the air in 1995. Today, historians who look at television and radio as history consider it one of the most influential reality shows of all time, ushering in our public obsession with in-depth media coverage of superstars and entertainers and sports figures and royals and the magnates of the business world.[1]

But our obsession with "lifestyle" doesn't stop with the rich and famous. We also talk about "active lifestyles" and "healthy lifestyles" and "minimalist lifestyles" and "maximalist lifestyles" and "urban lifestyles" and "rural lifestyles," just to name a few. It's safe to say we are fascinated with discovering which lifestyles represent the best way to live.

That brings us to the last portion of Ephesians 4 where Paul wants to talk with us about the lifestyle of a Christian. What should a Christian look like? What should his lifestyle be like?

It's interesting to note the way Paul talks about a Christian lifestyle. He doesn't talk about financial wealth or physical health or geographical location. Paul instead describes what we would call character or integrity—the ability to live with others in a virtuous and honorable way.

The qualities of character Paul writes about in this section are necessary qualities that a person must have to function within a group, within a church. They show us how it's possible to get along with one another. And they represent, in essence, the character of Christ. In these verses, Paul is going to call out five areas of life in which you and I have the opportunity to demonstrate our Christianity.

Here is the larger passage we're going to explore together:

Therefore, putting away lying, "Let each one of you speak truth with his neighbor," for we are members of one another. "Be angry, and do not sin": do not let the sun go down on your wrath, nor give place to the devil. Let him who stole steal no longer, but rather let him labor, working with his hands what is good, that he may have something to give him who has need. Let no corrupt word proceed out of your mouth, but what is good for necessary edification, that it may impart grace to the hearers. And do not grieve the Holy Spirit of God, by whom you were sealed for the day of redemption. Let all bitterness, wrath, anger, clamor, and evil speaking be put away from you, with all malice. And be kind to one another, tenderhearted, forgiving one another, even as God in Christ forgave you. (Ephesians 4:25-32)

Let's work through those verses together one at a time.

Our Morality

Paul began by writing about our morality as followers of Jesus. What we consider to be right and wrong should be different from the rest of the world, both in terms of philosophy and practice. Citing a specific example, Paul said we must put away "lying" and instead "speak truth" (Ephesians 4:25).

In the culture of Ephesus, lying was very much a part of everyday existence, even as it is today. As someone has said, lying for the Ephesians was a very present help in times of trouble. People used lies like they used the truth until most people could hardly tell the difference. But Paul's admonition to us is that when we become Christians, we are to put off lying and we are to speak the truth.

Bismark Mensah knows a thing or two about speaking the truth, even when it was costly for him. As an immigrant from Ghana, Mensah was an employee at Walmart in the greater Seattle area. His main task was collecting carts from the parking lot and returning them to the store. He made $9.05 an hour.

Because of his responsibilities, Mr. Mensah was used to finding items that had been left behind in shopping carts—

usually keys, bags, or even wallets. He had a system worked out where he simply passed each lost item over to the customer service desk so that customers could find them when they came back searching.

One day, however, Mensah helped a couple load their bags into their car. The couple had purchased two carts full of supplies, so it was a long interaction and took some effort to get everything loaded in properly. As the couple was driving away, Mensah noticed an envelope left in the cart. There was a plastic window or screen in the envelope that gave the young man a clear view of its contents: cash, and lots of it.

Turns out, there was $20,000 in that envelope. The couple had just removed it from the bank in order to pay the down payment on a house.

What did Bismark Mensah do? He ran toward the car, waving and shouting to get the couple's attention. It worked! When the vehicle came to a stop, the young immigrant handed over the envelope with a polite smile. When the woman took some money out of the envelope to offer as a reward, Bismark refused. He was just doing his job.

Later, reporters asked Bismark Mensah if he considered keeping the money. He replied that it never crossed his mind. "My conscience wouldn't allow it," he said. "I couldn't even drive home if I did that."[2]

Maybe right now you're thinking, *What's the big deal about lying? Everybody does it, at least a little bit.*

The problem is that Almighty God has labeled Himself as "truth." Jesus identified Satan as a liar and the father of lies

(John 8:44). When we lie, then, we are playing on Satan's turf instead of God's turf. We are acting antithetically to who God is.

Our Moods

Next, Paul moved from our morality to our moods. He wrote, "'Be angry, and do not sin': do not let the sun go down on your wrath, nor give place to the devil" (verses 26-27).

In *Wishful Thinking*, Frederick Buechner wrote,

Of the Seven Deadly Sins, anger is possibly the most fun. To lick your wounds, to smack your lips over grievances long past, to roll over your tongue the prospect of bitter confrontations still to come, to savor to the last toothsome morsel both the pain you are given and the pain you are giving back—in many ways it is a feast fit for a king. The chief drawback is what you are wolfing down is yourself. The skeleton at the feast is you.[3]

In this context, Paul wasn't talking about getting angry at things like traffic or the day's news. He was talking about getting mad at our "neighbor" (verse 25). When you're most tempted to lose your temper, it's often because of someone else, perhaps someone you love very much.

Interestingly, the Bible doesn't tell us never to be angry. Anger is a natural human response, but it must be governed. It's a dangerous emotion, as volatile as nitroglycerin, that must be controlled.

Aristotle reportedly said, "Anyone can become angry. But to be angry with the right person, to the right degree, at the right time, for the right purpose, and in the right way—this is not easy."

That's why Paul quoted Psalm 4:4, which says, "Be angry, and do not sin."

That may feel surprising because many Christians have been taught the idea that anger is always bad—that anger is always a sin. Yet, we know that can't be true for one simple reason: Jesus was angry.

Remember when Jesus made Himself a whip and cleared out the money changers from the temple? That's one of my favorite stories, although it's important to know the background of what was going on in that moment. People brought sacrifices to the temple as part of their worship. But the priests had to determine whether a sacrifice was "acceptable" or not. You can probably guess what happened. Some entrepreneurial thief convinced the priests (most likely through bribes) to declare many or most of the animals brought by the people as unacceptable. Then those scoundrels set up a booth where travelers could purchase acceptable sacrifices—at a huge profit, of course.

In short, there was fraud and greed and dishonesty right in the outer court of the temple. John 2:15 says, "When He had made a whip of cords, He drove them all out of the temple, with the sheep and the oxen, and poured out the changers' money and overturned the tables."

Jesus wasn't calm and collected in that moment. He was angry! Yes, Jesus expressed anger at injustice. He expressed anger at evil and its effect on other people—especially on those people who were unable to defend themselves.

The same should be true of you and me. How can we not be angry when we see babies being aborted in our culture? How can we not be angry at child abuse? How can we not be angry about domestic violence and drugs? How can we not be angry about politicians who profit from poverty and war?

Even so, Paul says we are to be angry, and then he qualifies that command with three negatives—three ways to make sure our anger is under control. In your anger …

- Do not sin.

- Do not let the sun go down on your wrath.

- Do not give a place to the devil.

John Phillips gave us this advice: "If you have to be angry— if the cause is righteous, the provocation severe—then let the storm burst but make sure the expression of your anger is not promiscuous or prolonged. Let calm follow the storm and be sure that your fellowship with God is not broken."[4]

We need to put off the old way of selfish, reactionary anger, and we need to put on the new way of self-control. As someone has said, "The more you grow up, the less you blow up."

Our Money

I remember reading a story about a Soviet factory worker who attempted to steal items from his workplace. Every day he filled a wheelbarrow with cylinders, iron ore, and tools—and every day as he left, he got caught and the stuff was taken away from him.

Finally, he was fired, and on his last day the commissar waited for him to come out with the contraband. When he arrived at the door, the commissar pulled back the cover from the wheelbarrow, and there was the usual stuff. He confiscated everything and said to the thief, "You are a fool! We caught you every single day. You got away with nothing!"

"Sir, Mr. Commissar," he answered, "You are the fool. I have been stealing wheelbarrows."

There is such a thing as stealing because there is such a thing as ownership. God dignifies us as His children by giving us work to perform, property to maintain, and rights to uphold.

There are only three ways to acquire property: work for it, receive it as a gift, or steal it. In verse 28, Paul addressed all three: "Let him who stole steal no longer, but rather let him labor, working with his hands what is good, that he may have something to give him who has need."

"Let him who stole steal no longer." Never has that instruction been more appropriate than it is today. In our day, stealing—what we call theft—has taken on a whole new meaning. Day after day we watch on television as gangs of young hoodlums crash into jewelry stores and department stores. Using hammers, they destroy display cases and stuff the products of the stores into bags and run out into the street having stolen everything they can get their hands on. They are getting away with it to the point that many such places of business are closing their doors.

The reigning rule in my own state of California is that any shoplifter can steal up to $950 without being arrested and prosecuted. There is no longer any penalty for taking that which is not yours.

I had a very real encounter with this new normal recently. While my wife was recovering from a recent surgery, I started doing the grocery shopping. Donna gave me a list, and I went on a search to find each item. Two times in a row I was assigned to bring back some Tide Pods, but when I went to the place where they usually were on shelves in the grocery store, I was surprised to see those shelves were empty. When I came home without the detergent, neither of us could understand how the stores could be out of that product.

Well, I returned on my mission a third time, and when once again I found the detergent shelves empty, I asked one of the workers who was stocking the nearby shelves what was going on. She explained, "We can no longer stock that product on the shelves because people have been reaching into the containers and stealing the pods, putting them into their pockets without paying for them. When honest customers buy the container of detergent, they would get home only to discover that the container was half full."

The worker then gave me a voucher and told me to give this to the cashier, and they would get my detergent for me when I checked out.

Stealing soap! Can you believe such a thing? Now I know why drug stores and grocery stores have so many products under lock and key!

The mentality in our culture seems to be: If you don't get caught, there is nothing wrong with shoplifting or stealing or theft. But the Bible says that stealing is a sin no matter how sophisticated the process might be. That's why Paul wrote,

"Stop stealing!"

Some of the Christians who first read this letter—the Ephesians—had come to Christ from a background of thievery. They were shoplifters, cheaters, even burglars. Paul was saying that if they stopped stealing and instead worked hard with their hands to earn a livelihood, then they would have something of their own to share with others.

About verse 28, one New Testament commentator said this:

> This verse may be the most striking description of conversion in the New Testament: "The thief is to become a philanthropist."

> Do not take what is not yours but work hard so that you may be able to give to others what is not theirs.

> The person who did wrong in order to meet his own selfish desires must now work in order to contribute to someone else's need. This is a compelling example of dying and rising with Christ.[5]

What a reversal! Instead of stealing from others, the former thieves were to give to others. Based on this verse, I advise you to work hard to earn a living and then use what you earn to care for those in need. The Christian life is about the aggressive pursuit of what is productive and beneficial.

Our Mouths

Next, we can demonstrate godliness through our mouths—through the way we speak. Paul said, "Let no corrupt word proceed out of your mouth, but what is good for necessary edification, that it may impart grace to the hearers" (Ephesians 4:29).

Interestingly, the word "corrupt" in the text actually describes the decaying body of an animal or putrid garbage. Paul was saying, "Get rid of your corrupt words. Get rid of that junk before it stinks up your life!"

Notice also the next verse: "And do not grieve the Holy Spirit of God, by whom you were sealed for the day of redemption" (verse 30).

If you want an example of unwholesome talk, just turn on the TV or radio. Listen to the conversations around you. Even better, listen to your own words for a day and evaluate them through the grid of Ephesians 4:29.

The Bible is filled with verses about how we speak—the words we say and the tone we employ. But Ephesians 4:29 is among the most practical and helpful passages in Scripture when it comes to the subject of our tongues. Nothing we say should be corrupt, which means unholy, unhealthy to others, destructive, or detrimental. Instead, our words should benefit others and build them up.

Many people are standing out in the rain of discouragement, as it were. Their hearts are soaked with heavy drops of disappointment and pessimism. For that reason, you and I should never underestimate the power of a kind word.

One way to practice this is to make a habit of complimenting at least one person every day. As you start your day in the morning, ask yourself, "Whom can I compliment today?" You'll be amazed at the gratitude that flows your way and fills your heart over time. People crave positive reinforcement. All of us do.

Abraham Lincoln wore a Brooks Brothers overcoat when he and his wife, Mary, attended a performance at Ford's Theatre on April 14, 1865. Shortly after 10:00 p.m., John Wilkes Booth crept behind him and fired the fatal shot that killed the President. Afterward, the personal belongings in his coat pockets were collected and given to his son, Robert Todd Lincoln, who put them in a box. They were later passed down to Robert's daughter, Mary, who donated them to the Library of Congress in 1937.

The box was unopened until 1976. Do you know what was in the box? What Lincoln had carried with him that fatal night in his Brooks Brothers coat? He had a couple pairs of eyeglasses, a pocketknife, a gold watch fob, a white handkerchief, a cufflink, a five-dollar bill, a brown leather wallet, and several newspaper clippings. One of them extolled his accomplishments and began with the words: "Abe Lincoln is one of the greatest statesmen of all time."[6]

Though he was truly one of the greatest statesmen of all time, Abraham Lincoln endured unceasing criticism. He needed encouragement and affirmation as badly as his most beleaguered soldiers, and he was carrying an article that reassured him of his worth in his pocket when he died.

From the greatest to the smallest, we all crave words and actions that will encourage us, edify us, and build us up. So let's take Proverbs 18:21 to heart: "Death and life are in the power of the tongue."

Put off destructive words; put on encouraging words. Sometimes it really is that simple.

Our Manners

How do we enable the holy man in our lives? By demonstrating godliness in our morality, in our moods, with our money, with our mouths—and finally, with our manners.

Look at Ephesians 4:30-31: "And do not grieve the Holy Spirit of God, by whom you were sealed for the day of redemption. Let all bitterness, wrath, anger, clamor, and evil speaking be put away from you, with all malice."

In verses 26 and 27, Paul said that when we stay angry over a period of time, we "give place to the devil." In verse 30, he indicated that when we let bitterness grow in our hearts, we grieve the Holy Spirit of God. A bitter spirit does two things at once: It grieves the Holy Spirit, and it delights the devil.

One New Testament scholar challenges us with these stinging words: "'Hostile Christian' is an oxymoron. We must replace hostility with helpfulness. The primary place hostility and cynicism appear is in our families, the assumption being that those closest to us are responsible for the problem, have failed to solve it, or are easy targets for revenge. Where families are marked by bitterness, anger, shouting, or worse, violence, no one may speak of Christian faith."[7]

Paul tells us to replace all bitterness, wrath, anger, clamor, evil speaking, and malice with kindness and forgiveness: "And be kind to one another, tenderhearted, forgiving one another, even as God in Christ forgave you" (verse 32).

Verse 32 modifies the Golden Rule. It doesn't say, "Treat others as you would like them to treat you." It says, "Treat others as God has treated you."

Notice how those terms fit together. Put off bitterness and wrath, and then put on kindness. Put off anger and clamor, and instead put on tenderheartedness. Put away evil speaking and malice, and then put on forgiveness.

Followers of Christ should be exceptional forgivers because we know how we have been forgiven. How did God forgive us? For Christ's sake, He forgave us unconditionally. He forgave us freely. He didn't say, "I'll forgive, but I won't forget!" The Bible says when He forgave us, He threw our sins into the deepest part of the sea (Micah 7:19). He put our sin behind His back as far as the east is from the west (Psalm 103:12). That is how we are to forgive—just as we are forgiven.

Let me ask you something: Have you been forgiven by God through Jesus Christ? All your sins nailed to His cross? All your sins of omission, commission, and disposition erased by the acid power of His blood?

Yes? Then why should you or I harbor resentful attitudes toward others? Toward someone in our home? Why do we carry around grudges? We are commanded to forgive because God has forgiven us, and we're to forgive as He has forgiven us. When we do so, renewed blessings come into our life.

To forgive someone is not to endorse or excuse their behavior. Many people have experienced terrible trauma in their lives. Perhaps you've suffered at the hands of someone else, and you've never been able to make peace with what happened to you. I don't want to be simplistic; sometimes we need lots of time, counseling, and help. But I believe with all my heart that the basis of all emotional turnarounds is found in the grace of Jesus Christ and the power of the Holy Spirit. That's your foundation. When you personally experience His forgiveness, it changes you. It enables you to understand forgiveness, and it gives you the power to forgive others as God has forgiven you in Christ Jesus.

Paul encourages us to think of kindness as a lifestyle, like a piece of clothing we wear all the time. It's the attitude of wanting to bless others, to lift their spirits, to meet their needs—and to do so in Jesus' Name.

Davyon Johnson was a sixth grader in Oklahoma who had a particularly remarkable day. It started when another sixth grader took a drink from a bottle of water—but got the cap stuck in his mouth, and then all the way in his throat. He was in trouble! Thankfully, young Davyon jumped up from his seat in the cafeteria and performed the Heimlich maneuver, successfully dislodging the cap from the other student's mouth.

That was a heroic act. A demonstration of extreme kindness and good morals. But Davyon wasn't through.

Later that day he and his mother noticed a home on fire. He also saw an elderly woman on that porch's home, struggling to move. Quickly, Davyon rushed to her side and helped her to her car to escape the blaze. He repeatedly told the woman, "It's going to be okay."

In short, young Davyon Johnson saved a student from choking *and* saved an elderly woman from a house fire—all on the same day.

In recognition of his bravery and citizenship, Davyon was recognized by the local school board, made an honorary deputy by the sheriff's office, and declared an honorary police officer to boot.

"He's just a very humble and old spirit," said his principal, Latricia Dawkins. "He's responsible, reliable, friendly, just a kind soul."[8]

May the same be said of you and I as we demonstrate our spiritual transformation and live for Christ each day!

CHAPTER 12

Walking in Love

EPHESIANS 5:1-7

Martin Douthwaite began walking on a crisp March afternoon in the region of Selby, England. His plan was to make a circuit around his village of Hensall, walking completely around its borders. And then another. And another. And another.

In fact, Douthwaite had committed to walking a full 24 hours in order to raise support for the children of Ukraine—children whose lives had been turned upside down by a brutal Russian invasion in the early months of 2022.

Like most of us during that season, Douthwaite regularly checked updates on the news about the war in Ukraine, hopeful that the destruction might soon come to an end. At that point, more than four million Ukrainians had fled their homes and become refugees, many of them children separated from fathers who stayed behind to fight. Cities were besieged and being destroyed.

After a month of continual bad news—and ever-increasing suffering—Douthwaite knew he had to do something. So he announced his intentions, set up his fundraiser, and started to walk.

He carried a flag throughout his vigil that represented both Ukraine and the United Kingdom, showing the friendship between those nations. And he received a great deal of support from his fellow villagers, many of whom joined him for different portions of his walk. "Villagers laid out tables of food and drink in various places and some left me boxes of food during the night," Douthwaite said. "A lady got up at 3 a.m. to bring me a hot chocolate."

In the end, Martin Douthwaite raised more than £5,000 (or $6,500) for the organization Save the Children.[1]

One reason I like that story is because it reminds me of how many times Scripture refers to our day-to-day experiences with Christianity as a "walk." Many followers of Jesus believe they are supposed to sprint everywhere—at least at first. Then the reality of their own limitations sets in, and they collapse. Others view the Christian life as more of a couch session. They are content to sit patiently and comfortably in their cozy lives until Christ returns. Both of those extremes are unhelpful.

Instead, we are called to "walk" in the footsteps of Jesus. The Christian walk is a day by day journey. It's not rushing ahead or lagging behind but rather a steady progress forward in the direction of Christ.

As we'll see in this chapter, Paul used that image of a walk to help the Ephesians wrap their minds around their own spiritual journeys. Specifically, he encouraged them to walk in love.

The book of Ephesians reminds us several times that the Christian life is like walking. In the fourth chapter we are exhorted to "walk worthy of [our] calling." In that same chapter we are commanded not to walk as the Gentiles. In the passage we are studying in this chapter, we are told to "walk in love." Later we will be discussing walking in the light. And then in verses 15-21 of Ephesians 5 we are admonished to walk in wisdom.

Walking is a great example of the Christian life. It is one step at a time. Each step is a step of faith, and the metaphor describes the progress.

Remember that these verses were addressed to Christians who had come to Christ while living in the sinful city of Ephesus. In that city, people accepted sexual perversion and even exalted that way of life. Ephesus is a picture of many of the world's great cities today—Hong Kong, Moscow, San Diego, and more. Therefore, these words have great application to our own experiences.

The Command About Walking in Love

Paul began by writing, "Therefore be imitators of God as dear children. And walk in love" (Ephesians 5:1-2).

The "therefore" that begins this chapter points us back to the last verse of chapter 4: "And be kind to one another, tenderhearted, forgiving one another, even as God in Christ forgave you" (Ephesians 4:32).

The word "imitators" is translated from the Greek term *mimetes*, which is where we get our English word *mimic*. Paul said we are to mimic God in the matters of kindness and tenderheartedness and forgiveness, and we are to walk in that kind of love.

The Bible says one day we are going to be like Jesus when we see Him just as He is (1 John 3:2). In the meantime, we have been called to be godly men and women, which means we are to be imitators of God. Notice, Paul said we are to do this "as dear children." Just as children imitate their parents, we are to be imitators of God our Heavenly Father.

Peter sounded the same note in his first epistle: "As obedient children, not conforming yourselves to the former lusts, as in your ignorance; but as He who called you is holy, you also be holy in all your conduct, because it is written, 'Be holy, for I am holy'" (1 Peter 1:14-16).

We become imitators of God when we read His Word and discover who He is and what He is like. Then, through the Holy Spirit, we pray that those characteristics will be formed in our life so that we can be more like our Father in heaven. This should be every believer's goal—to become like their Father.

If we follow Paul's reasoning back to the fourth chapter, we begin to understand that we are walking in love when we are forgiving one another. That's the point of Ephesians 4:32—"Even as God in Christ forgave you." When we imitate Him, we forgive others.

So if we want to know if we are walking in love, here is the question: Are we walking in forgiveness? Are we forgiving one another as God has forgiven us?

The Case for Walking in Love

But what does it mean on a practical level to imitate God? What does that look like? Paul answered that question in verse 2: "And walk in love, as Christ also has loved us and given Himself for us, an offering and a sacrifice to God for a sweet-smelling aroma."

Scripture says God is love, which means Jesus is a walking and talking definition of love—a walking and talking example of what it looks like to love. If we are in doubt as to how we should walk in love and in forgiveness, we have been given a role model in our Savior.

Jesus Himself said, "Greater love has no one than this, than to lay down one's life for his friends" (John 15:13).

The apostle Paul wrote, "For when we were still without strength, in due time Christ died for the ungodly .... But God demonstrates His own love toward us, in that while we were still sinners, Christ died for us .... When we were enemies we were reconciled to God through the death of His Son" (Romans 5:6-10).

Just as our Lord sacrificially gave up His life for us, we are to sacrificially (and continually) give up our lives for one another. When we are living in such a loving and forgiving way, we are a sweet aroma to the throne in heaven. Does this describe your life? Does it describe mine? These are questions we must answer as we seek to live a godly lifestyle.

The Counterfeit to Walking in Love

Next. Paul moves on to describe the opposite of walking in love: "But fornication and all uncleanness or covetousness, let it not even be named among you, as is fitting for saints; neither filthiness, nor foolish talking, nor coarse jesting, which are not fitting, but rather giving of thanks" (Ephesians 5:3-4).

That is quite an uncomfortable list of words:

- fornication

- uncleanness

- covetousness

- filthiness

- coarse jesting

- idolater

- empty words

- disobedience

Maybe you're wondering, *Why did Paul have to mess up this passage about love by bringing in all that junk?*

The answer is Satan. While we are called to be imitators of God, Satan is a counterfeiter of God. As such, our enemy has set up a counterfeit program of love—one that was evident in the world of Paul's day and remains evident in our own society. While God's love is filled with forgiveness and self-sacrifice and all manner of good things, Satan has set up a corrupted imitation of love that is destructive, disruptive, and sadly more and more dispersed in our culture and even in the Church.

We need to spend a little time identifying and delegitimizing that counterfeit so that we can more deeply appreciate God's love.

Immorality

For starters, Satan's counterfeit system of love is bursting with immorality. Paul wrote, "But fornication and all uncleanness or covetousness, let it not even be named among you, as is fitting for saints" (Ephesians 5:3).

While godly love seeks to give, lust seeks to take. While true love is self-sacrificial, lust sacrifices others for our benefit. While true love purifies and lifts us up, lust and fornication degrade us and drag us down. True love satisfies, but immorality leaves us with a gnawing emptiness in our hearts so that we continually hunger for more.

The word "fornication" is from the Greek term *porneia*, from which we get the word *pornographic*. This Greek term describes all kinds of sexual sin against God, but it especially refers to adultery and infidelity—sex outside of marriage.

The word "uncleanness" refers to anything that is unclean and filthy. It is used to describe the decaying of bodies in a tomb.

The third word Paul mentions under the category of immorality is the word "covetousness." Covetousness and greed are at the core of immorality, for immorality is self-centered lust bent on personal gratification. It is the exact opposite of love. Love seeks the best interests of the one loved. Lust is the desire to satisfy one's self.

There are many examples of this counterfeit system of love at work in our society, and I'm sure some of those examples have already crossed your mind. Pornography. Sex outside of marriage. Homosexuality and transgenderism. Divorce. Sexual abuse, including the abuse of children.

The Bible says such practices of immorality should not be so much as even named among those who are saints. This does not mean that they should not be talked about as they are in this letter but that they should never be associated with those who follow Christ.

Impurity

But it's not just our actions. Paul talked about the way impurity has infected our words, including what we say to one another and what we say to God. "Neither filthiness, nor foolish talking, nor coarse jesting, which are not fitting, but rather giving of thanks" (Ephesians 5:4).

Paul now turns from immorality to impurity. Immorality is a counterfeit walk, and impurity is counterfeit talk.

"Filthiness" is dirty or vulgar language. This is a term that signifies something obscene or shameful. In fact, Paul used this word again in verse 12 of this same chapter: "For it is shameful even to speak of those things which are done by them in secret."

"Foolish talking" comes from a Greek word that can be translated "buffoonery." It's the nonsense we hear so much in movies and TV shows these days.

And then "coarse jesting" describes taking something that was meant to be good and turning it upside down so that it becomes bad. It's when we drag an idea or the speech of others into an off-color arena for the sake of laughs.

Paul says that such speech is not fitting for followers of Christ. We should be known for gracious speech and for thankful words.

The Cost of Not Walking in Love

If you're like me, you have wondered why anyone would take a medicine that comes with so many warnings. Sometimes it actually seems like the warnings that come with health products are scarier than the disease we are trying to cure!

As crazy as some warnings sound, we all need warning signs in our lives. Warning signs on the road inform drivers of what is ahead. They warn of a stop light, a curve, or a deer crossing ahead. Those signs help prevent damage and even death on the highway.

On the spiritual highway, there are also danger signs. These signs warn us about our spiritual life.

Why is this a big deal? Why is this something we need to discuss? Because of Ephesians 5:5: "For this you know, that no fornicator, unclean person, nor covetous man, who is an idolater, has any inheritance in the kingdom of Christ and God."

In that verse, Paul uses three of the same words he just used in verse 3. He adds a fourth word to describe covetousness as idolatry. In doing so, Paul reminds us that people who are characterized by these things are not believers. He is not saying that if someone commits one of these sins, he is not a believer any longer. What he is telling us is this: You cannot be a child of God and live like a child of the devil. This is an impossible picture.

Here's why: "Therefore, if anyone is in Christ, he is a new creation; old things have passed away; behold, all things have become new" (2 Corinthians 5:17).

And here: "For the grace of God that brings salvation has appeared to all men, teaching us that, denying ungodliness and worldly lusts, we should live soberly, righteously, and godly in the present age" (Titus 2:11-12).

Christians are not sinless, but they do sin less and less and less as they grow in Christ. John Phillips has a powerful comment here:

> A cheap form of Christianity is in circulation today. It is not really Christianity at all, just a popular counterfeit. People make professions of faith that entail no repentance, no genuine conversion, no regeneration by the Holy Spirit, and no dynamic new life in Christ. Such people can be deceived into thinking that they are Christians, but they see no need—and feel no impulse from an indwelling Holy Spirit—to give up sinful practices or resist them. It is "business as usual" .... Such people are as lost as they were before they went through the meaningless motions of professing to believe, being baptized, and joining local churches.[2]

Paul concludes this part of his letter with a solemn warning: "Let no one deceive you with empty words, for because of these things the wrath of God comes upon the sons of disobedience. Therefore do not be partakers with them" (Ephesians 5:6-7).

In Paul's day there were some in the Church who had been influenced by pagan philosophers, and they were teaching that no physical act could harm the spirit. Therefore, the believer could continue to be sexually promiscuous and not be tainted in his relationship to God. Paul warns us that we should not listen to those who try to tell us we are all right if we are living in sin.

What a prophetic message! So much of what is going on in the Church today is simply and powerfully described in those short verses. We are standing up and telling each other that we are all okay, when in truth we are living in violation of God's Word.

Every time you turn around in our "Christian culture," someone is making a case for more toleration, for more freedom, and for more "understanding" when it comes to the absolutes of God's Word. Every time you turn around it seems like morality is being tried in the courts—and it is losing. If we are not careful, we can begin to buy into this relaxed attitude about God's moral standards. But Paul warns us not to be deceived and not to let others tell us that what God says is wrong is somehow okay.

Furthermore, we are admonished not to hang out with people who marginalize their Christian faith by living as children of the world. We are not to be partakers with them! Ephesians 5 begins with an encouragement to us to follow God and be imitators of Him, and this section ends with a reminder that we are not to be imitators of the world.

The Conclusion to Walking in Love

As I review our text in Ephesians 5:1-7, I see at least three commitments we can make as we seek to walk in love as imitators of Jesus.

Remember God's Love

Paul said we should love "as Christ also has loved us" (Ephesians 5:2). I like the way Bryan Chapell framed this in his commentary on Ephesians:

> We obey because we are loved; we are not loved because
> we obey. How would you turn others from sin? Should
> you warn? Yes. Should you command to avoidance? Yes.
> Should you condemn participation? Yes. But what first?
> First, remind those who love God and are grieving for
> their failure that they are his dearly loved children. Say,
> "You are a wonderful child, a precious child of God,
> dearly loved. You are precious to him. Live as one dearly
> loved. Be what you are in Christ."[3]

In an interview about spiritual vitality, Henri Nouwen said:

> I cannot continuously say no to this or no to that, unless
> there is something ten times more attractive to choose.
> Saying no to my lust, my greed, my needs, and the
> world's powers takes an enormous amount of energy.
> The only hope is to find something so obviously real and
> attractive that I can devote all my energies to saying yes.
> One such thing I can say yes to is when I come in touch
> with the fact that I am loved. Once I have found that in
> my total brokenness I am still loved, I become free from
> the compulsion of doing successful things.[4]

Respect God's Wrath

Paul used a critical phrase in Ephesians 5:6 that should catch our attention: "the wrath of God." That's a phrase that makes many people uncomfortable—especially when applied to ourselves—but it's one we should never ignore.

We may resist the biblical teaching of God's wrath in this passage, but consider this analogy from E. H. Gifford: "The more a father loves his son, the more he hates in *him* the drunkard, the liar, the traitor."[5] "Anger isn't the opposite of love. Hate is, and the final form of hate is indifference .... To be truly good one has to be outraged by evil and utterly and implacably hostile to injustice."[6]

That is what Paul is saying in Ephesians 5. God is angry at the things that destroy people. He is working against immorality and impurity. He wants us to fight against the things that destroy life, and He wants us to embrace the things that bring life!

N. T. Wright uses the following illustration to describe how we should avoid sin and embrace the new life we have in Christ:

Think of an animal you'd really be afraid of, whether it's an angry rhinoceros or a large spider. If you came round a corner and found yourself facing it, what would you want to do? Run away, of course. Well, as a Christian that's how you should feel about a lifestyle of greed, lust, jealousy, injustice, or another sinful pattern.

Then think how you'd feel if you saw the person you loved best in the entire world, who you hadn't seen for years, walking down the street. What would you do? Why, chase after him or her, of course. That's how you should behave when you think of Jesus and the new life that he is offering you and the whole world.[7]

Respond to God's Grace

Remember, rather than taking part in ungodliness, we are to be defined by "giving of thanks" (Ephesians 5:4), and that is one of the best ways we can overcome the temptation to sin.

Pastor Heath Lambert wrote:

Thankfulness is the opposite of lust because the thankful heart has stopped prowling around for everything it doesn't have and is overwhelmed with appreciation for all the good things it already possesses. The logic of lust requires you to be discontent with what you have and pay attention to all the things you don't have. The logic of thankfulness requires you to focus on what you have already received and to overcome with thanks. Gratitude is the opposite of sin.[8]

Have you been to the Louvre in Paris? It is one of the most famous museums in the world and perhaps the best loved by art patrons. Displayed within its walls are originals by such masters as Michelangelo, Rubens, da Vinci, Vermeer, and hundreds of others.

Interestingly, since 1973, the Louvre has encouraged established or aspiring artists to visit the museum and copy those masters—to repaint their own versions of famous pieces. Why? So those modern artists can become better painters by studying and doing their best to reproduce the work of those masters.

A man named Amal Dagher is a good example. He has been participating in these sessions at the Louvre for more than thirty years. He keeps coming back because he is in awe of what the ancient masters were able to achieve, and he wants to move in that direction. "If you're too satisfied with yourself," he says, "you can't improve."[9]

David C. Egner writes, "Like the Louvre copyists, we'll never reach perfection before we get to heaven. Even so, we must resist the temptation to be satisfied with our present imitation of Jesus. We need to keep looking to Him, learning from Him, and asking for His help. Let's copy the Master."[10]

FOR YOU WERE ONCE
DARKNESS, BUT NOW
YOU ARE LIGHT IN
THE LORD. WALK AS
CHILDREN OF LIGHT.

EPHESIANS 5:8

CHAPTER 13

Leave the Light On

EPHESIANS 5:8-14

Thomas Edison is normally given credit as the inventor of the light bulb, but there's a deeper story behind it all—starting with a man named James Prescott Joule.

Joule, a British scientist, discovered the first law of thermodynamics: Energy is conserved even as it is transformed from one form to another. In what eventually became known as the Joule Effect, he predicted that electricity, if passed through a resistant conductor, would glow white-hot when heat energy was transformed to light energy. As we now know, that's how lightbulbs work.

Joule eventually proved his point, but he faced a difficult challenge: finding a material out of which a thin filament could be made that would not burn up quickly when electricity was passed through it. He could create light, but only for a second or two before the resistant conductor burned up.

Between Joule and Edison stands a long line of tinkers and inventors who tried to extract all the oxygen from a glass bulb and find a filament that would provide just the right amount of resistance to an electric current so that it glowed and gave off light. From 1820 to 1879 filaments made out of platinum, charcoal, carbonized paper, carbonized bamboo, cotton, and other materials all worked to some degree. But it was left to the unflagging persistence of Thomas Edison to find and perfect the right filament.

Edison tried materials from all over the world while looking for a filament that would work: "Before I got through," he recalled, "I tested no fewer than 6,000 vegetable growths, and ransacked the world for the most suitable filament material."[1]

By October of 1879, using improved vacuum pumps and a carbonized cotton thread as a filament, he coaxed a light bulb into glowing for nearly 14 hours. With more improved filaments, by the end of 1880 he had a 16-watt bulb that gave off light for 1,500 hours. It was not until 1910 that tungsten, a material Edison tried but did not have the tools to perfect, was discovered to be the perfect filament, which resulted in the widespread use of the incandescent bulb that we used for years.

We learned in the previous chapter that we imitate God when we walk in love. That's one of the ways we imitate our Heavenly Father. Now we come to the next way, which is by walking in the light.

Paul wrote, "Walk as children of light" (Ephesians 5:8).

When Paul says that we are to "walk as children of light," he is reminding us that this light does not originate with us but with

God. The Bible is clear that God is the true light, and we are to reflect that light to others.

- "The Lord is my light and my salvation; whom shall I fear?" (Psalm 27:1)

- "The sun shall no longer be your light by day, nor for brightness shall the moon give light to you; but the Lord will be to you an everlasting light" (Isaiah 60:19).

- "Then Jesus spoke to them again, saying, 'I am the light of the world. He who follows Me shall not walk in darkness, but have the light of life'" (John 8:12).

- "This is the message that we have heard from Him and declare to you, that God is light and in Him is no darkness at all" (1 John 1:5).

Let's take a look at what happens when we allow the light of Christ to shine into our life.

A New Description

"For you were once darkness, but now you are light in the Lord" (Ephesians 5:8).

Note the words of contrast in this little verse: "once" and "now," "were" and "are." Earlier in this letter Paul conveyed the same truth when he wrote: "And you He made alive, who were dead in trespasses and sins, in which you once walked according to the course of this world, according to the prince of the power of the air, the spirit who now works in the sons of disobedience, among whom also we all once conducted ourselves in the lusts of our flesh, fulfilling the desires of the flesh and of the mind, and were by nature children of wrath, just as the others" (Ephesians 2:1-3).

Here are some important characteristics of the people we once were—the people we used to be before Christ.

We Were Once Darkness

Paul used the word "darkness" to describe the life of an unbeliever. What is the meaning of this term?

Darkness is an interesting concept. It is defined not by what it is, but by what it isn't. Darkness isn't the presence of something; it's the absence of light. It is the direct opposite of lightness—it is the lack of illumination or the absence of visible light.

There are four ways to discuss this existence the Bible calls darkness.

First, darkness is a *person*. Paul said *you* once were darkness, so darkness is personal. It applies to me and you as individuals.

In Ephesians 6, Paul wrote, "For we do not wrestle against flesh and blood, but against principalities, against powers, against the rulers of the darkness of this age, against spiritual hosts of wickedness in the heavenly places" (verse 12).

When the Bible speaks of darkness, it is often referring to Satan and his minions. Satan's kingdom is the kingdom of darkness, and under his control are very real personalities—powers, rulers, and spiritual hosts of wickedness in the heavenly places.

If you imagine the whole world being shrouded in darkness, like a pitch-black night, and Christians appearing as dots of light all over the world, you'll have a good idea of how darkness is the person of Satan and how he tries to influence the world.

Second, darkness is a *power*. As Paul wrote in Colossians, "He has delivered us from the power of darkness and conveyed us into the kingdom of the Son of His love" (1:13).

Darkness has an actual power over those who live under its dominion.

I remember visiting a man in the hospital who was dying of emphysema, the result of a lifetime of chain-smoking. Even while lying in his bed and breathing oxygen through a tube, he was still smoking. That is a picture of the power of darkness, when we are unable to free ourselves from destructive addictions and powers.

Darkness can exercise power not only over our bodies but our thoughts as well. We live under that power until Christ delivers us from it, conveying us into the kingdom of light.

Third, darkness is a *preference*. While no one likes to admit it, darkness is the preference of the natural man—it's what we often choose to choose.

John 3:19-21 says, "And this is the condemnation, that the light has come into the world, and men loved darkness rather than light, because their deeds were evil. For everyone practicing evil hates the light and does not come to the light, lest his deeds should be exposed. But he who does the truth comes to the light, that his deeds may be clearly seen, that they have been done in God."

In Ephesians 5:11 Paul referred to the practices of evil as "the unfruitful works of darkness," which people prefer to do when left on their own. Sin prefers darkness. Darkness is a picture of man's unwillingness to allow God (or anyone else) to shine a light and expose our unfruitful deeds of evil and immorality.

Fourth, darkness is a *place*. People who yield to the powers of darkness and prefer darkness to light are headed for a dark place where they will spend all eternity.

Jesus said, "But the sons of the kingdom will be cast out into outer darkness. There will be weeping and gnashing of teeth" (Matthew 8:12).

Can you imagine living in total darkness for eternity? I do not know if that is a literal reference Jesus makes to darkness, or a spiritual one. But in either case, the absence of physical or spiritual light forever is a gruesome prospect.

I have friends who minister in Alaska, and there is a period of the year when it is dark all day long. They have to leave for six weeks every year during that period because the darkness is so depressing. Imagine living in it for eternity!

We Are Now Light

What Paul is telling us is that darkness is a thing of the past for a true follower of Christ. Just as the moon reflects the light of the sun, so we are to reflect the light of the Son, Jesus Christ. We are to walk in that light!

In Jesus' words: "You are the light of the world. A city that is set on a hill cannot be hidden" (Matthew 5:14).

The apostle Peter described believers this way: "You are a chosen generation, a royal priesthood, a holy nation, His own special people, that you may proclaim the praises of Him who called you out of darkness into His marvelous light" (1 Peter 2:9).

Have you noticed that the word *gray* doesn't appear in these texts? It's either darkness or light—there is no middle ground. Too often, I see a desire to find a gray area, a middle ground, that is not so demanding. Too often, people seek a zone where they can be mostly in the light but still dabble a bit in the darkness.

That is not biblical. You are either in the darkness or called out of darkness into the light. There is no middle ground of compromise.

A New Direction

Those who have been called out of darkness are not just allowed to sit, soak, and sour in the light. We are called in order to pursue a new direction in life: "Walk as children of light (for the fruit of the Spirit is in all goodness, righteousness, and truth)" (Ephesians 5:8-9).

Paul's parenthesis in verse 9 is better translated "For the fruit of the Light is in all goodness, righteousness, and truth." In other words, if we are in the light, there is certain fruit that should be forthcoming. What does this fruit look like? First of all, it has to do with ...

Our Relationship With Others

Goodness, in all its simplicity, can be a troublesome concept. As Christians, we understand we are not saved by being good, so "good" gets a negative connotation. But it shouldn't! We are expected to be good: to be good people, do good things, and think good thoughts. Good is good!

Primarily, our goodness is manifested in our relationships with other people. While we may retain relationships with people we knew when we were in the darkness, we don't use relationships for dark purposes. We walk in the light and do good things to and for others.

First Thessalonians 5:15 says, "See that no one renders evil for evil to anyone, but always pursue what is good both for yourselves and for all."

We enjoy meeting and being around good people, don't we? People who are generous, dependable, and enjoy serving others. It's great to have a number of people you can count on as good friends. Every Christian is to be that kind of person—one who does good for his own benefit as well as the benefit of others.

As Paul wrote: "Fulfill all the good pleasure of His goodness and the work of faith with power" (2 Thessalonians 1:11).

Our Relationship With God

Righteousness has to do with our relationship to God. It means living in a way that reflects His character and desires. The righteous person does what is just or right according to God's Word.

Paul wrote to Timothy about some who strayed from the faith because of their love for money, and he told Timothy to "flee these things and pursue righteousness, godliness, faith, love, patience, gentleness" (1 Timothy 6:11).

What does it mean to "pursue righteousness"? It does not mean to take a passive approach to being honest and having integrity. It means "to chase after" and "to hunt down" what is right and godly. It means to swim against the stream of darkness in this world and pursue that which is not within easy grasp.

Unrighteousness is close at hand, but righteousness must be pursued. Scripture says, "Do not present your members as instruments of unrighteousness to sin, but present yourselves to God as being alive from the dead, and your members as instruments of righteousness to God" (Romans 6:13).

Our Relationship With Ourselves

Finally, the fruit of the light is "truth." This has to do with honesty, reliability, trustworthiness, and integrity—this is the light as opposed to the deceit and hypocrisy of the darkness.

If we are walking in the light, we will be people whose word is true, whose word is our bond. What we say will match up with how we live. Our relationship with ourselves will be defined by truth, which means there will be no conflict between our outward and inward persons.

A New Desire

The desire of those who walk in the light is "finding out what is acceptable to the Lord" (Ephesians 5:10).

This has to do with our continued growth in the light. We are to be learning as we are walking. The words *finding out* convey the idea of "trying to learn," or "proving or testing to determine what is right."

When Paul wrote to the Philippians, he expressed this desire for them: "And this I pray, that your love may abound still more and more in knowledge and all discernment, that you may approve the things that are excellent, that you may be sincere and without offense till the day of Christ" (Philippians 1:9-10).

As we continue to walk in the light, we will begin to see things differently. Indeed, we will begin to see things as Christ sees them. This change does not all happen at once—it happens day by day as we are in the Word of God and as we grow in grace and knowledge. The Christian life is a work in progress, and all of us are under construction.

But let me ask you this question: Are you trying to discover what the will of the Lord is for your life? So many people I meet are trying to find the least common denominator of the Christian experience. *What can I get by with? What's the minimum I need to do?* We do this instead of diligently seeking to know what the Lord wants of us so that we can do it!

The criterion for judging what is to be permitted in our lives is whether or not the conduct is acceptable to the Lord. That should settle all issues. Therefore, ask yourself that question each day.

A New Distinction

"And have no fellowship with the unfruitful works of darkness" (Ephesians 5:11).

It is impossible to be a Christian and not be in the world. But here we are reminded that while we are in the world, we are not to be of the world. We cannot help it that the people around us are wrapped up in the things of this world, and we must still love them and minister to them—but we cannot become partakers with them. That is the meaning of this admonition. We are to have a distinction as believers from others who are not believers.

Practically speaking, that means in our attempt to identify with the people we are trying to reach with the Gospel, we must never cross over the line and become partakers with them of the unfruitful works of darkness. And when it comes to those who profess to be followers of Christ and are practicing the works of darkness, Paul tells us in no uncertain terms what our attitude should be: "Have no fellowship."

We don't have to be weird or contentious when it comes to setting ourselves apart from the world. Some Christians think it's their job to act super-spiritual when turning down invitations from their old friends to join them in previously shared activities. You don't have to do that, but you can graciously share your testimony of what Christ has done in your life and why you need to excuse yourself from certain activities.

That's how Kimberly Shumate found Christ. Kimberly spent much of her life studying the occult and working as a psychic. At one point, she openly identified herself as a witch. She was into every type of dark and mysterious art she could find.

And she was miserable.

One day a friend invited her to church, of all things. Kimberly thought, *[That's] the only avenue I haven't pursued.* She agreed to attend a service but left feeling uncomfortable. But she went again. This time the pastor said Jesus was the only way to salvation, and Kimberly thought that was such an arrogant statement that she walked out.

Still, she came back the next week. And she kept attending. She even met a man named Scott who, in her words, had a Bible "held together by tape and highlight marks and ballpoint pen." Kimberly tried to argue with Scott about the truths contained in God's Word, but she had finally met her match.

"There was a sick feeling coming over me," she wrote, "and at that moment, the Holy Spirit came in and He showed me the truth. I couldn't believe what it was. It was Jesus!"[2]

We are not to separate ourselves from people who are in darkness but from "the unfruitful deeds of darkness." How will they ever hear the Gospel if we do not continue to love them, befriend them, invite them to church, and minister to their needs?

We can serve those in the darkness without participating in the deeds of darkness.

Paul's primary concern is Christians who bring the deeds of darkness into the Church—failing to draw a line after becoming Christians and putting those things behind them. He wants us to know that we can be in the world without being of the world.

A New Duty

"But rather expose them. For it is shameful even to speak of those things which are done by them in secret. But all things that are exposed are made manifest by the light, for whatever makes manifest is light" (Ephesians 5:11-13).

What do we do with those who are claiming to be followers of Christ but are practicing the works of darkness? In our day, the prevalent attitude is to leave them alone. After all, it's none of our business how they live. But wait a minute. If we are walking in the light, by the very virtue of our walk, we will expose the works of darkness.

Have you ever thrown open the shutters of a room on a bright sunny day, revealing all the dust and cobwebs that had been collecting for weeks in the darkness? The Christian who is willing to walk as a child of light has (or should have!) much the same effect on the works of darkness.

We've all seen illustrations of this in our life. When people know what we believe and how we live, it often makes them very uncomfortable with their own lifestyle. Our life exposes the works of darkness.

Tom Rees, an English evangelist, tells the story of a man who came to one of his crusades, received Christ, and moved dramatically out of the deep darkness he had been living in. He stopped being a drunkard, stopped abusing his wife and children, and started using his money for the good of his home and family. But all of his former drinking buddies gave him a hard time about the changes in his life. They even challenged him about his belief in the Bible.

"Do you really think Jesus turned water into wine?"

The newly converted man said, "I don't know a lot about the Bible yet, but I do know this: Jesus turned beer into furniture in my house."[3]

That's a good example of exposing the unfruitful works of darkness in a way that can't be contradicted. The change in your life is proof with which no one can argue; you really are a different person.

Don't be afraid to reveal the differences in your life. You may be the one who awakens others from their "sleep" to move into the light of Christ themselves (verse 14). The differences in your life may make others uncomfortable at first. But discomfort with the light at least is an indication of awareness. In time, they may recognize the source and join you in your walk in Christ.

But this goes even deeper. According to Paul we are to confront evil when we see it. He was talking about evil in the Church. We are not to just allow it out of a spirit of tolerance and acceptance. In the spirit of Christ, we are to confront. Paul also said that some things are not even to be discussed because they are so shameful. I think this is a reminder that we do not need to be so explicit when we are talking about the sins of others. We do not need to go into the sordid details.

Verse 13 is a difficult verse to interpret. Many commentators believe it is a motivational verse meant to inspire us to shine light into the darkness. Here is how the New International Version translates it: "But everything exposed by the light becomes visible—and everything that is illuminated becomes a light."

In other words, the first thing light does is expose the darkness. Then, second, it transforms the darkness into light. What an encouragement!

Our passage ends with this invitation: "Therefore He says: 'Awake, you who sleep, arise from the dead, and Christ will give you light'" (5:14).

This last verse is thought by many to be an Easter hymn of the Early Church. It is based upon a passage in Isaiah 60: "Arise, shine; for your light has come! And the glory of the Lord is risen upon you" (verse 1).

Today we talk about someone needing "a wake-up call"
when one seems oblivious to imminent consequences.
Paul issues this poetic wake-up call in the middle
of warning the church about the compromises with

darkness. Not only does he call the church to wake up, but also to "rise from the dead." The obvious reference to resurrection is a reminder that not to wake up to the dangers of the culture is to persist in what is fruitless and dead. But the contrary is also clear; that is, if you wake up from your slumber, Christ will shine on you.[4]

Let Your Light Shine

As we come to the end of this chapter, I think Jesus said best what it is really all about: "Let your light so shine before men, that they may see your good works and glorify your Father in heaven" (Matthew 5:16).

The renowned journalist Malcolm Muggeridge lived much of his life as an avowed atheist. He likened his attitude toward faith to a gargoyle on the top of a cathedral—looking down, grinning and laughing at the absurd behavior, the vain strivings of men on earth. But Muggeridge the skeptic became a Christian in 1969 after studying some of the great writers of the Christian faith—people like Saint Augustine, Blaise Pascal, and Søren Kierkegaard.

Toward the end of his life, the journalist wrote these words,

I am the light of the world, the founder of the Christian religion said. What a stupendous phrase! And how particularly marvelous today, when one is conscious of so much darkness in the world! *Let your light shine before men*, he exhorted us. You know, sometimes ... someone asks me what I most want, what I should most like to do in the little that remains of my life, and I always nowadays truthfully answer—and it *is* truthful—"I should like my light to shine, even if only very fitfully, like a match struck in a dark, cavernous night and then flickering out."[5]

That is our role in this world. We are to do everything in our power to shine with the light of Christ—to keep that light on and visible in our own communities. What a privilege, and what a calling!

CHAPTER 14

Walking in Wisdom

EPHESIANS 5:15-21

Yogi Berra passed away on September 22, 2015. He was a hall of fame player and coach for Major League Baseball, but in recent decades he was known more for his special combination of wit and hilarity than for his on-the-field achievements.

Here are some examples of his most famous "Yogi-isms":

- "Baseball is ninety percent mental. The other half is physical."
- "The game isn't over until it's over."
- "I'm not going to buy my kids an encyclopedia. Let them walk to school like I did."
- "Nobody goes there anymore because it's too crowded."
- "You can observe a lot just by watching."
- "It ain't the heat, it's the humility."

Of course, once people started asking Yogi about his famous quips, he replied with another of my favorites: "I never said most of the things I said."[1]

How would you categorize those quotes? Are they wisdom? Are they foolish? Something in between? I'm not sure, but I do know this: Our world today is in desperate need of true wisdom. Godly wisdom.

Robert Fulghum had this to say about wisdom:

Most of what I really need to know about how to live, and what to do, and how to be, I learned in kindergarten. Wisdom was not at the top of the graduate school mountain, but there in the sandbox at nursery school.

These are the things I learned: Share everything. Play fair. Don't hit people. Put things back where you found them. Clean up your own mess. Don't take things that aren't yours. Say you're sorry when you hurt somebody .... When you go out into the world watch for traffic, hold hands, and stick together.[2]

So far in Ephesians 5, Paul has instructed believers to be imitators of Christ by walking in love and by walking in the light. Now, as we explore verses 15-21, we'll see how to follow in Jesus' footsteps by walking in wisdom. Specifically, the wise walk of the Christian is diligent, disciplined, directed, and dynamic.

The Wise Walk Is a Diligent Walk

Paul used an interesting word in verse 15, which I want to highlight in context: "See then that you walk circumspectly, not as fools but as wise."

The Greek word *circum* means "circle or around," which is where we get the English word *circumference.* And the Greek term translated "spectly" means "to look"—as in spectacles. So to walk circumspectly means to look around in a careful way. If you were to imagine a cat walking across a fence with barbs sticking up at the top, you would see it stepping very carefully to avoid any obstacles or pain. That is walking circumspectly.

How does that type of walk benefit us as followers of Christ? In three ways.

Walking Diligently Keeps Us From Defection

In the Bible, the word *fool* is found several times. The psalmist defined a "biblical fool" like this: "The fool has said in his heart, 'There is no God.' They are corrupt, they have done abominable works, there is none who does good" (14:1).

Paul wrote this about fools and the foolish: "Because, although they knew God, they did not glorify Him as God, nor were thankful, but became futile in their thoughts, and their foolish hearts were darkened. Professing to be wise, they became fools" (Romans 1:21-22).

Titus 3:3-6 summarizes the transition from foolishness to wisdom that happens when we meet Christ:

For we ourselves were also once foolish, disobedient, deceived, serving various lusts and pleasures, living in malice and envy, hateful and hating one another. But

when the kindness and the love of God our Savior toward
man appeared, not by works of righteousness which
we have done, but according to His mercy He saved us,
through the washing of regeneration and renewing of
the Holy Spirit, whom He poured out on us abundantly
through Jesus Christ our Savior.

When you become a Christian, you move out of foolishness
and begin to walk in the wisdom of God, just as you move from
lust to love and from darkness to light. But it is possible to start
off on the way of wisdom as a new believer and find yourself
moving off that path and doing foolish things again.

In such cases, it is critical that we rectify that behavior
through repentance. We must confess our folly and turn back
toward God's wisdom.

Walking Diligently Keeps Us From Disobedience

As I've said many times, being a Christian does not make
anyone perfect—not yet. You can be walking in wisdom and
encounter a command from God, and if you're not walking
circumspectly, you can disobey.

Paul called the Galatians foolish when they began to
gravitate back toward the law after having been saved by grace:
"O foolish Galatians! Who has bewitched you that you should
not obey the truth, before whose eyes Jesus Christ was clearly
portrayed among you as crucified? … Having begun in the Spirit,
are you now being made perfect by the flesh?" (Galatians 3:1, 3)

Paul spared no words in his rebuke of their tendency.
They had lost sight of obedience and were tending toward
foolishness instead of walking in wisdom. When we choose to

walk diligently, however, we can avoid this kind of hypocrisy and maintain our forward progress.

Walking Diligently Keeps Us From Destruction

Did you know it's possible for us to self-destruct as Christians? It's true. Paul wrote to Timothy about one possible snare that can lead us down such a path: "Those who desire to be rich fall into temptation and a snare, and into many foolish and harmful lusts which drown men in destruction and perdition" (1 Timothy 6:9). Riches aren't the only source of temptation, of course, but they are a common one in our culture.

Any Christian can be tempted. If he yields to that temptation, he can find himself sidetracked and possibly destroyed. If you walk wisely and keep your focus on godly goals, that won't happen. To do that, you have to walk circumspectly—with your eyes wide open for the traps and snares that are in everyone's path. Living with your head buried in the sand of naivete is a quick way to stumble and fall.

Avoid that fate by choosing to walk diligently—by choosing to walk circumspectly, which is evidence of wisdom.

The Wise Walk Is a Disciplined Walk

Let's continue with Ephesians 5 and look at verse 16: "Redeeming the time, because the days are evil." Paul wrote something similar in Colossians 4:5, which says, "Walk in wisdom toward those who are outside, redeeming the time."

The older I get, the more important verse 16 becomes to me: "Redeeming the time, because the days are evil." Just what does this mean?

There are two words in the Greek language that are commonly translated as the word "time." The first is *chronos*. This is the word for clock time. We get our word *chronometer* from this Greek word. This is the word for hours, minutes, and seconds.

The second word for time is *kairos*. This is the word that Paul used here in Ephesians. It refers to a measured, fixed season or period of time. *Kairos* doesn't refer to the linear passage of time but to a set period of time. Paul didn't say, "Redeeming time;" he says "Redeeming the time"—a specific period of time. The time of which he speaks is the block of time allotted to each of us—our lifetime. He was talking about the time God has given us here on this earth to serve Him.

The psalmist put it this way: "The days of our lives are seventy years; and if by reason of strength they are eighty years, yet their boast is only labor and sorrow; for it is soon cut off, and we fly away" (Psalm 90:10).

I don't want to risk losing any of those years due to foolish choices and foolish living. Our lives are bounded by the bookends of birth and death, and God wants us to redeem our life as a whole, to make the whole thing count for Him. We do that, of course, by redeeming each *chronos*—each hour of the day that adds up to our *kairos*.

The Bible offers many metaphors to help us understand the preciousness and brevity of life:

- "Our days on earth are as a shadow" (1 Chronicles 29:15).

- "For my days are consumed like smoke" (Psalm 102:3).

- "As for man, his days are like grass; as a flower of the field, so he flourishes. For the wind passes over it, and it is gone, and its place remembers it no more" (Psalm 103:15-16).

- "Whereas you do not know what will happen tomorrow. For what is your life? It is even a vapor that appears for a little time and then vanishes away" (James 4:14).

God gives us these pictures so we will understand what a privilege we have to be alive—that life itself, in the grand scheme of things, is so fleeting.

I like what I read once about the gift of time: "There is a gift which comes to us from a royal source each day of our lives, bright and sparkling, absolutely untouched, unspoiled. What is this gift? The priceless gift of time. Each day we receive a fresh, new supply—24 hours, 1,440 minutes, 86,400 seconds. Twenty-four hours we have never lived before. Twenty-four hours we will never live again!"[3]

Paul said to "redeem" the time, a word that speaks of quickly snatching up a bargain you come across at the market, a special opportunity that comes rarely. It means to go into the marketplace, search out great deals, and buy them. The bargains would be the wise choices that embody the Christian life.

The more complicated life gets through increased opportunities, the more disciplined we have to become about what we choose to do. "So teach us to number our days, that we may gain a heart of wisdom" (Psalm 90:12).

The Wise Walk Is a Directed Walk

To walk in wisdom means choosing a diligent walk, a disciplined walk, and thirdly a directed walk. This is where we are coming finally to the good news of this section. Paul wrote, "Therefore do not be unwise, but understand what the will of the Lord is" (Ephesians 5:17).

Since our days are numbered, we need to make sure we don't take too many detours along the way. If we do not understand what the will of the Lord is for our life, we can lose many years wandering around just like the Israelites in the wilderness. Paul told us that we need to make sure we have a clear understanding of the will of the Lord or we will be spending our life foolishly.

The key question here is: How do I know what the will of the Lord is?

Imagine God in heaven saying to the angels, "I have a will for each of my children down on earth, but I'm going to hide it from them. I'm going to make them guess what it is." That's not the God we know, a Heavenly Father who loves His children. Granted, we're not going to get a special delivery letter telling us what His will is, but that doesn't mean it's completely hidden. The will of God is found in the Word of God in terms of basic principles. From there, through prayer, counsel, and other means, God fills in the details.

The first step is delighting yourself in the Lord: "Delight yourself also in the Lord, and He shall give you the desires of your heart" (Psalm 37:4).

Here's how that worked out in my life. Before God called me to pastor and preach, I wanted to be a radio broadcaster.

During college I worked at two different radio stations. I thought I would do that for the Lord all my life. Then God called me to preach, and I obeyed, though I didn't understand why since I thought He had put in my heart the desire to be in broadcasting. To make a long story short, I have been able to remain in broadcasting with our Turning Point programs. I never would have had that kind of impact for the Gospel had I remained solely in broadcasting. So God took a desire and worked it out according to His will in a way that was far more fruitful.

Once we delight ourselves in the Lord, we then have to unconditionally surrender to Him and to His purposes for our life. We do not get to discover the will of God and then make a choice to follow it or not. No, we come to God with total submission, and we say, "Lord I want to know Your will so that I can do it." When we do that, we will understand what the will of the Lord is for our life.

Jesus said, "If anyone wills to do His will, he shall know concerning the doctrine, whether it is from God or whether I speak on My own authority" (John 7:17).

While that verse was focused primarily on the doctrine of knowing who Jesus Christ was, there's a key principle present. The condition for knowing what God is doing in this world or in your life is wanting to know. If you want to know God's will, the first thing you need to say is, "Lord, I want to know Your will, and I am willing to do Your will whatever it is."

I think a lot of people are trying to find out God's will so they can decide if they want to do it or not—that's not how it works. God says, "Sign at the bottom first, then I'll fill in the top."

In the book of Psalms, for example, God says, "I will instruct you and teach you in the way you should go; I will guide you with My eye. Do not be like the horse or like the mule, which have no understanding, which must be harnessed with bit and bridle, else they will not come near you" (32:8-9). Walking in wisdom means we are directed by God, rather than by ourselves.

The Wise Walk Is a Dynamic Walk

The final key to walking circumspectly in wisdom and redeeming the time is to be filled with the Holy Spirit—to be empowered by, strengthened by, and controlled by the Spirit of God. In other words, walking with Christ is a dynamic experience.

"And do not be drunk with wine, in which is dissipation; but be filled with the Spirit" (Ephesians 5:18).

Paul compared being filled with the Spirit to being filled with alcohol, which begins to control you from the inside. When you allow the Holy Spirit full and complete access to your heart, soul, mind, and strength, He begins to control and empower you from the inside out. You will walk circumspectly in wisdom, and you will know the will of God.

What are some of the main results of the Spirit's control—of being filled with the Spirit?

A Dynamic Way of Speaking

"Speaking to one another in psalms and hymns and spiritual songs" (Ephesians 5:19). "Speaking" is a word that defines what happens when we are filled with the Holy Spirit. It is an outward-directed word, and it describes how we begin to touch others around us through our love, our fellowship, and our care and concern.

A Dynamic Way of Singing

"Singing and making melody in your heart to the Lord" (Ephesians 5:19). When you are filled with the Holy Spirit, you will naturally praise God and worship Him. There will be a new quality of joy in your life, and it will be supernatural.

R. Kent Hughes wrote:

Spirit-filled people overflow in song! This has been attested again and again in times of great spiritual blessing. That is the way it was in the awakening under St. Francis, the Troubadour of God. In the Reformation, Martin Luther brought hymn-singing to the Church. During the Wesleyan Revival, Charles Wesley wrote 6,000 hymns .... Think of the music that came with Moody and Sankey, and more recently during the spiritual harvest of the late 1960s. There is a sense in which when people are born again, music is born again in their souls. And if they remain full of the Spirit, life brings an ongoing symphony of soul.[4]

A Dynamic Way of Saying "Thank You"

"Giving thanks always for all things to God the Father in the name of our Lord Jesus Christ" (Ephesians 5:20). When we are filled with the Spirit of God, our life is characterized by a grateful spirit. We don't fall into grumbling and complaining.

We don't develop an agenda. Instead, we walk humbly and thankfully with the Lord and His people.

A Dynamic Way of Submitting

"Submitting to one another in the fear of God" (Ephesians 5:21). A person who is filled with the Spirit is not someone who's always looking to be first or to get on top. The characteristic of a Spirit-filled individual is that it's all right if someone else takes the lead. He doesn't always have to be first. She doesn't have to grab the spotlight.

Remember, no matter who we are within the Church, each of us must submit to Christ as our Head—as our Master. Therefore, submission is a vital part of our spiritual walk, and that submission must be empowered by God's Spirit.

How to Be Filled by the Holy Spirit

Look how Paul ends this particular section of Ephesians 5: "And do not be drunk with wine, in which is dissipation; but be filled with the Spirit, speaking to one another in psalms and hymns and spiritual songs, singing and making melody in your heart to the Lord, giving thanks always for all things to God the Father in the name of our Lord Jesus Christ, submitting to one another in the fear of God" (verses 18-21).

Walking in wisdom means being filled with God's Spirit. Again, that doesn't mean we are filled in the way that a glass is filled with water. Instead, being filled with the Spirit means being controlled by the Spirit. That's why Paul talked about being "drunk with wine." When you are drunk or high, you are controlled by an outside substance, which is destructive. On the other hand, being filled or controlled by the Holy Spirit is wise. We cannot walk this life of wisdom on our own, but we can walk this life in the power of the Holy Spirit. So how are we filled by the Holy Spirit?

Desire to Be Filled

James established the principle in his epistle that "you do not have because you do not ask" (James 4:2).

So desiring to be filled with the Spirit is the first step in experiencing His empowerment. Every Christian is indwelt by the Spirit (Romans 8:9), but not every Christian is controlled and empowered by the Spirit. The Holy Spirit wants to guide and direct us, not just reside in us. The Spirit, when given control of our life, warns us of impending temptation and strengthens us to resist it. But we must desire to live a holy life and desire to be filled with the Spirit.

Jesus talked about a thirst for the Spirit in John 7:37-39—a necessary prerequisite to His filling:

> On the last day, that great day of the feast, Jesus stood and cried out, saying, "If anyone thirsts, let him come to Me and drink. He who believes in Me, as the Scripture has said, out of his heart will flow rivers of living water." But this He spoke concerning the Spirit, whom those believing in Him would receive; for the Holy Spirit was not yet given, because Jesus was not yet glorified.

Denounce Sin in Your Life

Second, to be filled with the Spirit, we have to denounce sin in our life. After all, the Holy Spirit is the *Holy* Spirit. He is not going to compete with sin for control and direction in a double-minded lie.

First John 1:9 says, "If we confess our sins, He is faithful and just to forgive us our sins and to cleanse us from all unrighteousness."

What does it look like or sound like to denounce our sin? The easiest and perhaps most effective method is to make a verbal declaration. "By the power of Jesus' blood that was shed on the cross, I renounce the greed that has crept into my life." Or, "I renounce every single time I have indulged in lustful behavior."

Such renunciations can be a critical part of our prayer lives.

Dedicate Yourself Fully to Christ

Desire and denunciation are required for the filling of the Spirit at a point in time, but dedication is required for the Spirit's continual control and empowerment. Dedication to obedience, living a righteous life, and following the Spirit's lead will keep us from grieving the Spirit or quenching His work in us.

The New Testament translation by J.B. Phillips of Romans 12:1-2 is an excellent expression of this idea of dedication:

> With eyes wide open to the mercies of God, I beg you,
> my brothers, as an act of intelligent worship, to give him
> your bodies, as a living sacrifice, consecrated to him
> and acceptable by him. Don't let the world around you

squeeze you into its own mould, but let God re-mould your minds from within, so that you may prove in practice that the plan of God for you is good, meets all his demands and moves toward the goal of true maturity.

Have you made such a dedication in your life? Are you willing to do so as a step in being filled by God's Spirit?

Depend Daily on the Holy Spirit

Here's what Paul said to the Galatians about walking in the Spirit: "Walk in the Spirit, and you shall not fulfill the lust of the flesh" (5:16).

All of God's resources will be available to us if we simply let the Spirit of God take control of our life. For that reason, when we walk in the Spirit, we will not fulfill the lusts of the flesh.

Paul's use of the word "walk" is powerful. Walk means "step by step." The word is in the present tense, and it indicates a habitual way of life. The verb is also in the imperative mood, which means this is not an option but a command. Walk means "progress." Paul challenges us to keep moving in the Spirit.

It's said that while speaking to a large audience, D. L. Moody once held up a glass and asked, "How can I get the air out of this glass?"

One man shouted, "Suck it out with a pump!"

Moody replied, "That would create a vacuum and shatter the glass."

After numerous other suggestions Moody smiled, picked up a pitcher of water, and filled the glass. "There," he said, "all the air is now removed." He went on to explain that victory in the

Christian life is not accomplished by "sucking out a sin here and there," but by being filled with the Holy Spirit.

If you want to walk in wisdom, you have to be filled with the Spirit of wisdom (Acts 6:3). Desire Him, denounce your sin, and dedicate yourself to allowing God to mold your life, and you will make the most of each day that the Lord gives you!

CHAPTER 15

Marriage

EPHESIANS 5:22-33

Glynn "Scotty" Wolfe married for the first time in June of 1931. He was 22 years old and had met his wife Helen at a mixer near his hometown of Knox County, Indiana. From that very first moment, Scotty Wolfe knew that he loved being married.

"Everything was lovely," he said. "I realized right then and there that being married was the greatest thing in the world."

Staying married, however, was not one of Scotty's strong suits. He divorced Helen after only a few months, claiming a woman named Marjorie as his new bride. Then came Margie. Then Margie was replaced by one of her friends, Mildred.

When Scotty presented himself in front of a courtroom to seek an annulment for his marriage to Margie, the judge scolded him. "He told me if that was the way I wanted to act," Scotty said, "I should go to Hollywood."

That's exactly what Scotty did. He moved to Los Angeles, divorced poor Mildred, and then married Adele instead. When

Adele left him a year later, he married Mary. Then someone else. Then someone else.

All told, Scotty Wolfe was married 29 times. His final wife was Linda Essex-Wolfe, whom he married after discovering that she was the world's "most married" woman according to the *Guinness Book of World Records.*

One journalist had this to say about Scotty Wolfe, who started and ended more marriages than Zsa Zsa Gabor, Elizabeth Taylor, and Henry VIII combined: "He married teenagers and grandmothers, farm girls and drug addicts, virgins and prostitutes, preachers and thieves, taking and shedding partners casually as a square dancer."[1]

Despite his love of matrimony, Scotty Wolfe died alone at the age of 88. He had more than fifteen children, yet only one attended his funeral. None of his ex-wives were present.

Thankfully, the Bible offers us a better plan for marriage than what Scotty Wolfe and his 29 brides experienced. More than that, the book of Ephesians has a better plan for families than what many of us have experienced: for husbands, wives, children, and parents.

We're going to explore that plan together in this chapter.

A Word to Wives

Before we jump into the text, I think it's interesting to note that Paul's instructions for marriage in Ephesians 5:22-33 contains twelve total verses. Of that passage, nine verses are directed toward husbands, and just three are directed toward wives. Make of that what you will.

What I find most interesting, however, is that all twelve of those verses come after Ephesians 5:20-21, which says, "Giving thanks always for all things to God the Father in the name of our Lord Jesus Christ, submitting to one another in the fear of God." Remember that phrase "submitting to one another" as we jump into the marriage portion of Ephesians 5.

Here is Paul's word to the wives:

> Wives, submit to your own husbands, as to the Lord. For the husband is head of the wife, as also Christ is head of the church; and He is the Savior of the body. Therefore, just as the church is subject to Christ, so let the wives be to their own husbands in everything. (verses 22-24)

Obviously, the word that pops out for most people when they read this passage is "submit." That word can cause a great deal of consternation and confusion. In our day, as well as in Paul's day, the concept of submission is not positive. Culturally, submission tends to convey the idea of weakness, and nobody wants to be associated with weakness.

However, as we examine the text in these pages, I think we'll discover that a great deal of the resistance and fear connected to the idea of biblical submission in marriage is the result of misunderstanding what the Word of God actually says. If the Bible says "submit," then, of course, we'd better submit. It's God's Word! But as we explore this passage together, we'll see that God's instruction for wives and husbands really boils down to a different word altogether: love.

The Concept of Submission

First, let's look at the concept of submission, which we can see all the way back in verse 21. Paul wrote that all Christians should be concerned with "submitting to one another in the fear of God."

It's important for you and me to understand that the concept of submission goes beyond the boundaries of marriage. According to Paul, all of us who desire to walk in the Holy Spirit need to adopt this spirit of submission to one another in the fear of God. This is important because it sets the stage for each of the relationships we find within a family, including husbands, wives, children, and parents.

All of those relationships are founded on this idea of mutual submission. That's the concept we need to wrap our mind around.

The Center of Submission

Second, let's look at the center of submission. Paul wrote in verse 22, "Wives, submit to your own husbands, *as to the Lord*" (emphasis added). That's a key theme. Verse 21 calls us to submit to one another in the fear of the Lord. And now wives are called to submit to their husbands "as to the Lord."

There's a sense in which Ephesians 5 delivers a trinity of submission. It's not just wives to husbands, but it's also wives to the Lord. The primary relationship in a wife's life is not her relationship to her husband. Her primary relationship is with the Lord. The priorities in the life of every wife are the Lord first, her husband second, her children third, and everything else after that.

Therefore, when we obey at the top level of priority—if we are in submission to the Lord—then the rest of those things will be a lot easier. The concept of submission is to one another. And the center of submission is "as to the Lord."

The Context of Submission

Third, I want you to see the context of submission. The verse says, "Wives, submit to your own husbands."

Somewhere along the way, a certain subsection of the male population seems to have gotten the idea that this passage teaches all women to submit to all men. But that's not the case. The Bible never says all men have authority over all women. Instead, within the family unit, God has ordained that a wife should submit specifically to her husband.

Along those lines, let's not forget what Paul wrote in Galatians 3: "There is neither Jew nor Greek, there is neither slave nor free, there is neither male nor female; for you are all one in Christ Jesus" (verse 28).

Yes, Almighty God has established some structure within the context of a home. However, that does not mean a wife has any less standing before God than her husband or that a woman has any less standing before God than a man. We all stand as one before God; we all have the same position at His feet.

The Criterion of Submission

Then, in verse 24 we see the criterion of submission. Paul wrote, "Therefore, just as the church is subject to Christ, so let the wives be to their own husbands in everything." Scripture says that a wife is to be subject to her own husband just as the Church is subject to Christ.

Again, what we see here is a structure that God in His wisdom has put in place. Christ is head of the Church, and within the context of a home, the husband is head of his wife. But take a look at what Paul wrote in 1 Corinthians 11:3: "But I want you to know that the head of every man is Christ, the head of woman is man, and the head of Christ is God."

"The head of Christ is God." Isn't that interesting? Even Jesus has a "head." Even Jesus has Someone over Him, which is God the Father. And yet, as we know from the Gospels, Jesus is equal with the Father. He said Himself, "I and My Father are one" (John 10:30). God the Son and God the Father are equal and united. Yet within that equality, there is a structure in which Christ submits to the Father.

In a similar way, when a man and woman stand in front of the altar and commit before God to holy matrimony, they become united. They become "one flesh." Yet within the context of that one flesh, God has established that the wife submit to her husband. That is the criterion of submission.

The Consequence of Submission

And finally, there is a consequence to submission in the context of a family. What happens when a wife submits to her husband? What happens when a husband loves his wife? When both are doing their part, there is a beautiful tension that comes together to hold the marriage in a kind of trust. There is a give and take that naturally occurs.

For example, if a husband doesn't love his wife—if he doesn't nourish and cherish her as the Scripture says—the woman will find it much harder to submit. If the woman doesn't submit, her husband will find it much harder to love. Of course, that doesn't mean either one of them can get off the hook for doing what they've been called to do.

So husbands, if you think your wife isn't being as submissive as she ought, let me encourage you to quit worrying about her. Instead, ask yourself: Are you loving her as you should? Likewise, wives, if you think your husband isn't loving you as he should, let me ask you this question: Are you demonstrating a submissive attitude toward him as the Scripture instructs?

Do you see what I'm saying? These two pieces come together, and when you see them work in context one with another, it's a beautiful thing. God knew what He was doing when He gave us these instructions.

A Word to Husbands

Speaking of husbands loving their wives, that is the central message we find in Ephesians 5:25-33. Let's take a look together:

> Husbands, love your wives, just as Christ also loved the church and gave Himself for her, that He might sanctify and cleanse her with the washing of water by the word, that He might present her to Himself a glorious church, not having spot or wrinkle or any such thing, but that she should be holy and without blemish. So husbands ought to love their own wives as their own bodies; he who loves his wife loves himself. For no one ever hated his own flesh, but nourishes and cherishes it, just as the Lord does the church. For we are members of His body, of His flesh and of His bones. "For this reason a man

shall leave his father and mother and be joined to his wife, and the two shall become one flesh." This is a great mystery, but I speak concerning Christ and the church. Nevertheless let each one of you in particular so love his own wife as himself, and let the wife see that she respects her husband.

Let me say two things before we start to pull some principles out of those verses. First, there has been some confusion and debate among theologians for centuries about whether this passage is primarily about the family or the church. My strong opinion is that it is primarily about the family because the immediate context surrounding this passage focuses on the family. Paul was describing several important personal relationships—wives, husbands, parents, and children.

Second, sometimes people can stumble over this idea of "husbands, love your wives." There has been a sense in our culture for generations that love is a woman's territory—even a woman's job. The husband is supposed to be the breadwinner, while the wife pays attention to love and romance and keeping a nest and all that.

Please hear me: Those are cultural norms or cultural ideas, but they are not biblical truths. The Bible is clear that husbands are called to love their wives. More, husbands are commanded to love their wives in the same way that Christ loves the Church.

On that note, let's dig in to this passage and identify four principles that can help husbands accomplish just that.

Love Your Wife Unconditionally

The first question we need to ask ourselves after reading Ephesians 5:22 is: How did Christ love the Church? And the answer is, unconditionally.

Have you noticed that Jesus didn't say, "Hey, Church, when you get yourself cleaned up and straightened out, then I'll love you. I might even die for you." If that were the case, no church and no Christian would ever be the object of God's love because no person and no community of persons can ever achieve perfection.

Christ loves us anyway. He loves us just as we are, warts and all. That's why Romans 5:8 says, "But God demonstrates His own love toward us, in that while we were still sinners, Christ died for us."

I heard a story about a young lady who was preparing on her wedding day, but she was so nervous about her ability to get through the ceremony. She was having trouble with the idea of walking out in front of all those people in attendance.

The wedding coordinator tried to help her. She said, "Honey, there are only three things you have to remember. First of all, when you come into the auditorium, you have to walk down the *aisle*. Can you remember that? You start with *aisle*. Then you get down to the front, and there's a little place you need to stand while they give you away. That's the *altar*. And when you get done with that, you go up on the stage, and then you focus on your husband. Just focus on *him*. That's all you need to remember."

Well, this nervous young lady did her best to walk confidently from the back of the church to the front. But try to imagine the surprise of those in the audience when they heard her repeating three words out loud: "Aisle altar him." "Aisle altar him." "Aisle altar him."

That's what a lot of us think when we come into a marriage, isn't it? We believe we're going to change the other person. Make them different. But that's destructive, and it's not obeying Paul's command for husbands to love their wives as Christ loved the Church. Because Christ loved us just as we are.

Love Your Wife Sacrificially

Not only did Christ love us unconditionally, but also sacrificially. Paul wrote, "Husbands, love your wives, just as Christ also loved the church *and gave Himself for her*" (verse 25, emphasis added).

Jesus demonstrated His love for the Church through great sacrifice. Specifically, He demonstrated His love through His death on the cross. And it is with that same mindset that husbands are called to love their wives—that same willingness to pay any price.

Someone once said that it's not hard to give to your wife—but it is difficult to *give in* to your wife. Yet the healthiest marriages are built on that very act. The best husbands and wives know the value of giving in when it comes to their own priorities so that they can meet the needs of and intentionally serve their spouse.

When you love someone, there's nothing you aren't willing to give up for that person. And yes, you are even willing to give in when that is needed. Because true love requires sacrifice.

One of the great forces tearing marriages apart in our culture today is that we have become a selfish people. We are primarily concerned with getting what we want. Having our needs met. Receiving what we desire.

Let me tell you, selfishness in marriage is lethal. It will destroy your relationship. Therefore, husbands, take your eyes away from yourself and your own stuff, and focus instead on the object of your love. Choose to love her sacrificially.

Love Your Wife Purposefully

Next, choose to love your wife purposefully. Look at what Paul wrote in verses 26-27, speaking of how Christ loved the Church: "That He might sanctify and cleanse her with the washing of water by the word, that He might present her to Himself a glorious church, not having spot or wrinkle or any such thing, but that she should be holy and without blemish."

How do those verses apply to husbands today? Well, Christ loved the Church ultimately so that He might be able to present the Church to Himself one day as clean and washed and cleansed and sanctified. He had the purpose of presenting to Himself a glorious bride. In other words, Christ's immediate purpose is for the purity of the Church.

Now, what we need to glean from this as husbands can be phrased in this way: *My goal in loving my wife is that she might be all that she can be for God.* That's what it means to love purposefully.

As husbands, we should make it our goal to love our wives in such a way that they can become the godliest and most spiritually mature individuals they can be. We need to love in such a way that we are never guilty of holding our wives back from accomplishing everything God desires them to accomplish.

Here's a sad truth: There are many men who don't want their wives to be prosperous spiritually. Why? Because when their wives grow spiritually, it embarrasses them because they never take any time for spiritual things in their own lives. That's wrong.

Here's another thing. I have encountered men who are good at what they do—whether that's their careers or their role as a parent or their spiritual maturity in Christ—yet their wives are a little farther along. She is a little better at what she does than he is at what he does. For many men, that is a problem. They try to do everything they can to hold their wives back so that they don't feel stunted or shamed. What a tragedy!

Let me ask you this question: Do you think Jesus is worried about His bride, the Church, becoming too mature? Too spiritual? Too talented? No. Jesus is never jealous about the maturity of the Church. In fact, Jesus is anxious for the maturity of the Church.

In the same way, men, we cannot be jealous over the maturity of our wives. Instead, we must be anxious for the maturity of our wives. We must love them purposefully and do everything we can to ensure they become all that God desires them to be.

Love Your Wife Passionately

Husbands are commanded by God to love their wives unconditionally, to love them sacrificially, to love them purposefully—and finally, to love them passionately. Paul wrote, "So husbands ought to love their own wives as their own bodies;

he who loves his wife loves himself. For no one ever hated his own flesh, but nourishes and cherishes it, just as the Lord does the church" (verses 28-29).

Nourish your wife. I know a lot of men who are passionate about nourishing their bodies. Sometimes this is a form of gluttony, in that we fill ourselves with a lot of food. Other times this is more of a focus on health, where we spend a lot of time training muscles or developing our physiques. The point is not where you fall on that spectrum but rather to understand that most men invest a lot of effort and energy into the nourishment of their own bodies.

Well, in the same way, Scripture says we need to invest effort and energy into nourishing our wives. That means making sure her needs are met—and not just her physical needs but her emotional and spiritual needs as well. Nourishing your wife means doing everything you can to ensure that she is healthy and provided for.

Cherish your wife. More than that, Paul talked about the way Christ cherishes the Church, which is a picture for how we can passionately love our wives. *Cherish* is a word used elsewhere in the New Testament to describe the way a nurse cares for a sick patient or a mother cares for a newborn. This same tenderness is to characterize a husband's care for his wife.

This is one of the most important qualities that a husband can bring to his marriage. In our Rambo culture, it is hard for men to see the importance of tenderness.

Then Paul wrote,

We are members of His body, of His flesh and of His bones. "For this reason a man shall leave his father and mother and be joined to his wife, and the two shall become one flesh." This is a great mystery, but I speak concerning Christ and the church. Nevertheless let each one of you in particular so love his own wife as himself, and let the wife see that she respects her husband. (Ephesians 5:30-33)

Paul concluded this portion of his teaching on marriage with an interpretation of Genesis 2:24, which reflects the great mystery of the union between Christ and the Church. This illustration goes beyond mere analogy; it is a statement of reality. Just as a husband and wife become a new reality—one flesh— so the members of the Church become part of a new reality, Christ's Body!

I believe with all of my heart that for marriage to become the treasure the Bible says it can be, Jesus Christ must be at the center. That's the reason Jesus Christ came into the world: to tear down the barriers between a man and his God and ultimately to tear down the walls between a man and his fellow men and women. When Jesus Christ comes into a life, that individual gains the basic equipment necessary to become "one" with another person, to be a person secure in identity, someone who doesn't have to prove personal worth because he or she recognizes that worth in Jesus Christ. The best thing that can happen to any of our marriages is to come to know Jesus Christ as our personal Savior and to walk with Him by faith.

A Final Word

Let me remind you that Paul began this lengthy section with the truth about being filled with the Spirit of God. Remember his instructions to us all: "And do not be drunk with wine, in which is dissipation; but be filled with the Spirit" (Ephesians 5:18).

No one—not husband or wife—can love apart from the power of the Spirit. And there is no better place than marriage to test the reality of the presence of the Holy Spirit.

Norman Vincent Peale wrote:

There is nothing else like the closeness, the mutual support, the deep affection and companionship that grows between a man and a woman who have fought the battles of life together for years and years. Pleasures are brighter because you share them. Problems are lighter because you face them together. There's no describing these things, really; you have to experience them to know them. And the only way to experience them is to set a shining goal in marriage, permanence, and stick to it no matter what adversities you may encounter along the way.[2]

Hubert and June Malicote understood that closeness. When they first met in 1941, Hubert was impressed. "When I saw her, I said she'll be a good one," he later told interviewers. After Hubert served two tours during World War II, the couple were married in 1943.

They stayed married for 79 years! They moved to Ohio and had three children and eleven grandchildren.

Then, late in 2022, June became gravely ill. At age 100, she was admitted to the hospital and eventually transferred to hospice care. Seeing his beloved wife take such a terrible turn was too much for Hubert. According to their son, Hubert "broke down" and "fell apart." He, too, became gravely ill.

Soon, Hubert and June were reunited in that same hospice center. Unconscious but holding hands, the couple passed away in the same way they had maneuvered the majority of their lives—together.[3]

What an amazing story to hear about lovers united for nearly eighty years who passed into the next life side-by-side and hand-in-hand. And what a poignant picture of the power of marriage.

CHAPTER 16

Parents and Children

EPHESIANS 6:1-4

Over the years, I've come across several funny quotes about what
it means to be a parent. I often save these as potential sermon
illustrations, but I thought you might enjoy reading a few of
them here.

For example, one person said, "The quickest way for a parent
to get a child's attention is to sit down and look comfortable."

Another person said, "Raising kids is part joy and part
guerrilla warfare."

You might resonate with this clever insight: "Parenting
was much easier when I was raising my non-existent kid
hypothetically."

Or how about this description: "Parenthood is about guiding
the next generation and forgiving the last."

Just one more, and this one happens to be my favorite:
"Ever had a job where you had no experience, no training, you

weren't allowed to quit, and people's lives were at stake? That's parenting."

As we saw in the previous chapter, this particular section of Scripture begins in Ephesians 5 with the instruction given to the entire family of God concerning being filled with the Spirit. We are commanded to be filled with the Spirit, and we are told that when the Spirit of God controls our lives, we will be impacted in several ways. Namely:

- We will speak to one another in psalms and hymns and spiritual songs.

- We will sing and make melody in our hearts to the Lord.

- We will give thanks always for all things to God the Father in the name of our Lord Jesus Christ.

- We will submit to one another in the fear of God.

- Wives will submit to their husbands as to the Lord.

- Husbands will love their wives as Christ loved the Church.

Now, in Ephesians 6, we come to the next result of being filled with the Spirit: Children will obey their parents in the Lord and honor their father and mother. Additionally, fathers will not provoke their children to wrath but bring them up in the training and admonition of the Lord.

Let's take a look at what's next from the text itself:

Children, obey your parents in the Lord, for this is right. "Honor your father and mother," which is the first commandment with promise: "that it may be well with you and you may live long on the earth." And you, fathers, do not provoke your children to wrath, but bring them up in the training and admonition of the Lord. (Ephesians 6:1-4)

These four verses are a central passage in Scripture on the obedience of children and the oversight of parents.

The Obedience of Children

Obedience is a fundamental building block of the home. Whether there are Christians in that home or not, obedience is what makes a family work. In fact, there are two remarkable passages in the Word of God that tell us that obedience in the home is at the center of society.

The first of these Scriptures is found in Romans 1 where Paul is describing the iniquities that prevail in the heathen world. You will find disobedience to parents linked with the worst kinds of sin: "Being filled with all unrighteousness, sexual immorality, wickedness, covetousness, maliciousness; full of envy, murder, strife, deceit, evil-mindedness; they are whisperers, backbiters, haters of God, violent, proud, boasters, inventors of evil things, disobedient to parents, undiscerning, untrustworthy, unloving, unforgiving, unmerciful" (verses 29-31).

The same associations are revealed in 2 Timothy 3 where we are told what the world will be like just before Jesus Christ returns: "But know this, that in the last days perilous times will come: For men will be lovers of themselves, lovers of money, boasters, proud, blasphemers, disobedient to parents, unthankful, unholy, unloving, unforgiving, slanderers, without self-control, brutal, despisers of good, traitors, headstrong, haughty, lovers of pleasure rather than lovers of God …. From such people turn away!" (verses 1-5)

According to Paul, when the wheels begin to fall off a culture, one of the indicators is that there is no glue in the home.

Sometimes it amazes me to remember that our Lord Jesus Christ was also a child at one time—and that He had to submit to the authority of earthly parents. Did you ever stop to think that the God-Man was once a teenager? Do you ever think about the fact that He grew up in a normal home and went through the stages of adolescence?

Yet in Luke 2:51 we read these words about our Lord: "Then He went down with them and came to Nazareth, and was subject to them, but His mother kept all these things in her heart."

Think of this for a moment. The Ruler of the universe in submission to His mother, Mary. The God of creation willingly obeying two of His own creatures, a human mom and dad.

Now, if Jesus could obey Mary and Joseph, surely we can obey our parents in the Lord. How? By the power of the Holy Spirit.

Here are Paul's four good reasons for obeying our parents.

Because It Is a Principle of Morality

"Children, obey your parents in the Lord, for this is right" (Ephesians 6:1).

How plain and simple is this truth. We should obey our parents in the Lord because it is right. I know we are living in a time when many are saying that there is no such thing as right and wrong. But down deep in our hearts, whether we have been in church much or not, we know that some things are right and some things are wrong.

There is an order in nature, ordained by God, and it argues for the rightness of certain actions. Since parents bring a child into the world and since they have more knowledge and wisdom than the child, it is right that the child should obey his or her parents. Even young animals understand this!

In Paul's letter to the Colossians, there is a section that mirrors this passage in Ephesians, but when he comes to this command for children to obey their parents, he adds another phrase: "Children, obey your parents in all things, for this is well pleasing to the Lord" (3:20).

Do you want to please the Lord? Then do what is right. If you want to honor the Lord who formed you and gave you life and who sent His only Son into this world for your salvation, then obey your parents. Even as an adult, you can do what is right by honoring your parents.

Because It Is a Precept of Scripture

"'Honor your father and mother,' which is the first commandment with promise" (verse 2).

This is a very interesting text which refers back to Exodus 20:12. This is from the Ten Commandments. Here is how it reads in the Old Testament: "Honor your father and your mother, that your days may be long upon the land which the Lord your God is giving you."

God had given Moses four commandments up to this point, and there wasn't a promise attached to any of them. But when you get to this fifth commandment, something changes. Why the promise? If for no other reason, I believe it is evidence that God has placed great priority on this instruction. We are to obey our parents because this is God's design, and somewhere down the road we will look back and be glad that we did, even though we might struggle with it now.

Struggling with obedience to parents is part of the unhooking process we go through as we get older and ultimately learn to make our own decisions. But if we try to push that process ahead of schedule, we cause great harm to ourselves and to our families.

Because It Is a Protection for Children

"That it may be well with you" (verse 3).

I'm sure there are disobedient rebels out there who have violated this command and have somehow made it through life unscathed. But I have never met one.

Author Dave Stone wrote about an encounter he had while on a mission trip in the Dominican Republic with his young family. Traffic can be very dangerous in Latin America since drivers there have a tendency to be both aggressive and creative, which is a treacherous combination.

One evening Dave was watching his son, Sam, play a game where he jumped from a sidewalk, onto a narrow street, and then back to the sidewalk. He was zigzagging around, kind of playing in his own world.

Then, out of nowhere, Dave said in a firm voice, "Samuel, don't move!"

Here's what happened next in Dave's own words:

Immediately he froze. About a second later, a Moped zipped past him, going 30 mph with no lights on—right where Sam was about to step. My 6-year-old didn't ignore me, argue or blatantly disobey. I said freeze, and he froze. That obedience probably saved his life.[1]

The simple fact is that everybody has to report to somebody. That doesn't stop when a person turns twenty. Everybody has to learn the principle of submission to authority. If we don't learn it at home where it is supposed to be learned, then we will struggle with it all of our lives. Someday there will be a notation in a file with your name on it that says, "Struggles with authority," or "Has a problem with authority."

I can assure you that I never, ever thought of smart-mouthing my dad. Never even considered it! Intuitively, I knew what would happen to me if I ever did, and it just wasn't worth it. It was a good thing for me to grow up with that knowledge. It has helped me all the way through life.

Because It Is a Promoter of Long Life

"And you may live long on the earth" (verse 3).

Obedient children in the Old Testament did live longer. And discipline in a child's life is usually conducive to good health. Does that mean that a person who is disobedient always dies young and a person who is obedient always lives into his nineties? No, of course not! This is not an ironclad promise of Scripture. It is a proverb, and proverbs tell us what life will be like under normal conditions.

For instance:

- In the month of April in Portland, Oregon, you would do well to carry an umbrella.

- When you see a sleeping pit bull, you would do well not to yank on his ear.

Will it always rain in Portland on an April day? Will the pit bull always bite your arm off if you pull his ear? No, perhaps not. But these are truths of life you can generally count on!

Let's face it. A person who grows up rebellious against every fabric of control has put himself on a path that leads to discouragement and destruction, not a good life. These rebellious ways have a way of taking a toll on the years you spend on the earth. People who follow God's instructions have a much better chance of living a reasonably good life for a reasonably long period of time.

The Oversight of Parents

Several years ago, I decided to create a biblical theology of parents and parenting. I started at the beginning of the Old Testament, and I made note of every single reference that could be associated with families and parenting. I was surprised to discover that the negative examples in the Word of God far outweighed the positive examples.

For instance:

- Isaac pampered Esau, and it tore his home in two.

- Jacob allowed favoritism and jealousy in his home and set his sons against one another.

- Eli, a leader and priest, failed to discipline his sons and reaped a harvest of personal and national shame.

- David the king pampered Absalom and refused to discipline him, and that young man's rebellion and death turned the kingdom upside down and sent David to his grave a broken man.

Perhaps we learn more from the failures of others than we do from their successes.

Paul wrote, "And you, fathers, do not provoke your children to wrath" (verse 4). In case you mothers are sitting back thinking you are off the hook on this one because the word here is directed to the fathers, let me tell you something I discovered in the Bible. The word that is translated "fathers" here in Ephesians 6 is the same word found in Hebrews 11:23: "By faith Moses, when he was born, was hidden three months by his parents."

Meaning, the word "fathers" in Ephesians 6 and the word "parents" in Hebrews 11 are the same word in the Greek language. Paul was talking not exclusively to fathers but to all parents—to all who have oversight and authority in the lives of children.

Let's take a deeper look at four principles we can find in Paul's words to parents.

The Principle of Discouragement

"And you, fathers, do not provoke your children to wrath" (verse 4).

This is the only negative principle we'll find in these four verses. Paul begins by telling us what not to do as parents. He says, "Don't provoke your children to wrath. Don't irritate them! Don't discourage them by unreasonable demands."

There are some parents who are always on their kids' backs. No matter what their son or daughter does, it is wrong. Within the exercise of parental authority there is a need for understanding and love—for justice and fairness and self-control.

Sometimes a kid steps out of line, but then the father or mother steps even further out of line by overreacting. Small provocations should not set off major explosions.

When Paul was writing to the Colossian believers, he used this same instruction, but with this poignant added insight: "Fathers, do not provoke your children, lest they become discouraged" (Colossians 3:21).

Let me tell you something I've learned. For every time you have to say "No" as a parent, if you've worked hard to say "Yes" eight or nine times before then, the "No" will have much greater power. I've tried to teach people, not just in the family, but in administration, too, that even though we all have to say "No" at times, we ought to create the atmosphere where it's obvious we wish we could say "Yes." It is never "No" because we delight to say "No."

I'm reminded of the story of Alice Trillin. Alice was active in a camping program for children with cancer and other life-threatening diseases—a place where kids could just be kids, not patients, for a week each summer.

One year she became very drawn to "a sunny little girl who was," she wrote, "a magical child" despite the challenge of living with two genetic diseases that severely impacted her growth and her ability to eat.

One particular day the campers were playing a game of duck, duck, goose, and the little girl was tapped on the shoulder. As she struggled to get up to pursue the tagger, she handed some mail, which she had held tightly clenched in her hand, to Alice who was sitting behind her. Since it took the girl so long to run around the circle, Alice gave in to her curiosity about a note from the girl's mother that was on top of the bundle of letters.

Alice later wrote, "I simply had to know what this child's parents could have done to make her so spectacular, to make her the most optimistic, most enthusiastic, most hopeful human being I had ever encountered."

The line at the very end of the note grabbed Alice's attention. It read: "If God had given us all of the children in the world to choose from ... we would only have chosen you."

Alice showed the note to a coworker with the observation "Quick. Read this. It's the secret of life."[2]

Those words of love and encouragement certainly revealed the secret of that little girl's remarkable attitude despite her challenges.

The Bible insists that the little ones we have in our homes are from God. Children are not accidents that come to derail our career plans. They are not inconveniences or intrusions into the lives of busy parents. They are gifts to be treasured.

The Principle of Diligence

"But bring them up." (verse 4).

To "bring up" children is a biblical phrase that implies a serious responsibility for their spiritual, moral, mental, and physical wellbeing. This is a very encompassing term. In fact, in Ephesians 5:29, when Paul was speaking to the same group of people, he said: "For no one ever hated his own flesh, but nourishes and cherishes it."

The word "nourishes" in verse 29 is the same word for "bring …up" in Ephesians 6:4.

Parenting is a proactive assignment. Parent, God has put you in charge! If you have ever doubted or wavered in this knowledge, let me help you out: I do hereby, on the authority of the Word of God, empower you to be in charge of your family. Be in charge in a righteous, godly way. Take authority where God has given you authority, and bring up your children.

The Principle of Discipline

"In the training … of the Lord" (verse 4).

In the King James Version, the word here is "nurture," which means "correction." It is the same word used in Hebrews 12:6: "For whom the Lord loves He chastens, and scourges every son whom He receives."

We don't have time in this chapter to cover all the principles of discipline found in the Bible. But I want to underscore two basic principles about discipline that I think are critical to the exercise of godly parenting.

First, discipline should be reserved for disobedience in the home. It should not be the consequence parents use in response to mistakes.

Some of the craziest things happened in our family as our children entered the driving stage. I have to admit that is a scary time of parenting. One day when Jennifer was first getting started, she backed her Mustang out of the driveway—and straight into my van. That was an expensive little collision. We got two for one.

Now, should I get mad over that? Hey, it was a mistake. She just forgot to look. I remember saying, "It's okay; the only thing I am concerned about is you. Are you all right?"

Second, discipline should be applied in response to individual acts—what they do. It should never be an attack on a child's character, which is who they are.

Here's what I mean. If a child tells a lie, that doesn't necessarily make him a liar. When a kid impulsively swipes a piece of candy from the candy store, that doesn't make her a thief or a robber. Now, the child did an act that was wrong. Deal with the act, but don't create a character out of an act.

We are more than the sum of our individual failures.

So when you discipline your children, don't get caught up in creating an exaggerated image of their life. If you keep doing that, your child will become the fulfillment of your prophecies.

Authors Gary Smalley and John Trent once advised that all our criticism of our kids ought to be like a thin slice of meat in a sandwich, encompassed by thick slices of bread. The bread is praise and encouragement, which ought to both precede and follow any critical remarks.

The Principle of Direction

"Bring them up in the ... admonition of the Lord" (verse 4).

Training is correction. Admonition is instruction or teaching. We need to teach our kids. We are responsible to help them learn the difference between right and wrong. We are to help them learn the Scriptures and motivate them to follow what they learn.

Paul wrote a bit of exhortation to Timothy that sets the example for instructing our children: "But you must continue in the things which you have learned and been assured of, knowing from whom you have learned them, and that from childhood you have known the Holy Scriptures, which are able to make you wise for salvation through faith which is in Christ Jesus" (2 Timothy 3:14-15).

Many years ago, when our family lived on the East Coast, every summer we used to spend two weeks in Ocean City, New Jersey. A church family owned a duplex right on the ocean, and every August they handed us the keys to their house and said, "It's yours for two weeks."

I have photos showing us dragging down to the ocean all the paraphernalia required when you have little ones. From the cottage door to the ocean we lugged a bassinet and a crib and buckets bulging with toys—it seemed like hundreds of miles. We left in the morning and stayed all day because it was too hard to come back. We didn't want to do it more than twice a day. Every evening after dinner we took a walk on the beach. We spent many hours walking the beautiful, white sandy shores.

One night we decided to stroll to the boardwalk, about twenty blocks away. It was seven o'clock when we started toward the city; low tide was to be at seven thirty, and the ocean was busy depositing its debris on the sand. The whole bunch of us walked in bare feet, and we had to be careful not to step on broken shells or, worse, jellyfish. I gave the children a stern lecture about taking care where they walked.

By the time we reached our destination and decided to turn back, sea debris covered the shoreline. That day I must have been deep in thought, pondering the beauty of the evening and how much I loved the ocean, and I was walking rapidly in front of the rest of the family. Suddenly I realized someone was walking immediately behind me; I could almost feel his breath. I heard the crunch of feet not my own and looked over my shoulder to see one small son stretching his little legs to put his foot in the last footprint I left in the sand. He thought the only way he could be sure to avoid the broken shells, the jellyfish, and the crabs was to step exactly where I had been. As difficult as it was, he somehow made his feet fit inside the footprints I made, step by painful step.

That long-ago experience left a lasting impression on my soul. Walking behind me are four children trying hard to find my footprints so they can put their feet exactly where their father's have gone. That's what being a Christian parent is all about. That's why it's such an awesome thing. And that's why we often find ourselves on our face, saying, "God, who is sufficient for these things? Lord, help me not to be phony. Help me to embrace Your Word. But most of all, help me to live it. Help me to be the kind of parent who will infect my children with the desire to please You because that's what they see being lived out in my life."

For kids: Even when I don't feel like it, I'm going to honor my mother and father and be obedient to them. I'm going to live as Christ lived when He was a boy, submitting to the authority of my parents.

For parents: I'm going to hold the line where I need to, but I am going to do it without exasperating or discouraging my children with unneeded rules and regulations. I am going to love them so much in the process that the things I ask them to do will seem as nothing because of the love they feel for me and the nurturing I give them in their lives.

Here is God's standard for a Christian home!

CHAPTER 17

Honoring Christ From Nine to Five

EPHESIANS 6:5-9

Bill Hansen retired at the age of 97, having spent 32 years working as a permit coordinator for Hutchinson Plumbing, Heating, and Cooling in Cherry Hill, New Jersey. Prior to that, Hansen had spent almost 40 years working for other companies, including ExxonMobil.

In short, Bill Hansen spent 72 years of his life as an employee—and loved just about every minute of it. "I never had a job where I didn't want to go to work in the morning," he said. "I was blessed."

Three years after officially retiring, Bill Hansen had only one request for his one-hundredth birthday present: another day at work. "I hate being retired," he said. So he signed a one-day contract with Hutchinson Plumbing, Heating, and Cooling to spend his birthday doing what he loved.

The company made a big deal of the event, starting the day with a celebration and a cake to honor Bill. The other employees were there, including many whom Hansen had trained and worked with over his 32 years. CEO Fred Hutchinson presented Bill with his one-day contract to sign.

But Bill wasn't there for all the fuss. "He took off about fifteen minutes after we signed that agreement to get to work," said Hutchinson.[1]

Throughout these pages, we've been exploring the many blessings God pours over His people through the power of His Spirit as we follow Him. We've seen the blessings that come from belief in Christ, including salvation and inclusion in the Body of Christ. We've explored the opportunity for unity as members of God's household, and we've covered the different spiritual gifts we can receive as disciples of Christ. In recent chapters, we've learned how God's Spirit touches us and blesses us within the context of our marriages and our families.

Now, in this chapter, we're going to discover how the Holy Spirit extends His blessings even to our work. We're going to see that Christianity stretches even to the grit and grind of the marketplace.

The indwelling Spirit sits with us all day long at the terminal on our desk. He is with us as we stand behind the cash register or the check-out counter. He walks with us on the roofs of buildings as we build up or tear down. He crawls under the old house with us as we fix the plumbing. He cruises with us at night in the squad car. He makes a difference in the everyday experiences of life in our workplace, no matter where that workplace may be.

And yes, even for those who find themselves working in sweatpants and T-shirts from home, God's Spirit can reach us and bless us there.

Of course, there are many differences between the modern workplace of today and what people experienced in the ancient culture of Ephesus and the Early Church, and we're going to examine a few of those differences throughout this chapter. However, one thing remains similar in both cultures: What we think of as "work" is largely divided between two groups—employers and employees.

Work is a two-sided issue, which is why it's appropriate that Paul addressed that issue from both sides in Ephesians 6. In the space of just a few verses, this great apostle of the Lord, under the inspiration of the Holy Spirit, had a heart-to-heart talk with both labor and management. In essence, he gave us an employee's manual and an employer's manual. It is amazing to me how on target these instructions are even for today.

The Employee's Manual

Let's start with the employee's manual since in most market systems there are more employees than employers. Here's what Paul had to say to workers:

Bondservants, be obedient to those who are your masters according to the flesh, with fear and trembling, in sincerity of heart, as to Christ; not with eyeservice, as men-pleasers, but as bondservants of Christ, doing the will of God from the heart, with goodwill doing service, as to the Lord, and not to men, knowing that whatever good anyone does, he will receive the same from the Lord, whether he is a slave or free. (Ephesians 6:5-8)

That section begins with the Greek word *doulos*, translated as "Bondservants," which means we need to take a step back and look at the context of the ancient world. Specifically, we need to address the reality of slaves and slavery.

Paul wrote these instructions at the height of the Roman Empire, which was built on the foundation of slavery. During Paul's day, scholars estimate there may have been as many as six million slaves at work throughout that empire. Why so many? Partly because the leaders of the Roman Empire made it practically illegal for members of the aristocracy to engage in menial work, which means the vast majority of work was done by servants, also called slaves.

Indeed, almost all of what we describe as the "work force" in modern times fell under the label of slaves or servants in ancient Rome. I'm talking about farmers. Sanitation workers. Educators. Nannies and cooks and maids. Shopkeepers. Just about any other "job" you can think of, they were mostly performed by slaves.

Importantly, many of those slaves came to faith in Jesus during Paul's day. Christianity spread like wildfire among the poor and the mistreated, including servants—and that remains the case in our world. So Paul knew that many of his hearers in Ephesus and beyond were slaves and that they could be experiencing different types of treatment at the hands of different types of masters. Some masters (or employers) were cruel and heartless; others treated their servants like family.

Some masters were fellow Christians; others were hostile to the faith.

Paul's words in Ephesians 6 embrace all of those circumstances, as well as the circumstances of our work today. And in case you think Paul's instructions may be a little outdated—*After all, I'm not a slave!*—then look back at verse 8: "Knowing that whatever good anyone does, he will receive the same from the Lord, whether he is a slave or free."

These principles are all-encompassing.

The Worker's Action

Let's begin in verse 5 with what we might call the worker's action: "Bondservants, be obedient to those who are your masters." In other words, be submissive to those who are in authority over you.

Now, I understand that's not a popular principle. Remember what we saw earlier about submission in the context of marriage? Nobody likes to submit, but sometimes it is necessary. Paul wrote similar instructions in another epistle: "Bondservants, obey in all things your masters according to the flesh, not with eyeservice, as men-pleasers, but in sincerity of heart, fearing God" (Colossians 3:22).

What's interesting here is that the Bible tells us not only how to work but also why to work. Scripture shows us what our attitudes and actions should be like as disciples of Jesus who are also employees in the world. Specifically, when our attitudes are right and our actions are right—when they match with the Person and work of Jesus—then by our very work, we become witnesses to Almighty God.

Paul communicated something similar to Timothy, although in reverse. He said that if we don't obey those who have authority over us, we can do great damage to the cause of Christ: "Let as many bondservants as are under the yoke count their own masters worthy of all honor, so that the name of God and His doctrine may not be blasphemed" (1 Timothy 6:1).

Why should we guard our work ethic? Not because we are worried about others saying bad things about us, but because we are worried about others making wrong conclusions about our Lord.

There is a similar sentiment expressed in Titus 2:9-10. Notice what Paul wrote: "Exhort bondservants to be obedient to their own masters, to be well pleasing in all things, not answering back, not pilfering, but showing all good fidelity, that they may adorn the doctrine of God our Savior in all things."

In other words, we as followers of Jesus are to guard our work ethic, and our actions are to reflect obedience and submission to those who are in authority over us. Why? Because the way you work for your employer can actually make the Gospel of Jesus Christ more attractive to people—or less attractive. The Bible says you can change the opinion people have of Christ by the way you, a Christ-follower, go about your business.

That's the power of the worker's action.

The Worker's Assignment

Next, we can stay in Ephesians 6:5 and see what I call the worker's assignment: "Bondservants, be obedient to those who are your masters according to the flesh."

The required action is obedience. The assignment is to work for men or women that God has placed in authority over you. And this obedience isn't to be diminished because you and your employer both happen to be Christians.

Sometimes when Christians work for other Christians, they get the impression they don't have to work as hard or respond as well because, after all, "We're brothers in Christ." That may be true on the relational basis, but in the workplace, you are under the authority of the person who is your boss, and you are to treat that person with utmost respect.

Listen to what God's Word says on that very subject: "And those who have believing masters, let them not despise them because they are brethren, but rather serve them because those who are benefited are believers and beloved. Teach and exhort these things" (1 Timothy 6:2).

The Worker's Attitude

Paul was covering all the bases in his epistles about our relationships in the workplace. The worker's action is obedience, and the worker's authority is to anyone God has placed over us. Then, third, notice the worker's attitude in verse 5. It says we are to follow these instructions "with fear and trembling."

Now that doesn't mean you have to go to work every day shaking in your boots. That's not what Paul was talking about. Instead, this wonderful phrase is used several places in the New Testament, and it speaks of respect and honor. What Paul was saying is that we should take our work very seriously. Whenever we arrive at the office or our job site, our attitude should be: There is more at stake here than eight hours of work. There are eternal issues wrapped up in my thoughts and my actions as I go to work.

Sadly, that is not happening in our culture, even among Christians.

According to a recent Gallup poll, 18 percent of employees are "actively disengaged" from their work and/or their workplace. Meaning, they are physically present but mentally absent. They don't care whether they do a good job or a bad job; they are truly "working for the weekend" and for nothing else.

That's almost 1 out of every 5 workers. But, shockingly, a full 67 percent of workers are "not engaged" according to the same Gallup survey. The majority of workers in our culture! These women and men "are not your worst performers, but they are indifferent to your organization. They give you their time, but not their best effort nor their best ideas."[2]

May such a thing never be said of any worker who claims to be a follower of Christ! The majority of our lives are spent at work, which is precisely why we need to adopt an attitude of seriousness and respect in the workplace. We must use that time to glorify our Lord.

The Worker's Ambition

Verse 6 describes our ambition as followers of Jesus who also happen to be employees. We are to work "not with eyeservice, as men-pleasers, but as bondservants of Christ, doing the will of God from the heart."

That's the secret right there. The ambition that God rewards isn't that we just show up and punch the time clock but that we work at our jobs with all our hearts. This ambition aligns with another of Paul's more famous instructions: "And whatever you do, do it heartily, as to the Lord and not to men" (Colossians 3:23).

Martyred missionary Jim Elliot said it this way: "Wherever you are, *be all there.* Live to the hilt every situation you believe to be the will of God."[3]

When you are at work, are you all there? Or do you just bring a part of who you are to the marketplace?

Notice that phrase in Ephesians 6:5: "in sincerity of heart." Paul said we are to do our work "in sincerity of heart." Literally, the translation there is singleness of heart or with a single focus of heart. When we go to work, we are commanded to put other things aside and focus our attention on that which is our assignment for the day.

Now, you might be thinking, *Dr. Jeremiah, if you knew what my boss was like, you wouldn't expect me to listen to these instructions from Paul. After all, Paul never knew what I have to endure!*

Well, first of all, these instructions are not from Paul—not exclusively. For one thing, these instructions originated with the Holy Spirit, which is the case for all Scripture. Paul was merely the pen with which God's Spirit wrote these instructions down.

In addition, Paul wasn't the only biblical author who focused on these themes. Look at this passage from Peter, for example: "Servants, be submissive to your masters with all fear, not only to the good and gentle, but also to the harsh. For this is commendable, if because of conscience toward God one endures grief, suffering wrongfully" (1 Peter 2:18-19).

The Word of God is not giving us any loopholes here, is it? The instructions are clear. You don't like your boss? Well, that's too bad. She's not a Christian? That doesn't matter. He's harsh? That's not your problem. Your problem, if you are an employee, is to honor the person you work for and give him or her an honest day's work—to accomplish that work with all your heart. That's what the Word of God says. That is the worker's ambition.

The Worker's Aim

Next, let's focus on the worker's aim: our goal or purpose as we go about our work. Paul wrote that we should work "as to Christ; not with eyeservice, as men-pleasers, but as bondservants of Christ, doing the will of God from the heart, *with goodwill doing service, as to the Lord, and not to men*" (verses 5-7, emphasis added).

One of the things about this whole section of Ephesians that has gripped me is the way everything is connected to the Lord. In fact, here's a brief review. Look at the bullet points below, and you'll see Paul reminding us with every word he writes not to forget that we serve the Lord God and that all other relationships are secondary. If we can get our connection "to the Lord" right, everything else will fall into place.

Here's what I mean:

- In 5:19, it says we are to sing and make melody to the Lord.

- In verse 20, it says we are to give thanks in the Name of the Lord.

- In verse 21, we are to submit to one another in the fear of the Lord.

- In verse 22, wives are to submit to their husbands as to the Lord.

- In verse 25, husbands are to love their wives as Christ loved the Church.

- In 6:1, children are to obey their parents in the Lord.

- In verse 4, fathers are to bring their children up in the admonition of the Lord.

- In verse 7, servants are to obey their masters as to the Lord.

- And in verse 9, masters are to remember that they have a Master in heaven.

What is the central theme throughout those verses? We serve God!

Yes, you serve God when you come to church on Sunday. Yes, you serve God when you worship as a family, or when you praise Him together in your own home. But you also serve God when you arrive at work on Monday. We are all serving God every day, no matter what specific activity we happen to be doing.

That is the worker's aim.

The Worker's Award

And finally, in verse 8, we see the worker's award: "Knowing that whatever good anyone does, he will receive the same from the Lord, whether he is a slave or free."

This is an incredible principle and really an incredible promise. God will reward us for the work we do. Specifically, He will reward us in kind—good for good and poor for poor. Which means the good work we do for God is really good work we are doing for ourselves, as well.

A young man named Walter Carr discovered that principle on his very first day of work at a new job. A native of Alabama, Carr signed on with the Bellhops moving company and was supposed to be at a client's house at 8 a.m. for his first day of work. Sadly, Carr's car broke down the day before, leaving him stranded nearly twenty miles from that client's home.

Walter Carr had every opportunity to make excuses and ask for a mulligan. Instead, he set his alarm for midnight and started walking.

With about eight miles to go, Carr was forced to stop and rest for a moment. Thankfully, he received some assistance from local police officers, who took him out for breakfast before another officer dropped him off at the client's home around 6:30 a.m. Once there, the client offered Walter some food and the chance to lie down, but Carr insisted on getting to work instead.

"I didn't want to defeat myself," he said later. He wanted his first day on the job to go well, which in his mind meant he wanted to work hard.

Jenny Lamey was the client Walter had been assigned to help. She learned about his story from the police officer, and it blew her away watching him lift heavy boxes in the sweltering heat despite his restless night and long journey. "I burst into tears a couple times," she said. "He's like the poster boy for no excuses. He's just got this deep faith, he wasn't alone."

Lamey also contacted Luke Marklin, the CEO of Bellhop, to share how impressed she was with Walter Carr and his work ethic. In response, Marklin invited Carr out to lunch and then gave him a gift—his own SUV. Walter would never again need to walk to work.[4]

Have you heard the saying that "hard work is its own reward"? Well, that turns out to be true, and the source of that reward is God.

Maybe right now you're thinking, *Pastor Jeremiah, there are some days I just can't do it. I just don't feel like giving it everything I've got.* I've been there as well. We've all had that feeling. But you know what? There comes a time when we need to move Christianity beyond the level of feeling.

Because serving God is not primarily about our feelings, it's about being obedient to what God tells us.

You know what I've discovered? When we get obedience right, the feelings come along eventually. It's like the caboose at the end of the train. The drag of our working day may seem endless. It may seem like nothing will ever pay off. But if we continue in obedience and work "as to the Lord," the reward will come—and those positive feelings will come with it.

Remember, you're not working for the boss you can see. You're working for God. Which is why the apostle Paul wrote this reminder in another of his epistles: "And let us not grow weary while doing good, for in due season we shall reap if we do not lose heart" (Galatians 6:9).

The Employer's Manual

Paul has three specific instructions that he wants to get into the hearts of the masters or the employers.

Respect Your Employees

After plowing through these four verses that are addressed to the employees, we might be surprised to find that there is only one verse devoted to the employers. It looks like they are getting off easy, or that perhaps the main problems in the workplace are with the workers and not the bosses.

You could almost reason in that direction were it not for the first phrase in verse 9: "And you, masters, do the same things to them."

All that has been communicated to employees by way of attitude is also a requirement to the employers as well. Employers are to serve as to the Lord with sincerity of heart, not trying to please men but rather to do the will of God.

What should I check on this list if I am an employer? Answer: all of the above.

In other words, this is a reciprocal arrangement. You have men and women working under authority. You want them to work hard, you want them to show respect, and you want them to do an honest day's work. The Bible says if that's what you want, then you need to show them the same kind of respect with which you want to be treated.

That's what verse 9 is teaching by saying, "Do the same things." Give them what is due.

Paul says it this way in Colossians: "Masters, give your bondservants what is just and fair, knowing that you also have a Master in heaven" (4:1).

Refrain From Abusive Treatment

One way for employers to respect their employees is by "giving up threatening" (verse 9).

This term, "giving up threatening," suggests the idea of loosening up or releasing. The godly employer uses her authority and power as little as possible and does not throw her weight around or lord it over those under her. She is never abusive or inconsiderate.

Here is how one author describes a godly boss:

The good leader is one who will listen to you, stand up for you, trust you and not micromanage every aspect of your work. They communicate clearly, constantly, and in a collaborative manner. They seek your advice, listen to your concerns, and consult you on the best solutions for success.

They set high expectations and encourage you to be the best you can be ... striving for new heights of excellence. They also care about your life outside of work and want you to have good physical, social, and mental health.

Lastly, the good boss can be tough when needed. They live in reality and know there are some who will not respond to their leadership, and, may be required to use their authority to reprimand and/or terminate staff.

[H]owever, this is always a last recourse after all other positive strategies have failed. Overall … the good boss is one who lives sacrificially for the benefit of others, always desiring their success as well as the success of the agency.[5]

Remember to Whom You Report

"Knowing that your own Master also is in heaven, and there is no partiality with Him" (verse 9).

The Christian employer realizes that his own authority is from God, and that both he and his workers report to the same Lord. She also knows that before God she is no more worthy than her workers and that God does not show partiality.

The movie *Mr. Holland's Opus* follows the story of high school music teacher, Mr. Holland, who dreams of composing and directing on an international stage. He longs to stand under the spotlight in Paris or London, dressed in a formal tuxedo, conducting renowned orchestras. However, his dream never comes to fruition in that exact form. Instead, Mr. Holland finds fulfillment in his daily work, teaching ordinary students how to play and appreciate music in their own unique ways.

Toward the end of his career, Mr. Holland is surprised when he receives an unexpected invite to the school auditorium during school hours. As he enters the room, he is taken aback by the large crowd waiting for him—including current students and former students from his decades as a teacher. With their instruments in hand, they come together to perform a compilation of songs composed by Mr. Holland himself, with him as their conductor once again.

Mr. Holland eventually realizes that his life masterpiece—his *magnum opus*—wasn't a world-class composition but his faithful dedication as a teacher to inspire love and passion for music in his students. His true legacy was the countless lives he touched through his ordinary daily work.

In his book *Work Matters* Tom Nelson writes about that moment, saying:

> The *magnum opus* of most of our lives will not be seen under the bright lights of visibility, but will be the extraordinary impact of our ordinary day-to-day life, faithfully lived in extraordinary ways. It is in and through our vocations that the love of Christ shines bright … and where God desires our good work to be well done. It is where our Sunday faith and our Monday work meet.[6]

You and I have the same opportunity when we honor God with our work.

FINALLY, MY BRETHREN,
BE STRONG IN THE LORD
AND IN THE POWER OF
HIS MIGHT. PUT ON THE
WHOLE ARMOR OF GOD,
THAT YOU MAY BE ABLE
TO STAND AGAINST THE
WILES OF THE DEVIL.

EPHESIANS 6:10-11

CHAPTER 18

Spiritual Warfare

EPHESIANS 6:10-17

At around 10 a.m. on September 15, 2021, the town of Denton, North Carolina, went dark. More than 1,400 people found themselves without power, which is a big deal in a town with a total population of 1,660.

A little later that morning, Denton residents who still had some charge in their cell phones were able to read this message on the Facebook page of the Denton fire department: "Major Power Outage affecting the entire Town Limits and surrounding Duke Power Customers. Fire at the Duke Substation has been extinguished but major repairs will be needed to restore power."[1]

So a substation fire had caused the loss of power. But what caused the fire?

After a quick and thorough investigation, Duke Energy employees discovered that the source of the fire was not a falling tree branch, which is the most common cause of power outages in most municipalities. It wasn't a car striking a utility pole. It wasn't a piece of malfunctioning equipment, nor was it some kind of intentional sabotage.

No, the culprit behind the Denton power outage was a slithering snake.

Apparently, one of those critters had wriggled its way into the substation's inner workings, seeking warmth. It made contact with something sensitive, frying the snake and sending sparks in all directions. Thus the fire, and thus the loss of power for thousands of people.

This is not an uncommon occurrence in North Carolina and around the country. In fact, snakes often make it a point to seek out the covered areas of substations and other electrical buildings. "They will do anything to get in," said one Duke Energy employee.[2] And when they do get in, havoc is often the result.

There is another snake that has caused Christians to lose spiritual power for millennia. I'm talking of course about the ancient serpent we call Satan, or the devil. Like those slithering creatures around Denton, North Carolina, Satan will do anything to get into our midst as a church and sever our connection to God's spiritual power grid, throwing us into darkness.

Satan is determined to hinder and harm and ruin God's image in you and in me. He is here to kill and to destroy and to steal. The story of our lives as believers is the story of the long and brutal assault of the enemy on your heart and on mine by one who knows what we can be and fears it deeply.

Spiritual Warfare Is Real

"Finally, my brethren, be strong in the Lord and in the power of His might. Put on the whole armor of God, that you may be able to stand against the wiles of the devil. For we do not wrestle against flesh and blood, but against principalities, against powers, against the rulers of the darkness of this age, against spiritual hosts of wickedness in the heavenly places" (Ephesians 6:10-12).

Mark it down in your journal: We live in a spiritual war zone. There is a war going on for your heart and for mine. This comes as a surprise to many of God's people.

One New Testament scholar said:

It is, of course, a surprise to many people that there is a "struggle" at all. Yes, they think, we find it difficult from time to time to practice our Christianity. We find it hard to forgive people, to pray regularly, to resist temptation, to learn more about the faith. But as far as they're concerned that's the end of it. They have never thought that their small struggles might be part of a larger campaign.[3]

The War Is Satanic

People don't want to believe in the devil anymore. Even many people who say they are Christians don't believe in the reality of Satan. But Satan is the most bitter enemy of God and His people. Even his names tell you of his nature:

- the deceiver (Revelation 12:9)

- the murderer (John 8:44)

- the tempter (Matthew 4:3)

- the destroyer (Revelation 9:11)

- the liar (John 8:44)

- the accuser of the brethren (Revelation 12:10)

- the evil one (1 John 5:19)

Peter gave us a sober warning in his first epistle: "Be sober, be vigilant; because your adversary the devil walks about like a roaring lion, seeking whom he may devour" (1 Peter 5:8).

Look again at Paul's list of categories in reference to our enemies: principalities and powers and rulers of darkness and spiritual wickedness in high places. This is nothing less than the organizational chart for Satan's domain. The forces of evil in this world are led by Satan, and he has a great army of fallen angels that are well organized into a hierarchy.

Each of those terms tells us something:

- "Principalities" are the head officers,

- "Powers" describe staff officers,

- "Rulers" are divisional commanders, and

- "Spiritual hosts of wickedness" are rank and file minions.

John Phillips notes how carefully Paul defines our enemy:

Our enemies are not people. We must see beyond people. Satan may use people to persecute us, lie to us, cheat us, hurt us, or even kill us. But our real enemy lurks in the shadows of the unseen world, moving people as pawns on the chessboard of time. As long as we see people as enemies and wrestle against them, we will spend our strength in vain.[4]

The War Is Strategic

"Put on the whole armor of God, that you may be able to stand against the wiles of the devil" (verse 11).

The word "wiles" means "strategy" or "plans of war." The word in the Greek language is *methodia*. Satan has a well-developed strategy for this war, and he is implementing his strategy day by day. Even moment by moment.

Paul said, "Lest Satan should take advantage of us; for we are not ignorant of his devices" (2 Corinthians 2:11). The word for "devices" in this verse is translated everywhere else in the New Testament as "mind." The phrase here means that Satan has a very well thought-out plan for each of us. He attacks us in a mindful way.

The Bible says Satan's purpose is to hurt and discourage those who belong to God. He will stop at nothing to disturb the mind, deceive the heart, and defeat the life. If you read your Bible carefully, you will see that what he is doing today he has done from the beginning. He led Lot into Sodom, got Peter to deny Christ, caused Ananias and Sapphira to lie to the church, and even dared to attack Jesus Christ. If he isn't afraid to attack the Lord of Glory, you should not be surprised to discover that he is willing to attack the most mature of Christians.

The devil has three primary goals:

- To destroy the testimony of Christian individuals,

- To destroy the unity and purity of Christian homes,

- To destroy the ministry of Christian churches.

Here is the most frightening thing about spiritual warfare: Most Christians are not serious about it, if they even acknowledge it at all.

John Eldredge said, "To live in ignorance of spiritual warfare is the most naïve and dangerous thing a person can do. It's like skipping through the worst part of town, late at night waving your wallet above your head. It's like walking into an al-Qaeda training camp wearing an 'I Love the United States' T-shirt. It's like swimming with great white sharks, dressed as a wounded sea lion and smeared with blood. And let me tell you something: you don't escape spiritual warfare simply because you choose not to believe it exists or because you refuse to fight it."[5]

The bottom line is this: You are going to have to fight for your heart. Remember John 10:10, which tells us the thief is trying to steal the life God wants to give.

Spiritual Weapons Are Required

"Therefore take up the whole armor of God, that you may be able to withstand in the evil day, and having done all, to stand" (verse 13).

Spiritual warfare is real, but we do not have to be casualties of war. We can prepare for combat. God has given us what we need to be victorious. We can be strong in the Lord and in the power of His might.

I like what Peter O'Brien said about this passage: "Paul wants to see Christians strong, stable, and robust." So even though the enemy is a frightening prospect, this paragraph should not foster an attitude of fear. "The entire passage is suffused with a spirit of confidence and hope and the reader is left, not with a feeling of despair, but with the sense that Satan can be defeated."[6]

There are six pieces of armor listed by Paul in this passage. Each piece of armor deals specifically with an area of our lives that is a target of Satan's strategy. Let's inventory these six weapons of warfare and learn how to apply them to our own spiritual battles.

The Belt of Truth

"Stand therefore, having girded your waist with truth" (verse 14).

Paul begins with truth because that is Satan's primary target. From the Garden of Eden to our current culture, Satan has trafficked in deception and lies. Jesus described the devil's character to a T: "You are of your father the devil, and the desires of your father you want to do. He was a murderer from the beginning, and does not stand in the truth, because there is no truth in him. When he speaks a lie, he speaks from his own resources, for he is a liar and the father of it" (John 8:44).

William Gurnall wrote: "The devil has more temptations than an actor has costumes for the stage. And one of his all-time favorite disguises is that of a lying spirit, to abuse your tender heart with the worst news he can deliver—that you do not really love Jesus Christ and that you are only pretending, you are only deceiving yourself."[7]

The piece of armor that deflects Satan's lies is the belt of truth. Truth is always the answer for lies. A person of integrity with a clear conscience can face the enemy without fear. And the sword of the Spirit, which is the Word of truth, hangs from that belt. A person of truth who speaks the truth will win against Satan every time, but once a lie gets into the heart of the believer, everything starts falling apart.

Let me tell you something: Any time you allow a lie to live in your heart or your soul, you are giving a foothold to Satan. Because that's his domain. Don't do it! Don't cheat on your spouse, either in thought or deed. Don't cheat on your expense accounts. Don't say things you know are not true. Why? Because each time you give yourself to dishonesty, you walk in the domain of the enemy, and you give him free rein in your life.

Instead, put on the girdle of truth. Know the truth of God's Word. Live truthfully. Have integrity in your life. When what seems like a little lie starts to tickle your mind, stand up and say, "By the grace of God in the power of the Holy Spirit, I renounce that lie because Satan is the father of lies. Jesus Christ is the Author of truth, and I put on Jesus Christ, and I denounce that lie."

When we put on the girdle of truth, we acknowledge that God's Word is truth and that anything that contradicts God's Word is from the enemy.

We not only acknowledge the truth, but we live the truth. We gird up our loins with the truth. We lay aside every besetting sin, and we hold our ground against the enemy.

The Breastplate of Righteousness

It was a sunny day in the Kensington neighborhood of Philadelphia when SWAT officers approached an apartment building on West Lehigh Avenue. The time was about 12:40 p.m. Just after lunch. The officers had come to serve a warrant in what they knew could be a "high risk" situation. For that reason, the members of the SWAT team had fully equipped themselves in protective gear, including bullet-proof vests.

When the lead officer knocked on the door of the apartment in question, someone inside immediately opened fire, sending bullets through the wall. One bullet struck the lead officer directly in the chest, sending him backward. The perpetrator then tried to flee by jumping from a third-story window onto the second-floor roof, but he was quickly apprehended.

The officer who had been shot was taken to the hospital as a precautionary measure, but he was released that same day with no serious injuries. Why? Because he had been properly equipped during the moment of danger. He was wearing a bullet-proof vest.

"Thank God no one was injured today, thank God the officer was able to walk out of the hospital," said Philadelphia Police Commissioner Danielle Outlaw. "This was a SWAT team today," she added. "They have the equipment. They have the gear."[8]

As followers of Jesus, we need to equip ourselves with the same level of seriousness as that Philadelphia SWAT team.

Because we have an enemy who is not playing around. He will attack us without provocation, and he will shoot to kill.

Look at Paul's next instruction for followers of Jesus: "Having put on the breastplate of righteousness" (verse 14).

The Romans wore a breastplate that covered the body from neck to waist. In the context of this verse, the breastplate symbolizes Christ's righteousness, which is given to the believer at salvation. It pictures our daily walk with God in righteousness.

Satan is the accuser, and he loves to come at us with his darts of accusation. His purpose is to hurt us by attacking our imperfections. But when we put on the armor of God, we are clothed in the righteousness of Christ, and he cannot get at us.

"The night is far spent, the day is at hand. Therefore let us cast off the works of darkness, and let us put on the armor of light .... Put on the Lord Jesus Christ, and make no provision for the flesh, to fulfill its lusts" (Romans 13:12-14).

The Shoes of the Gospel of Peace

"And having shod your feet with the preparation of the gospel of peace" (verse 15).

Roman soldiers wore sandals with hobnails in the soles to give them better footing for the battle. They could actually dig those nails in the ground for more traction and better footing. In a similar way, if we are going to "stand" and "withstand" in our spiritual lives, then we need the shoes of the Gospel to help anchor us in place.

The Gospel of peace is the wonderful truth that in Christ, we are no longer enemies with God. We stand in the confidence of God's love for us and His commitment to us. We stand in the power of the Lord, and in His strength we resist the evil one.

The Shield of Faith

"Above all, taking the shield of faith with which you will be able to quench all the fiery darts of the wicked one" (verse 16).

The Roman shield was usually about four feet by two feet, made of wood and covered with tough leather. As the soldier held it before him, it protected him from spears and arrows. In Paul's day, arrows dipped in a flammable substance were ignited and shot at the enemy.

This is how our enemy comes at us today. He sends ugly thoughts, lustful thoughts, lies and rumors, and jealous and envious thoughts. If we do not, by faith, quench those darts, they will light a fire within us, and we will disobey God.

What are the fiery darts that Satan has been shooting at you recently? What kinds of ugly thoughts does he toss your way? What kinds of accusations? What memories or experiences from your past does he keep bringing up and flinging at you without mercy? What kinds of lusts or greedy desires or malevolent urges does he hurl at you when you least expect them?

If you have walked any amount of time as a disciple of Jesus, you have likely experienced all of those attacks and more. But here's the truth: You don't have to endure those attacks in passive silence. Instead, you can take up your shield of faith and say, "I deflect these attacks in the power of the Lord. I refuse to accept them. This is not who I am. I do not have an ugly, dirty heart. I have a clean heart that was bought and purchased at the price of Christ's blood. I reject this impulse or this memory or this urge."

Through faith in God and in His Word, you can deflect whatever Satan tries to throw your way. That's the power of the shield of faith.

"Every word of God is pure; He is a shield to those who put their trust in Him" (Proverbs 30:5).

"As for God, His way is perfect; the word of the Lord is proven; He is a shield to all who trust in Him" (Psalm 18:30).

The Helmet of Salvation

"And take the helmet of salvation" (verse 17).

Satan is after our minds, and the helmet is a protection for our minds. When God controls the mind, Satan cannot lead us astray. Once again notice that the point of attack on the part of the enemy is our salvation. Satan is the one who attacks the assurance of salvation. He is the one who assaults the security of the believer.

We can deflect and resist those attacks when God has placed His guard around our minds. "You will keep him in perfect peace, whose mind is stayed on You, because he trusts in You" (Isaiah 26:3).

The Sword of the Spirit

"And the sword of the Spirit, which is the word of God" (verse 17).

The swords that the Roman soldiers wore were short swords that could be used for hand-to-hand combat. Here, the symbolism is clear. Our sword is the Word of God—the *rhema* of God. It is the word of God for a given situation.

That's an important term that deserves some explanation. When Paul described the sword of the Spirit as the "word" of

God, he didn't use the Greek term *logos*, which is how John described the Word made flesh in his Gospel (John 1:14). *Logos* is a broad concept that communicates truth in a general way. But Paul used *rhema* to identify the Scriptures, which is important because *rhema* refers more to specific or immediate truths.

In other words, Paul said we don't attack Satan and his forces by swinging around something as broad and unwieldy as "the truth." Instead, we arm ourselves with specific truths—with precise examples of God's *rhema*: God's Word.

Ray Stedman has a helpful word concerning the way the sword of the Spirit works in our lives. He wrote:

> Sometimes when you are reading a passage of Scripture, the words seem suddenly to come alive, take on flesh and bones, and leap off the page at you, or grow eyes that follow you around everywhere you go, or develop a voice that echoes in your ears until you can't get away from it. Perhaps you have had that experience in some moment of temptation or doubt when you were assailed by what Paul calls "the flaming darts of the evil one." And immediately a passage of Scripture which supplies the answer comes flashing to mind.

> Or perhaps you have been asked a question that caught you off guard for a moment and you were about to say, "I don't know," when suddenly you had a moment of illumination, and a word of Scripture came to mind which gave the answer. Perhaps this experience has happened while you were sitting in a meeting where some message has come home to your heart with strange

and powerful effect. You were greatly moved and in that moment you made a deep and permanent decision.

All of this is the rhema of God, the sayings of God that strike home like arrows to the heart. This is the sword of the Spirit which is the word of God.[9]

The writer of Hebrews connects this sword to the Word of God: "For the word of God is living and powerful, and sharper than any two-edged sword, piercing even to the division of soul and spirit, and of joints and marrow, and is a discerner of the thoughts and intents of the heart" (4:12).

The best illustration of this truth is found in our Lord's encounter with Satan in the wilderness. Satan brought three temptations against Jesus, and each time the Savior answered with, "It is written" and then quoted from the Old Testament. Jesus was wielding the sword of the Spirit, which is the Word of God.

When you look back at the major wars that have been fought throughout history, there is almost always a single battle or event that served as the turning point—a specific, decisive moment that ultimately led to victory or defeat.

For example, most historians agree the Battle of Gettysburg was the turning point in the American Civil War; the North's victory in that battle was the key to victory in the war. Similarly, the Allied forces' surprise invasion of Normandy on D-Day was the beginning of the end of World War II.

As members of God's Kingdom, we have the comfort of knowing that a similar turning point has already taken place in the war between Satan and God. That turning point was the death and resurrection of Jesus Christ. Ever since that moment, God's victory has been assured—and Satan knows it.

I remember hearing a story about Napoleon Bonaparte during his attempt to conquer every civilization in the known world. While meeting with his various lieutenants, he spread out a large map of the world and pointed to a single spot. "Sirs," he said, "if it were not for that red spot, I could conquer the world." That red spot represented Great Britain—the same nation whose armies ultimately defeated Napoleon at the Battle of Waterloo.

In a similar way, I can imagine Satan surrounded by his minions and talking about his plans for spiritual domination. I can see our enemy pointing to the hilltop of Calvary where Jesus' blood was spilled, and I can hear him say: "If it were not for that red spot, I could rule the world!"

That red spot is what has made all the difference in our spiritual struggle against evil. The truth is that we don't have to live in fear of Satan, our enemy. Nor do we have to live in fear of the demons at his command.

All we must do as soldiers in God's army is take our place in the spiritual battle to which we have been called—and stand. And that's the wonderful news: We can stand because we've been armed with the truth that God's ultimate victory over Satan has already been won.

Right now, you and I are "more than conquerors through Him who loved us" (Romans 8:37). To that I say, "Thanks be to God, who gives us the victory through our Lord Jesus Christ" (1 Corinthians 15:57).

The greatest hymn that Martin Luther ever wrote, in my estimation, is "A Mighty Fortress is Our God." It's an Ephesians 6 anthem, and it sums up all we have talked about in this chapter.

A mighty fortress is our God,
a bulwark never failing;

Our helper He amid the flood
of mortal ills prevailing.

For still our ancient foe
doth seek to work us woe—
His craft and power are great, and armed with
cruel hate, on earth is not his equal.

Did we in our own strength confide,
our striving would be losing,

Were not the right man on our side,
the man of God's own choosing.

Dost ask who that may be?
Christ Jesus, it is He—

Lord Sabaoth His name,
from age to age the same,

and He must win the battle.

CHAPTER 19

All Prayer

EPHESIANS 6:18

After becoming England's prime minister, Winston Churchill grew concerned about the ability of his war cabinet to work effectively if Germany attacked from the air as expected. He wanted to know how the central core of the military could function with six-hundred tons of bombs falling all around it. Strategists devised evacuation plans for those in power, but Churchill didn't want to flee London.

So another scheme was used. A series of storage rooms beneath the Office of Public Works Building was refitted into a top-secret military command post.

Located between Parliament and Number 10 Downing Street, this building was the strongest structure in the area. Workers reinforced it with additional concrete and installed state-of-the-art systems to make sure unimpeded communication could continue even if London were bombed.

In May 1940, Churchill visited his underground bunker and declared, "This is the room from which I'll direct the war." Pointing a stubby finger at the desk, he added, "And if the invasion takes place, that's where I'll sit—in that chair. And I'll sit there until either the Germans are driven back—or they carry me out dead."[1]

For the next five years, those subterranean rooms were the nerve center for the war, and their existence was a tightly guarded secret. Communication flowed in and out of them in steady currents. From there, Churchill guided the conflict, called Allied leaders, and growled out his famous radio speeches to the nation. From there, he had direct access to the world.

Jesus told us in Matthew 6:6 to enter our "closets" and pray to our Father in secret. He was referring to the storage rooms in Israeli homes in the first century. In those days, houses were filled with children and animals, and there was little privacy. But most houses had a room for storing supplies. It would have been a small room, cluttered and unheated. But it was a place where one could find a few moments of peace and quiet for prayer.

For the believer, Jesus said, such a humble spot provides direct access into the presence of God Himself. It's a secure communications complex where prayers can be rendered and rewarded.

As you embrace the practice of prayer, you'll find many ways to fill your life with it. Pray in the ways that come naturally, then grow and mature your practice of prayer steadily. Fill your life with the joyful discipline of praying without ceasing. This is how to prepare yourself for communication with your Commander as you engage in life's daily battles.

The one necessity of every good soldier of Jesus Christ is to keep in constant touch with his great Captain and Commander through the ministry of prayer. If you study the wars of the Old Testament, you will discover that when Israel fought in her own strength, she was defeated. But when she cast herself upon God's mercy, victory always followed.

Abraham took his trained servants numbering only 318, and he conquered the coalition of kings that fought the kings of Sodom and Gomorrah (Genesis 14). Gideon's army was reduced from 32,000 to 300, yet he delivered Israel from slavery. Joshua led Israel to a mighty conquest over Jericho by simply marching around the city.

King Hezekiah conquered the Assyrians, and for all the victors who went before and after him he wrote these words, "With us is the Lord our God, to help us and to fight our battles" (2 Chronicles 32:8).

We should not be surprised, then, that moving on from Paul's instructions on the armor of God leads to this critical verse about prayer. And it is critical—one could construct a very concise doctrine of prayer from this one verse alone.

Here it is: "And pray in the Spirit on all occasions with all kinds of prayers and requests. With this in mind, be alert and always keep on praying for all the Lord's people" (Ephesians 6:18, NIV).

If you have any doubts about the importance of prayer, please consider its high place in the life and ministry of our Lord. Here is how S. D. Gordon described it:

Prayer ... was not only His regular habit, but His resort in every emergency, however slight or serious. When perplexed He prayed. When hard pressed by work He prayed. When hungry for fellowship He found it in prayer. He chose His associates and received His messages upon His knees. If tempted, He prayed. If criticized, He prayed. If fatigued in body or wearied in spirit, He had recourse to His one unfailing habit of prayer. Prayer brought Him unmeasured power at the beginning, and kept the flow unbroken and undiminished. There was no emergency, no difficulty, no necessity, no temptation that would not yield to prayer .... How much prayer meant to Jesus![2]

Prayer was central to Jesus' life when He walked the earth two thousand years ago. Did you know it is still central to His life today? Philip Yancey wrote: "The New Testament's only glimpse of what Jesus is doing right now depicts him at the right hand of God 'interceding for us.' In three years of active ministry, Jesus changed the moral landscape of the planet. For nearly two thousand years since, he has been using another tactic: prayer."[3]

Let's look more closely at this vital verse to glean several principles that will help us incorporate prayer into our lives as we seek to follow Jesus in godliness and holiness.

The Persistence of the Warrior's Prayer

Paul started Ephesians 6:18 with these two words: "Praying always."

If you will look again at verse 18, you'll note that the word "all" occurs three times. In fact, you might want to just underline it in your Bible: "Praying always with all prayer and supplication in the Spirit, being watchful to this end with all perseverance and supplication for all the saints."

In his letter to the Thessalonians, Paul told the believers in that city to "pray without ceasing" (1 Thessalonians 5:17).

"Praying always" means we are in a constant attitude of prayer and that we trust God at every moment. As somebody has said, "The receiver to heaven is left off the hook. You never hang it back up." You are always available to God and He to you. You never have to really say, "Lord, we come into your presence," because you are already in His presence.

Thomas Kelly explains: "There is a way of ordering our mental life on more than one level at once. On one level we may be thinking, discussing, seeing, calculating, meeting all the demands of external affairs. But deep within, behind the scenes, at a profounder level, we may also be in prayer and adoration, song and worship."[4]

How can you pray always in your life today? One way is to look for triggers—prompts throughout your day that remind you to pray. For example, I read of one man who prayed every morning while brushing his teeth that God would give him wise words to say. As he washed his face, he asked God for a cheerful countenance.

Today we also have smartphones with prayer apps you can download. You can use your phone to set up prayer reminders just as you do an alarm. In fact, any behavior, time, or event can prompt you to pray—if you make it a habit.

Someone has written,

[Satan] will use every device to keep us from praying. He
will cause physical fatigue and lethargy; unfit us mentally
for prayer through the cares and burdens of the home,
and of business; and destroy our power in prayer through
doubt, discouragement, and depression. So when we least
feel like praying is the time we most need to pray, for
Satan has gained a foothold in us.[5]

The enemy watches for our prayerlessness. He waits for the
moment when we have neglected our prayer life, and then he
takes advantage of us. We must be constantly in prayer because
we are constantly in danger.

The Possibilities of the Warrior's Prayer

"Praying always," said Paul, "with all prayer" (verse 18).

For such a tiny word, the term "all" has an expansive
meaning. It means everything that can be placed in the basket.
No limits. No exclusions. The entire gamut. Here describing the
word "prayer" means every kind of prayer you can think of.

Let me offer a few examples.

We Are to Pray on All Occasions

Whether you're sitting at a stoplight, waiting at school,
seeing the doctor or dentist, doing the laundry, or mowing
the lawn—any time you have a spare moment, keep the
communication lines open between yourself and the throne of
God. You can pray during any and all occasions.

If those occasions sound like they lack the reverence that should accompany prayer, consider when Scripture tells us to pray: when we're thankful (2 Corinthians 1:11; Philippians 1:3), when we need to confess a sin (James 5:16), when we're sick (James 5:14), when we're in danger (Acts 27:29), and when we're tempted (Matthew 26:41). We should pray at public occasions such as church meetings (Acts 12:5) and in prayer groups (Acts 12:12). We should pray at social and festive occasions such as weddings, parties, or dinners.

No occasion is too undignified for prayer.

We Are to Pray in All Places

Today, it's common for believers to pray around the dinner table, in Bible classes, at our bedside, while jogging or walking, and in our own personal devotionals. All are great times for prayer!

New Testament people (sometimes the Lord Himself) prayed in the following locations: in a solitary place (Mark 1:35), on a mountain (Matthew 14:23), in the temple (Luke 2:37), on a housetop (Acts 10:9), in a house (Acts 10:30), at a riverside (Acts 16:13), on a ship (Acts 27:29), and in prison (Acts 16:25). Believers are also encouraged to pray in their own rooms or, as the King James Version says, to pray in a "closet" (Matthew 6:6).

We Are to Pray at All Times

The New Testament records prayers being offered before daylight (Mark 1:35), on the Sabbath day (Acts 16:13), when alone (Luke 9:18), when together (Acts 2:42), all night (Luke 6:12), night and day (1 Timothy 5:5), and continually

(Acts 6:4). We're to pray in sickness and in health, in prosperity and adversity, and at any hour.

There's never a time when we cannot pray.

We Are to Pray for All Things

To make an exhaustive list of what New Testament people prayed for would be—exhausting!

But to name a few, they prayed or were encouraged to pray for: safety (Matthew 24:20), forgiveness (Mark 11:25), food (Luke 11:3), faith (Luke 22:32), other people (John 17:9), healing (James 5:14), spiritual wisdom (Ephesians 1:17), relief from suffering (James 5:13), rain (James 5:18), children (Luke 1:13), health and prosperity (3 John 2), and spiritual strength (Matthew 26:41).

In other words, there are no limits! We should pray for personal things, home things, business things, and work things. All things should be covered by prayer.

If it's something you're concerned about, it's something you should pray about.

Ole Hallesby, a Norwegian minister and devotional writer during the early twentieth century, wrote: "If it becomes difficult for you to pray, then offer this little prayer, 'Lord, teach me to pray.' There is nothing that He, the Spirit of prayer, would rather do."[6]

The Petition of the Warrior's Prayer

Paul continued with another important term: "Praying ... with ... supplication."

The word "supplication" simply means "to ask." It means to ask God for what you need. Surely we come with worship and thanksgiving and gratitude, but we also must come asking. The Bible says: "You do not have because you do not ask" (James 4:2).

It is surprising how easy it is for us to go on striving for that for which we have not yet asked, seeking for that for which we have not yet knocked.

I read a sermon by Charles Haddon Spurgeon, the great British preacher. He said this: "Asking is the rule of the kingdom .... It is a rule that never will be altered in anybody's case .... If the royal and divine Son of God cannot be exempted from the rule of asking ... you and I cannot expect to the rule to be relaxed in our favor."[7]

When the Bible tells us that we are to pray always in all prayer and supplication, it means that the things we have need of we are to ask God for. That is why we have prayer lists.

Can you imagine your children coming to you and asking for something they need, and while you have the wherewithal to supply it, you deny them their request? I dare say there is not a father or mother reading these words who, if they knew their son or daughter had a need and they could supply it, would choose not to. Especially if the son or daughter came and said, "Please, can you help me?" Wouldn't you go to any lengths to supply it?

In Jesus' parable in Luke 11, a man answered a knock on his door late in the night. This was likely a common experience, for in the hot summer climate of Israel, most travel of any distance was done at night. The hungry guest had to be fed, but the host's cupboard was bare. So he ran to a friend's house, banged on the door, and asked to borrow food.

His friend's family was asleep on their mats. "Go away," the friend replied. "Do you realize what time it is? My door is locked, we're all in bed, and we don't want to be bothered."

Then Jesus thrust home His point: "I say to you, though he will not rise and give to him because he is his friend, yet because of his persistence he will rise and give him as many as he needs. So I say to you, ask, and it will be given to you; seek, and you will find; knock, and it will be opened to you. For everyone who asks receives, and he who seeks finds, and to him who knocks it will be opened" (Luke 11:8-10).

Do you know what kind of imperatives Jesus uses in this passage? All three of His commands—ask, seek, knock—are present imperatives. They could be translated this way: "Keep on asking; keep on seeking; keep on knocking." Don't ever stop asking; don't ever stop seeking; don't ever stop knocking. Just keep at it. Keep bringing your prayers to God.

The Power of the Warrior's Prayer

Next, Paul wrote, "Praying ... in the Spirit."

What is the power source for your prayers? It is the power of the Holy Spirit who lives within you. The Holy Spirit within you determines not only the character but also the content of your prayer. How can I know that what I pray for is the will of God? The Holy Spirit, who wrote the Word of God, is the same Spirit who lives within my heart. As I submit myself to that Spirit, He directs me to the things which God has already promised in Word of God, and the Spirit who controls me and the Spirit who wrote the Word of God come to agreement, and when I pray, God answers.

"Likewise the Spirit also helps in our weaknesses. For we do not know what we should pray for as we ought, but the Spirit Himself makes intercession for us with groanings which cannot be uttered. Now He who searches the hearts knows what the mind of the Spirit is, because He makes intercession for the saints according to the will of God" (Romans 8:26-27).

Watchman Nee explained the power of prayer like this: "Our prayers lay the track down on which God's power can come. Like a mighty locomotive, his power is irresistible, but it cannot reach us without rails."[8]

The Precision of the Warrior's Prayer

Next we come to, "Being watchful to this end."

The word "watchful" means "to be awake or vigilant"; it means "to keep awake in order to guard." It has to do with a close observation, to be on the alert. It means to stay alert spiritually and to keep guard. It means to stay awake in prayer. It means to pray correctly. One must be mentally alert and vigilant, for much prayer is hampered by a dull, drowsy frame of mind.

Some commentators believe the apostle is encouraging us to be alert, watching in expectation for the Lord's coming—and not only watching expectantly but praying expectantly.

"O Lord, come!" (1 Corinthians 16:22)

"Come, Lord Jesus!" (Revelation 22:20)

There are three places where Jesus told his followers to watch and pray.

- When we watch and pray, we can win over the world. "Take heed, watch and pray; for you do not know when the time is" (Mark 13:33).

- When we watch and pray, we can win over temptation. "Watch and pray, lest you enter into temptation. The spirit indeed is willing, but the flesh is weak" (Matthew 26:41).

- When we watch and pray, we can win over persecution. "Watch therefore, and pray always that you may be counted worthy to escape all these things that will come to pass, and to stand before the Son of Man" (Luke 21:36).

Here in Ephesians 6:18 Paul is essentially saying, "Watch and pray, and you will defeat the devil."

Watch and pray. Do you remember Nehemiah in the Old Testament? He defeated the enemy by watching and praying. We read in Nehemiah 4:9, "We made our prayer to our God, and because of them we set a watch against them day and night."

Let me tell you one of the battles I have fought in this. I used to get into my study for my time of prayer, get on my knees, and before I knew it, I was resting in the Lord. Do you know what I mean? I found out I am a better walker than sitter. I have been looking hard and long for a verse that says, "Walk and pray." I think the Lord understands that because He wants me to be vigilant. I walk, and I talk to the Lord.

What about you? What is your most-effective method for remaining watchful and vigilant during your prayers? "Continue earnestly in prayer, being vigilant in it" (Colossians 4:2).

The Perseverance of the Warrior's Prayer

What's next in our list of prayer principles? "Praying ... with all perseverance."

The Early Church was dedicated to praying with perseverance:

- "These all continued with one accord in prayer and supplication" (Acts 1:14).

- "And they continued steadfastly ... in prayers" (Acts 2:42).

- "We will give ourselves continually to prayer" (Acts 6:4).

- "Rejoicing in hope, patient in tribulation, continuing steadfastly in prayer" (Romans 12:12).

When it comes to praying, we need to hold on and hold out! Don't faint, don't quit, don't yield to discouragement, don't be deflected by the pressure of other things, don't ever give up, and don't ever quit. When you stop doing it for a little while, start doing it again; because if you don't do it, you are headed for trouble.

Some of you are discouraged about your prayer life. There are two things that Satan will tell you about your prayer life.

1. If you have two good days, he will try to get you to believe it will be like that for the rest of your life.

2.   The third day, when it does not work the same, Satan will come back and say, "Well, you've blown it now; there is no use trying anymore." The devil is a master at getting you to believe that because you missed a day of prayer, you might as well cancel your prayer life.

I like what Philip Yancey wrote about the practice and perseverance of prayer:

> As life changes, [our] prayer practice will no doubt change with it. A person battling chronic illness will pray differently than a college student who mainly worries about final exams and a noisy roommate. Taking a mission trip, getting married, managing a houseful of kids, giving care to an aging parent—every major life change will have its effect on prayer, both its practice and its content. The only fatal mistake is to stop praying and not begin again.[9]

If you did not pray yesterday, pray today. If you did not pray all last week, start this week.

The Purpose of the Warrior's Prayer

Next, Paul wrote, "Praying … for all the saints."

Jesus set the example when He prayed for His disciples: "I pray for them. I do not pray for the world but for those whom You have given Me, for they are Yours" (John 17:9).

Paul regularly prayed for those in the churches he visited, making mention of them always in his prayers (Romans 1:9;

Ephesians 1:16). Job's three friends angered God with their presumptuous judgments, but we read, "The Lord restored Job's losses when he prayed for his friends" (Job 42:10).

The Bible says a key purpose of our praying is to intercede for one another.

When we pray for one another, everybody in the army is praying for everybody else in the army, and in that way we all have each other's back. While I may not be praying for myself, I am praying for you—but I don't have to worry because you are praying for me.

D. Martyn Lloyd Jones told a story about the power of praying for others. Before the start of the Spanish Civil War, there used to be large clinics that treated patients dealing with different forms of psychosis and mental illness. These patients were often heavily medicated, and they came back week after week, month after month in search of treatments and psychoanalysis and other procedures.

Strangely, though, when the Spanish Civil War broke out, those clinics almost immediately became empty. The patients who used to frequent there constantly were all of a sudden anxious about much bigger issues—whether their homes would still be standing, whether their husbands or sons would be sent to war, whether they would be placed in physical danger, and so on. Those greater anxieties "cured" the little maladies that had been troubling those same people for years.

Here's what D. Martin Lloyd-Jones had to say about this interesting phenomenon:

A greater fear drives out lesser fears; and I am applying that principle to this whole question of prayer. When you feel that you are in a kind of vortex, and you cannot forget yourself; when you are sorry for yourself and feeling that you are having an unusually hard time with everything against you and [it's] almost enough to drive you to despair, one of the best remedies is to sit down and say, "What about so-and-so? What about this person, what about that person, what about Christians in other countries?" Get down on your knees and pray for them, and you will soon get up finding that you have forgotten yourself. You will find that in praying for them you are solving your own problems and obtaining release.[10]

The Practice of the Warrior's Prayer

R. A. Torrey is known for his exceptional books on prayer, but there was a time when even he struggled with his prayer life. Then, one day, Torrey realized that prayer was more than just a duty—it was an opportunity to communicate with God and receive His blessings. This realization transformed his attitude toward prayer, changing it from a chore to a cherished privilege.

"Before that," Torrey wrote, "prayer had been a mere duty, and sometimes a very irksome duty, but from that time on prayer has been not merely a duty but a privilege, one of the most highly esteemed privileges of life. Before that the thought that I had was, 'How much time must I spend in prayer?' The thought that now possesses me is, 'How much time may I spend in prayer without neglecting the other privileges and duties of life?'"[11]

Ben Patterson has a similar story of discovering the power of prayer. As pastor and chaplain for Westmont College, Ben had a "regular" prayer routine for most of his life. But after rupturing a disc in his back, he was forced to lay still while on bed rest. Unable to do anything else, he began to depend on prayer.

During this time, he devoted nearly two hours every day to praying for each member of his congregation. As the weeks passed, the prayer time became sweet and meaningful. And when Ben's recovery neared its end, he prayed and told God it had been wonderful spending so much time together.

The Lord replied, "Ben, you have just as much time when you're well as when you're sick. It's the same twenty-four hours in either case. The trouble with you is that when you're well, you think you're in charge. When you're sick, you know you're not."[12]

Are you still trying to take control of your life? Let go. Instead, take control of your time and attention by focusing it in prayer.

PEACE TO THE BRETHREN,
AND LOVE WITH FAITH,
FROM GOD THE FATHER
AND THE LORD JESUS
CHRIST. GRACE BE WITH
ALL THOSE WHO LOVE
OUR LORD JESUS CHRIST
IN SINCERITY.

EPHESIANS 6:23-24

CHAPTER 20

Final Greeting

EPHESIANS 6:18-24

In September of 2019, Gerald and Veronica Rush gathered their families together for a memorable Labor Day celebration in Georgia's Coweta County. What made it so memorable wasn't the number of people who attended, but the generations represented by each individual guest.

I'll explain. Gerald and Veronica both hosted their mothers at the event: Emma Rice and Elizabeth Rush. In addition, Gerald and Veronica invited their three daughters, eleven grandchildren, and three great-grandchildren.

When you add it all together, each side of Gerald and Veronica's family had five generations present at that celebration. "I think it's really cool we both have five generations on both sides of the family," said Veronica. "I've just never seen it."[1]

Imagine the family picture! What history represented in a single moment. What a pleasure to enjoy such a richness and breadth of familial connection.

As we've seen throughout these pages, the Christians in Ephesus enjoyed a similar level of connection and commitment to one another. The Ephesians weren't part of a single biological family, but they were joined together within a spiritual family— the Ephesian congregation and, more broadly, the Church as a whole. As brothers and sisters in Christ, they cared for each other and sought ways to love each other, just as they cared for and loved Paul and their other spiritual parents.

As we conclude our study on the book of Ephesians, it's appropriate that the final verses of that letter address the blessing of spiritual friendship. Take a look:

> Praying always with all prayer and supplication in the Spirit, being watchful to this end with all perseverance and supplication for all the saints—and for me, that utterance may be given to me, that I may open my mouth boldly to make known the mystery of the gospel, for which I am an ambassador in chains; that in it I may speak boldly, as I ought to speak.
>
> But that you also may know my affairs and how I am doing, Tychicus, a beloved brother and faithful minister in the Lord, will make all things known to you; whom I have sent to you for this very purpose, that you may know our affairs, and that he may comfort your hearts.
>
> Peace to the brethren, and love with faith, from God the Father and the Lord Jesus Christ. Grace be with all those who love our Lord Jesus Christ in sincerity. Amen. (Ephesians 6:18-24)

These verses represent Paul's final greetings to the church he loved so deeply and had invested so much of his life and energy to maintain. But this passage is more than a generic conclusion or a polite postscript. It offers three specific ways we can love and care for one another as the family of God.

Specifically, those of us in the Church can show love to one another through prayer, by giving comfort, and with the intentional act of offering blessings whenever possible.

Believers Pray for One Another

"Praying always with all prayer and supplication in the Spirit, being watchful to this end with all perseverance and supplication for all the saints—and for me, that utterance may be given to me, that I may open my mouth boldly to make known the mystery of the gospel, for which I am an ambassador in chains; that in it I may speak boldly, as I ought to speak" (verses 18-19).

We explored verse 18 in the previous chapter, and we saw many of the specific ways that prayer functions as a foundation for our spiritual lives as individual followers of Jesus. Now I want to broaden our view and explore the importance of prayer within the spiritual community. We don't just pray as isolated individuals. We often pray together and pray for each other within the Church.

Look at those three words at the start of verse 19: "And for me." Paul asked the Ephesians to pray for him. For *him!*

We've seen evidence of Paul's brilliance and spiritual maturity throughout all six chapters of his epistle to the Ephesians. For that reason, it would be easy to assume Paul was such a saintly saint that he had no need for other believers—no need for reinforcement or reassurance.

Such an assumption would be wrong. Paul was aware of his need for prayer, and he asked for it often.

Look at his letter to the believers in Rome: "Now I beg you, brethren, through the Lord Jesus Christ, and through the love of the Spirit, that you strive together with me in prayers to God for me, that I may be delivered from those in Judea who do not believe, and that my service for Jerusalem may be acceptable to the saints" (15:30-31).

Paul commended the Corinthians for "also helping together in prayer for us, that thanks may be given by many persons on our behalf for the gift granted to us through many" (2 Corinthians 1:11).

"Finally, brethren, pray for us," he wrote to the Thessalonians, "that the word of the Lord may run swiftly and be glorified, just as it is with you, and that we may be delivered from unreasonable and wicked men; for not all have faith" (2 Thessalonians 3:1-2). In his first epistle to that church, he wrote simply, "Brethren, pray for us" (5:25).

Over and over again, Paul sought, requested, and even begged for the prayers of other Christians on his behalf. He was constantly conscious of his need for the support of his spiritual family through prayer.

Speaking personally, I've felt the same need throughout my decades of ministry as a pastor and in everything we do at Turning Point. I need prayer! I crave the prayers of my congregation, my family, my friends, and many more. Every time we start something new as a church or as a ministry, we

feel the opposition of our enemy. We are constantly aware of
the intensity of spiritual warfare that surrounds our efforts to
serve Jesus, and so we constantly depend on prayer to carry us
through.

Before we move on, I want to highlight two specific elements
of prayer that Paul mentioned at the end of Ephesians 6:
boldness and specificity.

Praying for Boldness

As we look again at Paul's request for prayer in verses 19-20,
there's one word that stands out because he emphasized it twice:
"And for me, that utterance may be given to me, that I may open
my mouth *boldly* to make known the mystery of the gospel,
for which I am an ambassador in chains; that in it I may speak
boldly, as I ought to speak" (emphasis added).

Paul asked the Ephesians to pray that he would have
boldness. That he would speak boldly whenever he proclaimed
the Gospel.

The Greek root of that word "boldly" is *parrēsia*, which
means "to speak with freedom and confidence." Paul didn't want
to be confined by cultural expectations or doubt or the fear of
rejection. He wanted to speak freely and confidently about the
salvation available through the death and resurrection of Jesus
Christ. He wanted to speak boldly.

Peter and John made a similar request when the religious
leaders in Jerusalem attempted to prohibit them from declaring
the Gospel. Looking to heaven, they cried out: "Now, Lord, look
on their threats, and grant to Your servants that with all boldness
they may speak Your word, by stretching out Your hand to heal,

and that signs and wonders may be done through the name of Your holy Servant Jesus" (Acts 4:29-30).

Boldness was a necessary quality for believers in the Early Church. They faced persecution of all kinds because of their belief in Jesus—physical, social, financial, and even spiritual. They were often harassed. They had many reasons to feel afraid. Therefore, they needed boldness to take their stand for truth.

We need boldness in our world, as well. We need the confidence to speak freely in a culture that seems increasingly interested in restricting speech—especially speech connected with morality and the Bible and absolute truth.

Let's pray for one another that we would have everything we need to speak boldly about the Gospel of Jesus Christ, as we ought to be doing.

Praying With Specificity

The second thing that strikes me about Paul's request for prayer is how much he wanted the Ephesians to know the specifics of his situation. Look again at verses 21-22: "But that you also may know my affairs and how I am doing, Tychicus, a beloved brother and faithful minister in the Lord, will make all things known to you; whom I have sent to you for this very purpose, that you may know our affairs."

The great apostle was very interested in the Ephesians having direct knowledge about the details of his life and how he was doing. Was this the ancient equivalent of a Facebook post? Was Paul trying to get clicks or likes on his social media pages by displaying what he ate for lunch?

No. Paul wanted the Ephesians to know the details of his life so that they could pray for those details—so that they could pray in a specific way. In fact, Paul felt this was so important that he sent Tychicus, a fellow servant of the Gospel, to share with the Ephesians about everything Paul had experienced and expected to experience.

Have you noticed how often we settle for vague prayers? "Lord, I pray for my spouse." "Heavenly Father, please watch over my mother." Such prayers are common in the Church today—but are they effective? Do they carry any kind of spiritual power?

I wonder.

Paul wanted the Ephesians to pray for him in a specific way. Once again, this aligns with how we see Paul requesting prayer elsewhere in God's Word.

Look here, for example: "Continue earnestly in prayer, being vigilant in it with thanksgiving; meanwhile praying also for us, that God would open to us a door for the word, to speak the mystery of Christ, for which I am also in chains, that I may make it manifest, as I ought to speak" (Colossians 4:2-4).

Writing to the church in Colossae, Paul asked the believers there to pray for a specific, detailed request. He needed a door to open in the community through which he could share the mystery of Christ and His Gospel. Paul didn't ask for general support; he wanted them to pray for a specific need.

We see the same thing in Romans 15, which we explored a moment ago: "Now I beg you, brethren, through the Lord Jesus Christ, and through the love of the Spirit, that you strive together with me in prayers to God for me, that I may be delivered from those in Judea who do not believe, and that my service for Jerusalem may be acceptable to the saints" (verses 30-31).

Once again, Paul asked for prayer in specific ways—that he would be delivered from the hands of unbelievers, and that he would be able to reach Jerusalem in order to benefit the church.

Let's follow Paul's example by being specific both in how we express our needs for prayer and how we pray for the needs of others.

Believers Comfort One Another

"But that you also may know my affairs and how I am doing, Tychicus, a beloved brother and faithful minister in the Lord, will make all things known to you; whom I have sent to you for this very purpose, that you may know our affairs, and that he may comfort your hearts" (Ephesians 6:21-22).

Tychicus is an interesting character in the New Testament in that he is relatively unknown among Bible readers, yet he seems to have played an important role in the Early Church. His name is mentioned five times in Scripture, and those mentions paint the picture of a loyal friend and committed servant of Christ.

The first time we encounter Tychicus in Scripture comes in Acts 20:4, where he is identified as one of the members present during Paul's third missionary journey. Tychicus is specifically described as "of Asia," which means he was probably from Asia Minor, which is modern-day Turkey. Importantly, he was part of the entourage that accompanied Paul from Corinth to Jerusalem to deliver a financial gift to the church in that city.

In both Colossians and Ephesians, Paul described Tychicus as a "beloved brother" and "faithful minister." We know that

Tychicus was entrusted to deliver those epistles to the churches of Colossae and Ephesus, respectively. So he was trustworthy.

During that trip to Colossae, it's likely that Tychicus also accompanied a runaway servant named Onesimus as he returned to his former master. Tychicus was mature enough to play a role in that restoration. Finally, we know from Titus 3:12 that Paul considered sending Tychicus to Crete to replace Titus there as the primary spiritual shepherd of that community.

With all that in mind, what can we learn from Tychicus about operating as the family of God? Comfort. One of Paul's main reasons for sending Tychicus to the church at Ephesus was "that he may comfort [their] hearts" (6:22).

Why would the Ephesians need comfort? Well, remember that the book of Ephesians is one of Paul's prison epistles. The apostle wrote that letter while he was under guard in Rome. Therefore, it makes sense that the believers in Ephesus were worried about their spiritual father—the founder of their church.

As mentioned earlier, one of the reasons Paul sent Tychicus to Ephesus was to explain the details of his life and ministry so that they could pray for him in specific ways—so that they could pray for his specific needs. But Tychicus also served to comfort those in Ephesus who were frightened for Paul's present and future condition as an inmate of Rome. Because Tychicus had been with Paul and served him in that city, he was an excellent source of information and of comfort. At that time, Paul's imprisonment was not severe. He was being treated relatively well, and his ministry to the church of Rome continued forward.

Here's an important question: Where do you have opportunities to encourage your fellow believers today? What are some sources of worry or anxiety present in your community, and what can you do to offer comfort? Support? Encouragement?

In another epistle, Paul taught that one of the reasons God comforts and supports us during our difficult seasons is so that we will be able to offer that same comfort and support to others. "Blessed be the God and Father of our Lord Jesus Christ, the Father of mercies and God of all comfort, who comforts us in all our tribulation, that we may be able to comfort those who are in any trouble, with the comfort with which we ourselves are comforted by God" (2 Corinthians 1:3-4).

Where do you currently have an opportunity to offer that kind of comfort to those who are hurting?

Believers Bless One Another

"Peace to the brethren, and love with faith, from God the Father and the Lord Jesus Christ. Grace be with all those who love our Lord Jesus Christ in sincerity. Amen" (verses 23-24).

Did you know November 13 has officially been designated as World Kindness Day? (I'm not sure who decides these designations, but it's true.) Each year, people from all over the world take a moment to intentionally demonstrate kindness to others. That can include people they know or random strangers.

Among those celebrating World Kindness Day in 2023 was a group of high school students from the southwest suburbs of Chicago. Specifically, nearly two dozen student athletes representing ten different schools gathered in downtown La Grange, Illinois, to spread kindness using a multitude of methods.

Those students handed out donuts and flowers. They shouted encouraging statements to passersby. They even held up signs along the main road that read, "Honk for kindness!"

"It's always nice to show some act of kindness," said Hamzah Bedeir, a junior at Westmont High School.

Kim Reed was on the receiving end of that kindness when she was handed a flower as she walked downtown. "I just think you never know what anybody is going through," she said, "and even just a little flower like that is really day brightening."[2]

For followers of Jesus, of course, every day is World Kindness Day—or it should be. We are called to be a light in the darkness. We become all things to all people so that we might save some. We are commanded to love our neighbors even as much as we love ourselves. These are basic biblical principles.

That's why I like the way Paul ended his epistle to the Ephesians—with a blessing. "Peace to the brethren," he wrote, "and love with faith, from God the Father and the Lord Jesus Christ. Grace be with all those who love our Lord Jesus Christ in sincerity. Amen."

Regarding that verse, John MacArthur writes. "This beautiful benediction sums up the major themes of this very personal letter, reminding readers of the peace (v. 15; 1:2; 2:14, 15, 17; 4:3), love (1:15; 4:2, 15, 16; 5:25, 28, 33), and faith (v. 16; 1:15; 2:8; 3:12, 17; 4:5, 13) from God and Jesus Christ."[3]

It's interesting that Paul ended most of his letters with a similar blessing—a similar benediction. Consider:

- "Finally, brethren, farewell. Become complete. Be of good comfort, be of one mind, live in peace; and the

God of love and peace will be with you. Greet one another with a holy kiss" (2 Corinthians 13:11-12).

- "And as many as walk according to this rule, peace and mercy be upon them, and upon the Israel of God …. Brethren, the grace of our Lord Jesus Christ be with your spirit. Amen" (Galatians 6:16, 18).

- "The grace of our Lord Jesus Christ be with you all. Amen" (Philippians 4:23).

Paul understood the power of blessings, and he used them often. Shouldn't we do the same?

Certainly that includes the types of blessings people offer on World Kindness Day and other occasions—small gifts, delicious treats, paying for a stranger's meal, and other random acts of kindness. But like Paul, we as followers of Jesus should also take advantage of the power of spoken blessings. Words of affirmation, encouragement, and support.

In fact, we have a special advantage in this department because we have access to Scripture. We have access to a treasure trove of divine blessings that are custom made for the trials and tribulations of life. Here are just a few examples:

- "The Lord bless you and keep you; the Lord make His face shine upon you, and be gracious to you; the Lord lift up His countenance upon you, and give you peace" (Numbers 6:24-26).

- "Fear not, for I am with you; be not dismayed, for I am your God. I will strengthen you, yes, I will help

you, I will uphold you with My righteous right hand"
(Isaiah 41:10).

- "Now may our God and Father Himself, and our Lord
  Jesus Christ, direct our way to you. And may the Lord
  make you increase and abound in love to one another
  and to all, just as we do to you"
  (1 Thessalonians 3:11-12).

- "And my God shall supply all your need according to
  His riches in glory by Christ Jesus" (Philippians 4:19).

As a citizen of God's Kingdom, you have the power to bless
others through your words, your actions, and your prayers.
Be intentional. Be active. Choose to be a blessing in every way
possible.

Remember, blessings are what the book of Ephesians is all
about. One of Paul's primary goals in writing this letter was to
remind the Early Church—and by extension, all Christians—
about the many blessings we have received through Christ.
Those blessings include our salvation, the presence of the Holy
Spirit, our inclusion in the Body of Christ, inner strength,
spiritual transformation, meaningful work, and more. Much
more!

These are not future blessings. We have received them now.
We have access to them now. Therefore, we can be a blessing
to a world in need—not in our own strength, but through the
empowerment of the Holy Spirit.

Years ago I was invited to speak at a conference in upstate
New York. This was just after I began my ministry at Shadow
Mountain Community Church, so my children were still

relatively young. They were excited about this speaking opportunity because they got to join me and attend a camp a few hours from where my conference was being held.

One day during that week I had some free time, so I decided to drive over and see my children at the camp. One of the staff members at the conference was kind enough to lend me his car, which was an Oldsmobile. In fact, it had "Oldsmobile Diesel" stamped onto the front hood. When I got behind the wheel, I saw a note on the fuel gauge that said, "Diesel fuel only."

All right, I thought. *Good to know.*

Sure enough, during the middle of my drive, I needed to get some gas. So I filled up this Oldsmobile with diesel fuel. As I got back on the road, however, it pretty quickly became apparent that something was wrong. The engine started stuttering. Then sputtering. Then smoking.

Then it quit. Right there in the middle of the street in the middle of this small town in upstate New York.

Apparently there was quite a commotion because several people came out to the street to see what was happening. A little crowd gathered around me, and an old farmer took the lead. He came up to my window and asked, "What's going on, son?"

"I'm not sure," I said. "This is a borrowed car, and it died."

He asked, "Is this a diesel?"

"Yes it is," I told him, quite confidently. I even showed him the note still taped to the fuel gauge.

Well, this old farmer lifted up the hood of the car and poked around for about a minute, then he came back to my window. "Son," he said, "diesels don't have spark plugs. You got yourself a gasoline engine here."

The whole situation ended up being quite a catastrophe. They had to tow the car to a local garage and drain the whole thing until all the diesel was gone, which took a long time. I had to borrow another car in order to keep going and see my family. Then I had to retrieve my borrowed car in that same town and tell the same story all over again.

It was a thoroughly humiliating experience. It was so humiliating, in fact, that I decided to learn a lesson from it. And the lesson I learned is that I and every other follower of Jesus used to run on diesel fuel. Meaning, we used to be empowered by the things of this world because we were worldly people. We had "flesh" and "human being" written all over us.

But that was our old way of living. Our old way of being. Now that we are members of Christ's Kingdom, we have been transformed into something new. For that reason, we no longer run on our old fuel. Instead, we have new fuel. We are filled with the Spirit of God. We move by faith in God. We are empowered by His presence and His blessings—all the many blessings we've explored within these pages.

Just like I experienced in New York, problems arise when we attempt to run a new engine with an old type of fuel. Therefore, as we take advantage through faith of all the blessings now available to us through Christ, let us always remember that we are new creations. Let us forever let go of our old lives and our old sources of power, and let us cling to the One whose mercies are new every morning.

Notes

INTRODUCTION

1. Samantha Locke, "Man Who Became Millionaire Due to Bank Error Sentenced to Prison," *Newsweek*, June 28, 2021, https://www.newsweek.com/man-became-millionaire-bank-error-sentenced-prison-1604672.

CHAPTER 1: EIGHT SPIRITUAL BLESSINGS

1. Allison Klein, "A Dying Man Bought 14 Years Worth of Christmas Gifts for His 2-Year-Old Neighbor," *Washington Post*, December 18, 2018, https://www.washingtonpost.com/lifestyle/2018/12/18/twitter-weighs-after-neighbors-death-give-all-presents-now-or-one-year/.

2. Ryan Denham, "Viral Video of College Acceptance Letter Brings Joy To B-N Family and Beyond," *WGLT.org*, July 6, 2021, https://www.wglt.org/local-news/2021-07-06/viral-video-of-college-acceptance-letter-brings-joy-to-b-n-family-and-beyond.

3. Catesby Paget, "A Mind at Perfect Peace With God."

4. Mark Lungariello, "Oregon Woman Died Homeless While She Had $884K in Unclaimed Funds," *New York Post*, June 3, 2021, https://nypost.com/2021/06/03/oregon-woman-died-homeless-while-she-had-884k-in-unclaimed-funds/.

CHAPTER 2: THE SECRET TO SPIRITUAL POWER

1. "Florida Woman Without Power for 15 Years," *UPI*, February 19, 2007, https://www.upi.com/Florida-woman-without-power-for-15-years/26071171913391/.

2. Andrew Bisharat, "This Man Jumped Out of a Plane With No Parachute," *National Geographic* July 29, 2016, https://www.nationalgeographic.com/adventure/article/skydiver-luke-aikins-freefalls-without-parachute.

3. Dallas Willard, *The Divine Conspiracy: Rediscovering Our Hidden Life in God* (New York, NY: Harper Collins, 1998) 30-31.

CHAPTER 3: SALVATION PURE AND SIMPLE

1. Susan Scutti, "Meet the Baby Who Was Born Twice," *CNN*, October 20, 2016, https://www.cnn.com/2016/10/20/health/baby-born-twice-fetal-surgery/index.html.

2. R. Kent Hughes, *Ephesians* (Wheaton, IL: Crossway, 1990), 66.

3. James Montgomery Boice, quoted by Casey Lute, *But God: The Two Words at the Heart of the Gospel* (Minneapolis, MN: Cruciform Press, 2011), Introduction.

4. "Is This the Secret Coke Recipe?" *ABC News*, February 14, 2011, https://abcnews.go.com/Business/coca-colas-secret-formula-revealed/story?id=12914877.

5. Adapted from Denise Banderman, "Professor Takes Students' Tests for Them," *Preaching Today*, accessed October 14, 2022, https://www.preachingtoday.com/illustrations/2003/march/14238.html.

6. Charles Spurgeon, "A Sermon to Open Neglectors and Nominal Followers of Religion," *The Spurgeon Center*, March 24, 1867, https://www.spurgeon.org/resource-library/sermons/a-sermon-to-open-neglectors-and-nominal-followers-of-religion/#flipbook/.

7. Max Lucado, *Shaped by Grace* (Nashville, TN: Thomas Nelson, 2012), 44.

CHAPTER 4: CREATED FOR GOOD WORKS

1. Valerie Strauss, "Chadwick Boseman Praised Student Protesters in 2018 Commencement Speech at Howard University," *The Washington Post*, August 29, 2020, https://www.washingtonpost.com/education/2020/08/29/chadwick-boseman-praised-student-protesters-2018-commencement-speech-howard-university-watch-video/.

2. Calvin Miller, *Into the Depths* (Cincinnati, OH: Bethany House, 2001), 135.

3. Ken Gire, *Shaped by the Cross* (Downers Grove, IL: InterVarsity Press, 2011), 22-23.

4. Pat Williams with Jim Denney, *Your Formula for Success: Finding the Place Where Your Talent and Passion Meet* (Grand Rapids, MI: Revell, 2017), 15.

5. Warren Wiersbe, *Be Rich* (Wheaton, IL: Victor Books, 1976), 49.

6. Pat Williams with Jim Denney, *Your Formula for Success: Finding the Place Where Your Talent and Passion Meet* (Grand Rapids, MI: Revell, 2017), 19.

7. Lewis Drummond and Betty Drummond, *Women of Awakenings: The Historic Contribution of Women to Revival Movements* (Grand Rapids, MI: Kregel, 1997), 293.

8. Arthur T. Pierson, *The Heart of the Gospel: Sermons on the Life-Changing Power of the Good News* (Grand Rapids, MI: Kregel, 1996), 229.

9. Michael P. Green, *Illustrations for Biblical Preaching* (Grand Rapids, MI: Baker Books, 1989), 354-355.

CHAPTER 5: BEFORE AND AFTER

1. Adapted from Allen Langam, "Jesus Gave Me What Boozing and Brawling Couldn't," *Christianity Today*, May 17, 2019, https://www.christianitytoday.com/ct/2019/june/allen-langham-taming-villain-jesus-boozing-brawling.html.

2. Scott Hubbard, "Remember Who You Were Without Christ," *Desiring God*, September 4, 2020, https://www.desiringgod.org/articles/remember-who-you-were-without-christ.

3. Bertrand Russel, *The Free Man's Worship,* accessed October 28, 2022, https://users.drew.edu/~jlenz/br-free-mans-worship.html#:~:text=That%20Man%20is%20the%20product,can%20preserve%20an%20individual%20life.

4. Dena Yohe, *You Are Not Alone* (New York, NY: WaterBrook, 2016), 141-142.

5. Harold Hoehner, quoted in *The Bible Knowledge Commentary: Acts and Epistles* (Colorado Springs, CO: David C. Cook, 2018), Kindle Edition.

6. Corrie McKee, "Asian Students Tear Down Walls," *Urbana Today*, December 31, 2009, 6.

7. Bryan Chapell, *Ephesians* (Phillipsburg, NJ: P&R Publishing, 2009), Kindle Edition.

8. John MacArthur, *The MacArthur New Testament Commentary: Ephesians* (Chicago, IL: The Moody Bible Institute of Chicago, 1986), 80.

9. John R. W. Stott, *God's New Society* (Downers Grove, IL: InterVarsity Press, 1979), 104.

10. Charles H. Spurgeon, "The Quotable Spurgeon," *Christianity Today*, Vol. 39, no. 3.

11. Dr. Paul Brand and Philip Yancey, *Fearfully and Wonderfully Made* (Grand Rapids, MI: Zondervan Publishing House, 1987), 47.

12. Clarence Edward Macartney, *Macartney's Illustrations* (New York, NY: Abingdon-Cokesbury Press, 1945), 61.

13. Adapted from Gerald Sittser, *Love One Another: Becoming the Church Jesus Longs For* (Downers Grove, IL: IVP Books, 2008), Kindle Edition.

CHAPTER 6: UNITY

1. David B. Barrett, George T. Kurian, and Todd M. Johnson, *World Christian Encyclopedia* (Oxford: Oxford University Press, 2001), 16-18.

2. Lee Iacocca, *Iacocca: An Autobiography* (New York, NY: Bantom Books, 1984), 60.

3. Annabel Graham, "Music Written for the Broken Instruments That Public Schools Couldn't Afford to Fix," *Garage*, December 6, 2017, https://garage. vice.com/en_us/article/qvz8yx/symphony-for-broken-instruments?callback= in&code=ZTIZMDFHYJYTMWM0MS0ZOWM1LTKWOTETNJM4NZA2O GM5NGVJ&state=dffc3d300f994c7c9d646205724fdc03.

CHAPTER 7: A PRAYER FOR INNER STRENGTH

1. Gregory Thomas, "Ultrarunner Dean Karnazes on Recovery, Aging, and Running in Every Country on Earth," *San Francisco Chronicle*, February 6, 2019, https://www.sfchronicle.com/travel/article/Podcast-Ultrarunner-Dean-Karnazes-on-recovery-13595254.php#photo-16886151.

2. Dean Karnazes, *Ultramarathon Man* (New York, NY: Penguin Publishers, 2006).

3. Robert J. Morgan, *The Strength You Need* (Nashville, TN: W Publishing, 2016), Kindle Edition.

CHAPTER 8: THE "ONENESS" OF OUR FAITH

1. Sangeeta Ojha, "Here's Why Burger King Is Urging Customers to Order From McDonalds, Other Rivals," *Mint*, November 4, 2020, https://www.livemint. com/companies/news/here-is-why-burger-king-is-urging-customers-to-order-from-mcdonald-s-other-rivals-11604452528607.html.

2. Paul E. Billheimer, *Love Covers* (Minneapolis, MN: Bethany House Publishers, 1981), 7.

3. Daniel James Brown, *The Boys in the Boat* (New York, NY: Penguin Books, 2013), 179-180.

CHAPTER 9: THE DIVERSITY OF UNITY

1. Pat Foran, "Ontario Man Purchases $800 Worth of Gift Cards That Turn Out to Be Empty," *CTV News*, February 25, 2022, https://toronto.ctvnews.ca/ontario-man-purchases-800-worth-of-gift-cards-that-turn-out-to-be-empty-1.5796844.

2. F. F. Bruce, *The Letter of Paul to the Romans* (Grand Rapids, MI: Wm. B. Eerdmans Publishing Company, 1985), 214.

3. John MacArthur, *The MacArthur New Testament Commentary Series: Ephesians* (Chicago, IL: Moody Press, 1986), 140.

CHAPTER 10: THE NEW AND THE OLD

1. James Clear, "How to Break a Bad Habit and Replace It With a Good One," *James Clear*, February 17, 2023, https://jamesclear.com/how-to-break-a-bad-habit.

2. Mark Batterson, *Do It for a Day* (Colorado Springs, CO: Multnomah, 2021), 21.

3. Klyne Snodgrass, *The NIV Application Commentary: Ephesians* (Grand Rapids, MI: Zondervan Academic, 1996), 229-230.

4. Rosalind Picard, "An MIT Professor Meets the Author of All Knowledge," *Christianity Today*, March 15, 2019, https://www.christianitytoday.com/ct/2019/april/rosalind-picard-mit-professor-meets-author-knowledge.html.

5. R. Kent Hughes, *Ephesians* (Wheaton, IL: Crossway, 1990), 142.

6. John Stott, *The Message of Ephesians* (Downers Grove, IL: InterVarsity Press, 1979), 178.

7. Jim Matthews, *Saved But Stuck: 30 Days to Personal Revival* (U.S.A.: Xulon Press, 2004), 98-99.

8. Grant R. Osborne, D. Stuart Briscoe and Haddon Robinson, consulting editors, *Romans: The IVP New Testament Commentary Series* (Downers Grove, IL: InterVarsity Press, 2004), 321-322.

9. R. Kent Hughes, *Disciplines of a Godly Man* (Wheaton, IL: Crossway, 1991), 76-77.

CHAPTER 11: A NEW LIFESTYLE

1. Ed Koch, "Remembering Robin Leach," *Las Vegas Sun*, April 24, 2018, https://lasvegassun.com/news/2018/aug/24/remembering-robin-leach-lifestyles-of-the-rich-and/.

2. Erik Lacitis, "Hero with a $20,000 heart: Walmart Worker Honored for Returning Cash Left in Cart," *The Seattle Times*, April 5, 2013, https://www.seattletimes.com/seattle-news/hero-with-a-20000-heart-walmart-worker-honored-for-returning-cash-left-in-cart/.

3. Frederick Buechner, *Wishful Thinking: A Theological ABC* (New York, NY: Harper & Row, 1973), 2.

4. John Phillips, *Exploring Ephesians and Colossians* (Grand Rapids, MI: Kregel Publications, 1995), 133.

5. Klyne Snodgrass, *The NIV Application Commentary: Ephesians* (Grand Rapids, MI: Zondervan, 1996), 250.

6. Adapted from David Jeremiah, *Everything You Need* (Nashville, TN: W Publishing, 2019), 146-147.

7. Klyne Snodgrass, *The NIV Application Commentary: Ephesians* (Grand Rapids, MI: Zondervan, 1996), 263.

8. Diane Herbst and Steve Helling, "Faced With Deadly Danger, Davyon Johnson, 11, Sprang Into Action: 'I Saved 2 People's Lives In 1 Day,'" *People*, January 26, 2022, https://people.com/human-interest/davyon-johnson-11-sprang-into-action-i-saved-two-peoples-lives-in-one-day/.

CHAPTER 12: WALKING IN LOVE

1. Mike Laycock, "Man Walks for 24 Hours Round His Village and Raises £5,000 for Ukraine," *The York Press*, March 21, 2022, https://www.yorkpress.co.uk/news/20008276.man-walks-24-hours-round-village-raises-5-000-ukraine/.

2. John Phillips, *Exploring Ephesians & Philippians* (Grand Rapids, MI: Kregel, 1995), 143.

3. Bryan Chapell, *Ephesians* (Phillipsburg, NJ: P&R Publishing, 2009), Kindle Edition.

4. Richard Foster and Henri Nouwen, "How Can a Spiritual Leader Keep His or Her Faith Vital?" *Christianity Today*, accessed January 24, 2024, https://www.christianitytoday.com/biblestudies/bible-answers/spirituallife/spiritualleader.html.

5. E. H. Glifford, quoted in Rebecca Manley Pippert, *Hope Has Its Reasons* (Downers Grove, IL: InterVarsity Press, 2001), 100.

6. Rebecca Manley Pippert, *Hope Has Its Reasons* (Downers Grove, IL: InterVarsity Press, 2001), 101.

7. N. T. Wright, *Paul for Everyone: The Pastoral Epistles* (Louisville, KY: Westminster John Knox Press, 2003), 76.

8. Heath Lambert, *Finally Free* (Grand Rapids, MI: Zondervan, 2013), 126.

9. David C. Enger, "Copy the Master," *Our Daily Bread*, November 10, https://odb.org/US/2003/11/10/copy-the-master.

10. Ibid.

CHAPTER 13: LEAVE THE LIGHT ON

1. "Edison's Lightbulb," *The Franklin Institute*, accessed January 30, 2024, https://fi.edu/en/science-and-education/collection/edisons-lightbulb.

2. "Never Too Far From God's Love: A Witch Comes to Christ," *CBN*, December 10, 2022, https://www2.cbn.com/article/not-selected/never-too-far-gods-love-witch-comes-christ.

3. John Phillips, *Exploring Ephesians & Philippians* (Grand Rapids, MI: Kregel, 1995), 145.

4. Bryan Chapell, *Ephesians* (Phillipsburg, NJ: P&R Publishing, 2009), Kindle Edition.

5. Malcolm Muggeridge, *Vintage Muggeridge* (Grand Rapids, MI: William B. Eerdmans Publishing Company, 1985), 17.

CHAPTER 14: WALKING IN WISDOM

1. "Yogi Berra Quotes," *Baseball Almanac*, accessed March 31, 2022, https://www.baseball-almanac.com/quotes/quoberra.shtml.

2. Robert Fulghum, *Preaching Today*, accessed March 17, 2023, https://www.preachingtoday.com/illustrations/1996/june/1811.html.

3. Original source unknown.

4. R. Kent Hughes, *Ephesians* (Wheaton, IL: Crossway, 1990), 172.

CHAPTER 15: MARRIAGE

1. J. R. Moehringer, "Marrying Marathoner Died Alone," *The Baltimore Sun*, August 15, 1997, https://www.baltimoresun.com/news/bs-xpm-1997-08-16-1997228033-story.html.

2. Norman Vincent Peale, "Worth Fighting For," *Guideposts*, February 1977, 13.

3. Adriana Diaz, "Couple Married 79 Years Die Hours Apart: 'They Went Out Together,'" *New York Post*, December 7, 2022, https://nypost.com/2022/12/07/couple-100-die-hours-apart-from-each-other-after-79-year-marriage/.

CHAPTER 16: PARENTS AND CHILDREN

1. Dave Stone, "Teaching Respect Within the Home: Ephesians 6:1-3," *Preaching.com*, accessed April 5, 2022, https://www.preaching.com/sermons/teaching-respect-within-the-home-ephesians-61-3/.

2. Calvin Trillin, "Alice, Off the Page," *New Yorker*, March 19, 2006, https://www.newyorker.com/magazine/2006/03/27/alice-off-the-page.

CHAPTER 17: HONORING CHRIST FROM NINE TO FIVE

1. Erin Coleman and David Chang, "Retired NJ Man Celebrates 100th Birthday by Going Back to Work," *NBC Philadelphia*, March 29, 2017, https://www.nbcphiladelphia.com/news/local/haddon-township-new-jersey-work-cherry-hill-100-years-old-man-birthday/43815/.

2. Jim Harter, "Dismal Employee Engagement Is a Sign of Global Mismanagement," *Gallup*, accessed April 6, 2022, https://www.gallup.com/workplace/231668/dismal-employee-engagement-sign-global-mismanagement.aspx.

3. Elisabeth Elliot, *Through Gates of Splendor* (Wheaton, IL: Tyndale, 1981), 20.

4. Dominick Proto, "Young Man Walked Miles for First Day of Work, Gets Car From CEO," *ABC News*, July 17, 2018, https://abcnews.go.com/US/young-man-walked-miles-day-work-car-ceo/story?id=56642518.

5. Dr. Steven R. Cook, "Being the Good Boss," *Linkedin*, October 31, 2019, https://www.linkedin.com/pulse/being-good-boss-dr-steven-r-cook.

6. Tom Nelson, *Work Matters* (Wheaton, IL: Crossway, 2011).

CHAPTER 18: SPIRITUAL WARFARE

1. Anabelle Doliner, "Entire Town Nearly Left Without Power After Snake Started Electrical Fire," *Newsweek*, September 16, 2021, https://www.newsweek.com/entire-town-nearly-left-without-power-after-snake-started-electrical-fire-1629986.

2. Xavier Walton, "Snake Knocks Out Power Outage to Thousands of NC Homes," *WCNC*, May 21, 2019, https://www.wcnc.com/article/news/snake-knocks-out-power-outage-to-thousands-of-nc-homes/275-e0d6e33b-773b-4ceb-9450-c413a5edfee0.

3. N. T. Wright, *Paul for Everyone: The Prison Letters* (Louisville, KY: Westminster John Knox Press, 2004), 73.

4. John Phillips, *Exploring Ephesians and Philippians: An Expository Commentary* (Grand Rapids, MI: Kregel Publications, 1995), 187.

5. John Eldridge, *Waking the Dead* (Nashville, TN: Nelson Books, 2016), 159.

6. Peter T. O'Brien, *The Pillar New Testament Commentary: The Letter to the Ephesians* (Grand Rapids, MI: William B. Eerdmans Publishing Company, 1999), 461.

7. William Gurnall, quoted by John Eldridge, *Waking the Dead* (Nashville, TN: Nelson Books, 2016), 159.

8. Rudy Chinchilla, "Philadelphia SWAT Officer Saved by Bulletproof Vest in Shooting," NBC Philadelphia, February 11, 2022, https://www.nbcphiladelphia.com/news/local/watch-live-police-reveal-details-of-shooting-involving-philly-police-officer/3143253/.

9. Ray C. Stedman, *Spiritual Warfare: Winning the Daily Battle With Satan* (Portland, OR: Multnomah Press, 1975), 116.

CHAPTER 19: ALL PRAYER

1. James Leasor, *War at the Top: What Went on Behind the Closed Doors of the Cabinet War Rooms* (Cornwall, UK: House of Stratus, 2001), 56.

2. S. D. Gordon, *Quiet Talks on Prayer* (New York, NY: Fleming H. Revell Company, 1904), 233.

3. Philip Yancey, *Prayer: Does It Make Any Difference?* (Grand Rapids, MI: Zondervan, 2006), 88.

4. Thomas Kelly, quoted by Richard J. Foster, *Celebration of Discipline* (San Francisco, CA: HarperCollins, 1998), 45.

5. Ruth Paxson, *The Wealth, Walk, and Warfare of the Christian* (Old Tappan, NJ: Fleming H. Revell Company, 1939), 177.

6. Ole Hallesby, *Prayer* (Minneapolis, MN: Augsburg Fortress, 1994), 175.

7. Charles Spurgeon, "Ask and Have," accessed December 7, 2010, http://www.spurgeongems.org/vols28-30/chs1682.pdf.

8. Watchman Nee, *The Collected Works of Watchman Nee* (Anaheim, CA: Living Stream Ministry, 1993), 141.

9. Philip Yancey, *Prayer: Does It Make Any Difference?* (Grand Rapids, MI: Zondervan, 2006), 163.

10. D. Martyn Lloyd Jones, *The Christian Soldier* (Grand Rapids, MI: Baker, 1977), 357-358.

11. Reuben A. Torrey, *The Power of Prayer and the Prayer of Power* (Grand Rapids, MI: Zondervan, 1955), 75-77.

12. Ben Patterson, quoted by Philip Yancey, *Prayer: Does It Make Any Difference?* (Grand Rapids, MI: Zondervan, 2006), 169.

CHAPTER 20: FINAL GREETING

1. "Five Generations of Families: Gerald and Veronica Rush Each Have Five Living Generations in Their Families," *The Newnan Times Herald*, September 8, 2019, https://www.times-herald.com/five-generations-of-families-gerald-and-veronica-rush-each-have-five-living-generations-in-their/article_74139e1a-f8f0-590a-8ce8-9d85ac15bef5.html.

2. Christian Piekos, "Southwest Suburban High School Students Share Random Acts of Kindness Ahead of World Kindness Day," *ABC 7 Chicago*, November 12, 2023, https://abc7chicago.com/world-kindness-day-la-grange-random-acts-of-buddys-helpers/14048808/.

3. John MacArthur, *The MacArthur Bible Commentary* (Nashville, TN: Thomas Nelson, 2005), 1707.

Additional Resources from
David Jeremiah

FURTHER YOUR STUDY OF THIS BOOK

Belief That Behaves Resource Materials

To enhance your study on the book of Ephesians, we
recommend the correlating CD or DVD albums and
two-volume study guide for *Belief That Behaves*.

CD or DVD Albums

The material found in this book
originated from messages preached
by Dr. Jeremiah. These messages are
conveniently packaged in accessible
CD or DVD albums.

Study Guides

These 144-page study guides correlate
with the messages from the *Belief That
Behaves* series by Dr. Jeremiah. Each
lesson provides an outline, an overview,
and personal and group application
questions. These study guides are
perfect for personal or small group
study.

Also Compered to the Teaching
of David Jeremiah

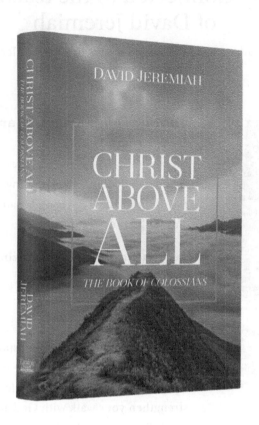

Christ Above All

No subject will expand your mind, deepen your heart, or inflame
your hope like the glorious personality of Jesus Christ. The
apostle Paul compresses the greatest truths about Christ into
his small letter to the Colossians—4 short chapters, 95 precious
verses. In *Christ Above All*, Dr. Jeremiah takes you verse by verse
though this rich apostle, and the truths you discover will set you
free to find all you need in Christ—and all you will ever need.

Stay Connected to the teaching of David Jeremiah

Take advantage of three great ways to let David Jeremiah give you spiritual direction every day!

Turning Points Magazine and Devotional

This monthly magazine includes relevant articles, daily devotional readings, *Turning Point* Radio and Television broadcast schedules and Bible study resource offers.

Request *Turning Points* magazine today!
DavidJeremiah.org/Magazine

Daily E-Devotions

Find words of inspiration and spiritual motivation in your inbox every morning. Each e-devotional from David Jeremiah will strengthen your walk with God and encourage you to live with authentic faith.

Sign up for your free e-devotional today!
DavidJeremiah.org/Devo

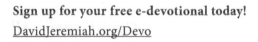

Turning Point Mobile App

Access Dr. David Jeremiah's video teachings, audio sermons, and more . . . whenever and wherever you are.

Download the free app today!
DavidJeremiah.org/App